The War Diary of Clare Gass
1915–1918

The War Diary of Clare Gass
1915–1918

EDITED AND INTRODUCED

BY SUSAN MANN

McGill-Queen's University Press

Montreal & Kingston • London • Ithaca

© McGill-Queen's University Press 2000
ISBN 0-7735-2126-7

Diary for the years 1915 and 1916
© Elizabeth Anderson 2000

Legal deposit third quarter 2000
Bibliothèque nationale du Québec

Printed in Canada on acid-free paper

McGill-Queen's University Press acknowledges the financial
support of the Government of Canada through the Book
Publishing Industry Development Program (BPIDP) for its
activities. It also acknowledges the support of the Canada
Council for the Arts for its publishing program.

Matron MacLatchy's recollections (Appendix 6) are published
by permission of the editor, *The Canadian Nurse.* Nursing Sister
Clint's recollections (Appendix 7) are published by permission
of the Alumnae Association of the Royal Victoria Hospital
Training School for Nurses.

Canadian Cataloguing in Publication Data

Gass, Clare, 1887–1968
The war diary of Clare Gass
(McGill-Queen's/Associated Medical Services (Hannah
Institute) Studies in the History of Medicine ; 9
Includes bibliographical references
ISBN 0-7735-2126-7

1. Gass, Clare, 1887–1968—Diaries. 2. World War,
1914–1918—Medical care—France. 3. World War,
1914–1918–Medical care—Canada. 4, Canada. Canadian
Army. Royal Canadian Army Medical Corps—Biography. 5.
Nurses—Canada—Diaries. 6. World War, 1914–1918—
Personal narratives, Canadian. I. Mann, Susan II. Title. III.
Series.

D630.G38A3 2000   940.4'7571'092   C00-900431-9

This book was designed by David LeBlanc and typeset in
10.3/13 New Baskerville

Contents

For Elizabeth Anderson
Who introduced me to Aunt Clare

Abbreviations

ADMS	Assistant Director Medical Services
ASC	Army Service Corps
Batt	Battalion
CAMC	Canadian Army Medical Corps
CB	Confined to Barracks
CC	Convalescent Camp
CCS	Casualty Clearing Station
CMR	Canadian Mounted Rifles
CRT	Canadian Railway Troop
Can	Canadian
Capt	Captain
Col	Colonel
DCM	Distinguished Conduct Medal
DDNS	Deputy Director Medical Services
DSO	Distinguished Service Order
MGH	Montreal General Hospital
NB	New Brunswick
NCO	Non-commissioned Officer
NS	Nova Scotia
OC	Officer Commanding
PPCLI	Princess Patricia's Canadian Light Infantry
QAIMNS	Queen Alexandra's Imperial Military Nursing Service
RAMC	Royal Army Medical Corps

RTO   Railway Transport officer
RVH   Royal Victoria Hospital
Reg   Regiment

Acknowledgments

Editing Clare Gass's wartime diary has been a delight. From the first hint of the existence of such a document to the last footnote for this publication, I have been surrounded by people as intrigued as I with the topic. In order of appearance they are Pamela Miller of the Osler Library at McGill, Philip Cercone of McGill-Queen's University Press, and Elizabeth Anderson, Nova Scotian niece of Clare Gass and owner of the major portion of the diary. Those three were the ring-leaders of this project. Individually and collectively they provided encouragement, information, connections, surprises, and support. Through Elizabeth Anderson I was able to meet other Nova Scotian relatives of Clare Gass: nephew John Gass, who has his aunt's wartime photograph album; niece Geraldine Brenton, proprietor of the last two years of the diary and some correspondence; niece Trudy Henderson, who has her aunt's scrap-books and other memorabilia; niece Roslyn MacPhee, who has a prewar photograph album as well as the Gass-Miller family Bible; and cousin Marion Walsh, who shared some childhood letters of Clare Gass with me. In Ontario were two other nieces, Catherine Germa and Mary Brown and a family friend, Coreen Flemming. All of these people had memories and stories of a Clare Gass special to each of them in different ways. Their candour, good humour, and openness – family traits I suspect – were heartwarming and I thank them for permission to use their material in this book.

Heart warming as well was the welcome I encountered in the many public institutions a historian frequents. At the National Archives, the National Library, the Canadian War Museum, la Bibliothèque nationale du Québec, the Public Archives of Nova Scotia, and the Archives of the Canadian Nurses' Association, the staff was unfailingly generous with time and leads and knowledge.

I have been fortunate, too, in my connection with four educational institutions. King's-Edgehill School in Windsor, Nova Scotia, through Linda Davison-Landymore, the director of Development and Alumni Affairs, provided documents of Clare Gass's early twentieth-century schooling. My home institution, York University, supported the post-presidential leave that gave me the time to renew my love of research and writing. And my temporary home at the McGill Centre for Research and Teaching on Women has the ideal conditions for a visiting scholar. Director Dr Shree Mulay and Administrator Blossom Shaffer have been enormously helpful. At McGill too, Desmond Morton happily shared his encyclopedic knowledge of military history while Johanne Pelletier opened obscure and fruitful corners of the university archives. I am glad to be able to repay McGill's hospitality with a book that adds to the history of the university and, I hope, to the lustre of McGill-Queen's University Press. At the Press, Aurèle Parisien's legal-diplomatic skills guarded the manuscript from many a pitfall. Joan McGilvray guided the manuscript with great interest and a sharp pencil through the multiple post-writing and pre-publication stages. During those stages I had the opportunity to develop a new course on women in the First World War for the Institute of Women's Studies at the University of Ottawa. One paragraph in particular of the introduction reflects that experience.

Finally, gratitude for domestic hospitality and intellectual stimulation during research trips is owing to Margaret Conrad in Halifax and Britt-Mari and Kimball Sykes in Ottawa. Indeed some of the introduction to the Gass Diary was written while we all awaited the arrival of Susan Hannah Sykes, my grand-daughter.

Introduction

CLARE GASS WENT TO WAR AS A PATRIOTIC CANADIAN, a dutiful daughter, a devout Anglican, a loving sister, a dear friend, an adventurer, a romantic, – and a nurse. Indeed, only as a nurse could she, a woman, go to war at all. Two thousand other women preceded, accompanied, or followed her overseas between 1914 and 1918, nursing sisters with the rank of lieutenant in the Canadian Army Medical Corps (CAMC). A varying number, between four hundred and eight hundred – Clare Gass among them – saw service in France, and an even smaller number – Gass there too – served close to the line of fire. All expected to be home soon, and home alive. The war belied the first expectation: in Clare Gass' case her time in Europe stretched to almost four years. The second expectation she and most of her colleagues did achieve. Thirty-nine did not. The experience of the military nurses and the aura surrounding them contributed in large part to the quadrupling of the number of nurses in Canada between 1911 and 1921.[1]

Nothing in Clare Gass's background or upbringing suggested a career at all, much less one in military nursing. Born in Nova Scotia in 1887 to small-town, middle-class parents of Scottish origin, Clare was the oldest living child and only girl in a family of ten, three of whom did not survive infancy or childhood. Her father, Robert, owned a general store and lumber mill in Shubenacadie; her mother, Nerissa, came from the Miller brickmaking family just across the river. Clare and her father were kindred spirits – quiet,

Clare Gass age seven

dreamy, poetic – and they doted on each other. Her mother was more practical, forthright, a force to be reckoned with in the household. The later diary-keeping nurse is clearly a daughter of both. The only hint of a future diarist, however, are Clare's childhood letters to vast numbers of relatives, letters full of fun and mischief and misspellings. Clare retained all of these characteristics in later years. She was a reader from a young age and had free rein in her father's extensive library (except for Rabelais). Might she have encountered there, or at school, Florence Nightingale and the origins of military nursing in the Crimea in the mid-nineteenth century? Although she lived at a time when thousands of young Nova Scotian girls were moving about, to the cities, to the "Boston states," for jobs in service, in industry, even in nursing, Clare's future was probably more circumscribed due to her parents' position: an only Gass daughter ought not to work and should marry. Her future would then look much like her mother's life: a large, noisy household, presence in the community, and pregnancies every two years for almost twenty years. Did she wonder about that? We simply do not know. All we know is that she eventually did work and that she never married.[2]

Part of solidifying a family's middle-class status in the late nineteenth century was providing prestigious schooling for daughters. As Clare reached adolescence and outgrew the local school, her parents chose Edgehill, a private Church of England school for girls in Windsor, Nova Scotia, for her secondary schooling. In 1901, when she went as a boarder, Edgehill was only ten years old but was already

Gass family, Shubenacadie, late nineteenth century.
Clare is centre front.

attracting the daughters of prominent families from Quebec City, Montreal and Ottawa, Bermuda, and the United States. If part of the parental concern was the effect of so many rowdy brothers on a young girl, they could not have chosen better. Four years in the company of ninety other girls spread across the six "forms" of a school consciously modelled on "the leading English schools for girls" provided a superb education and all the feminine proprieties of the upper middle-class. By 1905 Clare knew scripture and history, literature and languages, geography, mathematics, and natural science. She could draw and recite, play the piano, and appreciate art and music. She won a prize for needlework, a bronze medal for proficiency, and completed her studies First Class with distinction in four subjects in the "associate in arts" (Senior Matriculation) examination at King's College, also in Windsor at that time. Like her counterparts elsewhere in the English-speaking world, she was an accomplished and disciplined young woman. Had she been a boy in England, such a background would have taken her straight into the army as a junior officer. As a girl, in Canada, marriage remained the more likely option.

Inadvertently, Edgehill provided Clare Gass with more scope. In the all-female teaching staff Clare encountered single career women. Almost all of them had "Higher Certificates" from Cambridge, a concession to women's post-secondary education at a time when the university did not grant degrees to women, and one had a licentiate from the Royal Academy of Music. Two of the teachers remained linked to Clare for years, long after they had all left Edgehill. One, Miss Lefroy, shows up in her diary. While at school, Clare followed a school routine that made her eventual choice of nursing and then of the military that much easier. Through the pattern of the school day, with its "rising bell" at 7 A.M. to "lights out" at 9.15 P.M., the girls were acquiring orderly, accepted discipline. Ten years later réveillé and last post would not be much different. Besides the highly structured academic program, the girls also had sports and games under the direction of a teacher certified, among other things, in "Military Drill." Through it all, strict obedience to the "Lady Principal" was merely ini-

Clare Gass, Edgehill schoolgirl

tiation for the same requirement by the "Lady Superintendent" at nursing school and then by the matron and commanding officer in the military.[3]

The reasons behind her decision to go into nursing remain obscure. Three years elapsed between the end of her schooling at Edgehill in 1905 and her going to Montreal. During that time she was at home, perhaps awaiting the suitor expected for such young women and most likely assisting her mother with the younger children. Two more had joined the family while she was at Edgehill. Clare was allowed to name the first as recompense for his not being the sister she longed for and chose the name Athelstan. The second necessitated her being summoned home from school in 1904 when the birth of this last brother threatened to take the lives of both mother and child. And two years later her twelve year-old brother John died. So she was surrounded by birth and death and people needing care. Moreover, not until she was twenty-one, early in 1908, was she old enough for nursing school.

Once she decided to go into nursing, she had to choose among American training schools and any one of the seventy Canadian schools – all at that time attached to hospitals. The more obvious choices were Halifax's Victoria General Hospital, with its waiting list of up to two years, and the two big English-language city hospitals in Montreal.[4] The latter drew their nursing students from all across the country, women ranging in age from twenty-one to thirty-eight. Most, like Clare, marked "Nil" under the heading "Vocation" on their application, but a fair number declared themselves as accountants, governesses, or clerks. In short, middle-class women wanting or needing a profession, one which, by then, was both respectable and recognized. Perhaps following a family reminder of distant, unmet cousins in Montreal, Clare Gass shows up in January 1909 among the incoming student nurses at the Montreal General Hospital (MGH).[5]

There followed three years of all-female residential life and a regimen of work, discipline, and obedience that would have won the admiration of any militia officer. Along with the other students, Clare offered her services to the hospital in return for board, instruction, and a small monthly stipend. "On pain of expulsion" she promised to have no personal dealings with any of the (male) medical staff and students. The same fate awaited her should she fail the "Junior exam" or injure a patient. Before completing her training she had to work without pay for three months for the Montreal Maternity Hospital, an obligation she fulfilled in the late winter and early spring of 1912.[6] Apart from illness (scarlet fever in 1909 and the removal of a neck gland in 1910, the scar of which is recorded on her military attestation papers), she spent three years rotating among the wards of the hospital, learning by doing. Photographs of these hospital wards show that they were remarkably similar to the later military hospital wards, as was the use of alphabetical letters to name wards. Through surgical, medical, and children's wards, in the operating room, the diet kitchen, or the maternity hospital, Clare perfected the nurse's particular combination of skill, authority, and deference.[7] Both her character and her competence were part of the School's assessment of her: the competence summarized as "practical work," the character as "efficiency."[8] Through it all she had just enough time off to meet the Montreal Gass relatives and to take a particular liking to her second cousin Laurence, a young engineering student at McGill. He is the "Laurie" of her diary. By June 1912, with her "time expired," she was ready to earn her living – like most other graduate nurses of the time – in private duty nursing or, should the need arise, in military nursing.

Few people foresaw that need in the summer of 1912. Indeed, Canada's permanent military force, tiny in itself, had only five nurses.[9] Some of them were veterans of the South African War (1899–1902), when twelve Canadian nurses had gone overseas. One of them, Margaret Macdonald, was subsequently matron-in-chief of Canada's military nurses during the First World War. As a lieutenant in the Permanent Army Medical Corps as of 1906, Macdonald instigated some personnel planning, but even she could not predict the need for, nor interest in, military nursing.[10] When it developed, in the late summer of 1914 and throughout the four years of war, with military nurses at home and abroad numbering just over 3,000, there were always more applicants than places. In a limited job market, and with graduate nurses increasing in number, the war offered an unusual opportunity. Nurses had to be British subjects (as all Canadians were at the time) and single (some widows do appear – Mrs Austin and Mrs Giffin of the diary), in good health, graduates of a recognized school of nursing, and between twenty-one to thirty-eight years of age,[11] with the graduate requirement effectively ensuring that the nurses were at least twenty-four. Competition for the initial jobs in 1914 involved old-fashioned political favouritism, new-fangled professional lobbying through the Canadian National Association of Trained Nurses,[12] and the young women themselves pleading with hospital authorities to speed up their final examinations so they could enlist, now.[13]

Clare Gass's enlistment involved a more circuitous route, via McGill University rather than directly to the Ministry of Militia and Defence. By 1915 she was almost twenty-eight, an experienced nurse with the maturity and stamina required of army nurses. In her decision to enlist, she was likely encouraged by her recruiting officer father and the example of two of her brothers, Gerald and Cyril, who had already enlisted (two more, Blanchard and Athelstan, would follow) and just perhaps by a sense that her family would disapprove of what may have been a budding romance with cousin Laurence. Whatever the motivation – and pay, friends, travel, adventure, and the call of the British Empire would also have played their part – she became one of the original members of the McGill University hospital overseas, known formally as No. 3 Canadian General Hospital (McGill). The first such entity in the imperial war effort, the hospital was the dream of the dean of Medicine at McGill, Dr H.S. Birkett, who happened also to be a colonel in the Canadian militia. He persuaded Sir William Peterson, McGill's principal, and Sam Hughes, the Canadian minister of the Militia, of the benefits of a university-based hospital. It would have the best surgeons, drawn from McGill's faculty, the best technology, and the best nurses, chosen equally from the graduates of the two major teaching hospitals in Montreal, the General and the Royal Victoria. Male medical students would even ensure that it had the best orderlies. Moreover, McGill's status and alumni would ensure private support for the hospital. It took Birkett many months to convince both Canadian and British authorities of his plan; to persuade the British he called upon McGill's distinguished graduate and former professor, then at Oxford, Sir William Osler. By the spring of 1915 he had succeeded and the unit set sail for Britain early in May. By August the hospital, under canvas at Camiers on the north eastern coast of France, was ready to receive its first patients. Early in 1916 it moved to more substantial quarters on a hill above Boulogne, where it remained until May 1919. Both locations were about forty miles behind the front lines in Flanders. As commanding officer during most of the period, Colonel Birkett continued his public relations campaign for the hospital. He insisted it remain as a single unit and not be broken up to reinforce the numerous British hospitals nearby. He demanded that only McGill doctors and medical students come as reinforcements. And he made sure the hospital's successes were known. Eventually Canada produced eight such university-based hospitals – four of the six General Hospitals and four of the six Stationary Hospitals. By all accounts, its own included, McGill was one of the best.[14]

The war diary of Clare Gass begins with her month of military training in Quebec City in March 1915. The common background of the nurses – Clare's training overlapped with that of twenty-six of the thirty-six MGH graduates – explains both the easy camaraderie of the women and the occasional difficulty. They were among friends. They were also returning to the residential, uniformed, disciplined, hierarchical life of school and hospital.[15] The additional training in Quebec was more military than medical, as the nurses absorbed the etiquette, law, and administration of their new employer,[16] to whom they had contracted their services for the duration of the war. At $2 a day (plus "field" and "messing" and travel allowance when overseas) they were receiving better pay than private duty nurses[17] and were embarking on an unusual adventure for women. They intended to make the most of it. Whether they were in tents, huts, or billets, doing month-long night duty as the convoys of wounded came in, or shielding their patients from bombardments, the nurses displayed a female version of esprit-de-corps. Friendship, humour, escapades – whether in work or play the nurses combined seriousness of purpose with sheer delight. These women enjoyed each other's company and they loved their work, "if it were only possible," added Clare, "to forget its cause."[18] But the cause for which the war was being fought, interpreted by political, military, and religious leaders of the time as the defence of civilization, righteousness, and justice, they neither forgot nor questioned. Indeed, that cause gave their work a higher moral purpose, one involving religion, morality, and the family. With brothers and cousins in the fighting ranks, this war was a family affair, the ties of empire and religion as strong as those between siblings.

The presence of the nurses themselves added to the moral force of the war. That women would be willing to leave their homes to share at least part of the agony of warfare emphasized both the worthiness of the cause and the appropriateness of contemporary male-female divisions of labour. Even the original justification of the war – the defence of small, helpless Belgium against strong, brutal Germany – had overtones of gender. Those overtones continued throughout the war. Young men were encouraged to enlist to protect *their* women and children from the outrages purportedly inflicted upon the women and children of territory overrun by the Germans. A drowning nurse figured prominently in the on-going campaign to present Germany as a monster. Even the financial purpose of Victory Bonds – that the Canadian public pay its own war costs – was camouflaged as the provision of security for women. As for bad women – those preying prostitutes of England corrupting young Canadian soldiers – their existence merely accentuated the moral superiority of "good women." Nurses were the only good women anywhere near active duty soldiers; they thus had a substantial image and reality to uphold.[19]

In their military work, the nurses maintained very strict female-male distinctions. The symbolism of language and dress is the most revealing but so too is the myriad of detail in the Gass diary about expected and cheerily undertaken female behaviour. The nurses were "Sisters" with all the familial and religious connotations of the title. They were swathed in garments that combined a matron's light blue housedress with a schoolgirl's collar and cuffs, a child's white pinafore (or a servant's apron), and the hair-covering white veil of a nun. Thus garbed, they tended to "lads" and "boys," words that turned the young soldiers (often considerably younger than the nurses) into brothers or children. To add to the distancing, the nurses had a dress uniform of brass-buttoned dark blue, complete with hat and great-coat, boots, and gloves, the whole outfit so distinctive and unusual as to have Londoners wondering who these women were. Policewomen? Suffragettes? In any case, formidable.[20]

To the mix, the army added the rank of lieutenant, complete with stars on the shoulder strap of the nurses' uniform. The rank placed

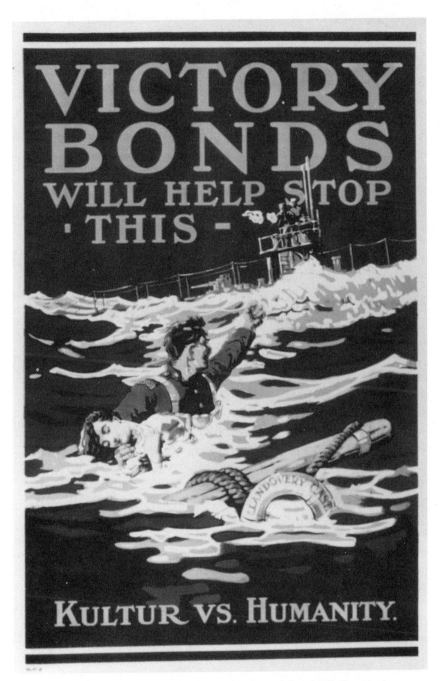

(McGill University Libraries, Rare Books and Special Collections)

the nurses squarely in an hierarchy of command (albeit limited to the hospital): they owed deference to the captains, majors, colonels, and generals above them and deference was their due from the non-commissioned officers and privates below them. They took orders from their seniors and gave orders to their subordinates. Men of all ranks seemed to find this latter puzzling: women exercising authority outside the household or the schoolroom was a novelty, and it appeared even stranger if, as often happened in the hospital, the orders given were to perform household tasks. One of the doctors at the McGill hospital observed that some of the nurses were rather "picayune" in commanding male medical students – mere sergeants – to do the sweeping.[21] For the nurses it must in fact have been a bit of a lark. But it clearly did not always work. In 1917 and again in 1918 senior military personnel had to reiterate that the nurses had authority and were due the obedience and respect of their rank.[22]

Everyone was more comfortable with traditional roles. If military nursing allowed women to exercise some unusual authority as well as to spread their professional wings in distant settings, army life also ensured the maintenance of rigid nineteenth-century lines of separate female and male spheres of activity and propriety. The nurses themselves took for granted their segregated and familial functions within the army hospital structure. In their sharply demarcated living quarters, they expressed indignation if any males intruded. And they expected male protection from any undue advances. In their "lines," which included a "Mess" tent for eating and an "Ante-tent" for socializing, they revealed the portability and durability of women's culture. They decorated and embellished, they planted gardens, and, when wind and cold got the better of them, they also hammered and repaired. They organized parties and entertainments for their patients, themselves, the officers, and the men. They held afternoon teas and "at homes" to which the male officers of the McGill unit and the many other nearby hospitals were invited. Often one of the men would play the piano. Under the matron's beaming and watchful eye – she seems to have been a combination of administrator, hostess, and chaperone – mutual admiration held sway.

More formal occasions were equally stylized. The many high-ranking visitors to the McGill hospital took tea with the matron and nurses, then dined with the male officers in their separate mess. One Hallowe'en, referred to in the Gass diary, the sisters proposed a masquerade for the men, much to the commanding officer's consternation. With their fellow officers, it might be acceptable, but with the men? Surely a breach of military etiquette. The nurses deferred and then the colonel relented. Once the lines of military etiquette were crossed, the masquerade itself allowed the indulgence of numerous displays of cross-dressing. But it all just proved the rule. At Christmas the sisters outdid themselves with ward decoration, stocking stuffing, serving dinner to the "other ranks" (the men below them), and then dining and dancing – dress uniforms de rigueur – with the male officers, complete with a receiving line of colonels and, once again, the matron.[23]

The dancing raised an eyebrow or two but not among the Canadians. It seems that English nurses, organized in a unit quite separate from the British army – Queen Alexandra's Imperial Military Nursing Service (QAIMNS) – were forbidden the easy association with brother officers that the Canadians enjoyed. The dancing therefore added to the rivalry occasionally discernible between the Canadian and English nurses. A nurses' dance at the McGill hospital to mark Dominion Day, for example, could draw officers from near and far. There is a hint of disapproval, perhaps reflecting some jealousy in the ranks, in a report of the British matron-in-chief: "Members of the C.A.M.C. are permitted by their regulations to dance with officers in their own messes," she remarked archly, glad of a thorough discussion of the topic at a conference of overseas matrons-in-chief in late 1917. The Canadian representative, Matron Margaret Macdonald, was forthright: "dancing [was] a necessary and very legitimate exercise ... nurses who were surrounded with an atmosphere of depression needed the recreation both mentally and physically."[24]

On the nurses' part, some of the strict adherence to gender roles may have been camouflage. In the CAMC the nurses were finding valued, satisfying, and demanding work, work that they accomplished with energy and enthusiasm. Moreover, the army allowed them to concentrate on that work by tending to all their other requirements. Lodging, food, laundry, health care, entertainment, transportation, vacations and travel, freindships, even servants in the form of "batmen" and "home sisters," were all provided as part of the nurses' contract – and opportunity – to work. There was nothing like it at home, either in private duty nursing or in the household. No wonder they loved their work. But perhaps no wonder, too that they spoke so little of it. For the nurses were breaking a middle-class gender code that cast them, as women, in the role of supporting actor to someone else's work. While that is one way of seeing nursing itself in relation to the medical profession, it belittles the actual work of the nurses and ignores the propitious circumstances of that work in the army. The fact that so many of the nurses remained single after the war suggests that at some level they knew what was happening. They may simply have chosen to hide that knowledge in the role-playing of gender.

The semblance of normality provided by adherence to gender roles of family and class occurred in the midst of the worst human carnage the world had seen. Perhaps it was necessary to surviving a war whose only sure winner was technology. Even Clare Gass's spelling, awkward and inconsistent as it is, reflects the novelty of shrapnel, gas masks, machine guns, anti-aircraft guns, airplanes themselves, dirigibles, torpedoes, bombs, shells, even trucks and cars. Curiously she mentions neither of the nineteenth-century's standard soldier's equipment of rifle and bayonet nor the bumbling beginnings of the tank. What she sees all too clearly is the effect of these inventions on human flesh. She knows her physiology and the proper medical term for gas gangrene but before going to Europe she would never have encountered its appearance or its stench. Long before the war touched her own kin, she had seen how it shattered limbs and innards and minds. The wounds appal her; they pierce the normal gentility of diary-keeping, they numb and eventually silence her. Neither her training nor her gender allowed her to share the scientific interest of her medical colleagues (on one occasion indeed, the nurses served the refreshments before the doctors read their research papers to the Boulogne Base Medical Society). At the same time her nursing practice was facilitated by technological improvements in health care. Keeping pace with weaponry were X-rays, blood transfusions, and bone splints.[25]

Before a wounded soldier could profit from any of the medical inventions or skilled care, he had to run an obstacle course designed to have him repaired in the shortest possible time. From no-man's land, between the opposing lines of trenches, he would hobble, if able, to the first aid post in his own line, hoping that the line was still there. If unable to get there on his own, he would await the cover of darkness and the chance of stretcher bearers locating him. With luck they might get him to a field ambulance or advanced dressing

Horse ambulance collecting wounded at advanced dressing station, 1916
(National Archives of Canada [NA] PA 680)

Stretcher cases arriving at No. 3 CGH, Boulogne
(Pirie, *No. 3 Canadian General Hospital*)

station in time for preliminary assistance. From there, a vehicle, horse-drawn or motorized, would take him over impossible roads to the nearest Casualty Clearing Station (CCS), usually three or four miles behind the front. Depending on a medical officer's judgment, and the period of the war, he might be operated on then and there and kept under nursing surveillance until he could be moved further back "down the line" that he had come "up" on his way to the front. Or he might die there and never get any farther. The nature of the wound or the repair could also send him straight on through, often by ambulance train this time, to a larger and more fully equipped hospital – a two-hundred-and-fifty-bed Stationary Hospital or a five-hundred to fifteen-hundred-bed General Hospital – far enough back to permit him to sleep in peace. Subject still to decisions about how soon he could make the reverse journey back to the front, he could stay in such a hospital as a surgical or medical case from a few days to a few months. He would then move on to a convalescent camp before returning to his unit or to a longer-stay hospital in England. A good word in his favour (Clare Gass records one such occasion) might get him to England faster, as would the imminence of a major battle that required emptying the hospitals before the next wave of wounded. Even in England, there were still decisions about reparability, except in cases of amputation or blindness: either condition would send him home, if Canada-bound, aboard a hospital ship.[26]

Except for the very first stages of his journey down the line, nurses accompanied him all the way. They were originally never intended to be so close to the front, but as of 1915 ten or twelve nurses were at each Casualty Clearing Station. At least two were on the ambulance train. Sixteen awaited him at a Stationary Hospital and as many as seventy-two at a General Hospital. In all units numbers expanded with the need: a wounded soldier in 1918 might find as many as one hundred and forty nurses at the McGill hospital. Nurses were on the hospital ships from Boulogne to England and again from England to Canada. Here, too, they were not intended to be in danger, but in fact a torpedoed hospital ship caused the greatest single number of Canada's nursing dead. Fourteen nursing sisters, all in the same lifeboat, went down with the *Llandovery Castle* as it returned from a trip to Canada in June 1918. Clare Gass records this too.[27]

To repair the wounded, nurse the sick, and ease the dying, nurses performed a multitude of tasks. All the ward preparation was theirs, from making and equipping beds to obtaining stores from the central supply, stocking the tiny ward kitchen, and arranging space for the charge nurse to make her reports. The nurses prepared all the dressings, pads of clean cotton gauze, in advance, enough, literally, for an army. Most of the actual changing of dressings – the replacement of blood-soaked, pus-laden bandages, the washing of the wound with a sterile (and stinging) solution, and its covering up again with a clean dressing fell to the nurses.[28] So too did the feeding of soldiers too weak or incapacitated to feed themselves. The nurses checked pulses and temperatures, brought down fevers, stopped hæmorrhages, and watched for the ever-lurking gangrene. They tended to the aftermath of operations, occasionally participating in the operation itself as surgical nurse or anæsthetist (this latter a Canadian première).[29] And they carried out the "the small attentions to patients" – a smile, a word, a pat, a cigarette, a query, a chat, a treat from the town pastry shop – that sustained everyone's spirits, both the patients' and their own.[30] The nurses brought lads back from the brink of madness and accompanied them to the edge of death. When the latter took over, the nurses conveyed the soldier's final state and last wishes to his family.

The nurses did all this, year after year, day and night, the rhythm of their work regulated by the ebb and flow of blood from battle. They treated patients from England, Scotland, Australia, New Zealand, Canada, South Africa, even Portugal – more than 140,000 over the life of the McGill hospital – whoever was sent to them sick or

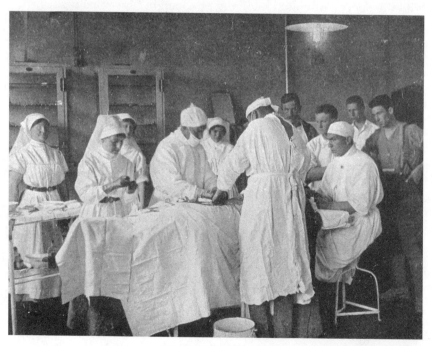

Operating room nurses
(Pirie, *No. 3 Canadian General Hospital*)

wounded down the British "lines of communication" from camp or trench or battlefield. Although Clare Gass mentions many of those battlefields, her interest and that of other nurses seemed to be more the country of origin and the name or number of a soldier's unit (for possible connections with relatives and friends) than the battle that marked his wound and appeared in history books. The nurses cared for these soldiers in tents and huts, where heat, lighting, and water could be less constant than they. They waded through the mud, rain, and wind of north-eastern France with chilblains and backache from the low-slung hospital cots and even lower stretchers that filled available floor space after a major battle. According to one account, the physical labour required of Canadian nursing sisters was greater than that of their English counterparts whose trained (male) orderlies took on more of the routine care. But the Canadians had male assistance too, privates (and the occasional sergeant) acting as ward masters, orderlies or general duty providers. Privates Lapp and Valentine are examples from the Gass diary. In the McGill hospital, most of the male assistants were medical students and Clare despaired of them initially. But in fact their task was to do things considered not quite proper for women to undertake: washing the "dirty, bloody, lousy boys" who came in from the trenches, sending "their grimy uniforms for disinfection," and presumably – although no one mentions this – fetching and carrying bed-pans. As the war went on and medical students returned to their studies in Canada or transferred to fighting units, recuperating patients often took on some of the ward duties. One of Clare's favourites was the English lad "Blanch" and she may well have prolonged his life by having work for him to do in her ward. In fact there were never enough people to do the work.[31]

With all the military activities requiring careful organization, time seems to have been crucial. The nurses' time was carefully structured. If, on occasion, they had to do double duty, they were seldom run ragged. A normal day shift had "hours off," enough time for a bicycle sprint into town or a walk in the neighbouring countryside. A half-day, or the more occasional entire day, off allowed for longer ventures, dedicated sight-seeing (these nurses were travellers along

Office of Matron-in-Chief MacDonald, London (NA, PA 680)

with everything else) in surrounding towns and villages, picnics in valleys and on hillsides, lunch in a café. Every three months or so a stint of night duty of about four weeks duration – the interval and length shorter at a Clearing Station – required adjusting personal time to hospital time. Clare Gass never did get used to sleeping during the day; she always marked the early morning transition with a sea bathe, a walk, or a bicycle ride. Because there were so few nurses on night duty, the breaks were fewer, but on a quiet night a nurse could slip away to her "lines" for a few moments. About every six months, a nurse could apply for leave, a ten-day to two-week permission to be away from the hospital, almost always to go to England.

Along every step of these activities, the army kept track of its nursing personnel. Rarely did a nurse go anywhere alone; permission slips littered her path and when in London she had to report in to the office of the matron-in-chief. To carry out all this supervision the matron or assistant matron in a unit could count on the nurses' own upbringing and training. These disciplined women knew how to behave. This gave the matron a slight advantage over other army officers in their similar supervision of citizen soldiers, a rather more recalcitrant group. For the nurses, however, the army accepted a gendered obligation: protection was due its female members. This entailed not allowing them into the fighting zone, leaving guards should they be alone in camp, and watching out for any moral danger that might befall them. The commanding officer of the McGill unit was particularly adamant about the latter danger. During a change of hospital sites Colonel Birkett did not want his nurses billetted in Boulogne for fear of urban influences on discipline and morale.[32]

In return for this moral and physical protection, the army expected speedy and efficient repair of its soldiers. In Birkett's mind, protection of the women and repair of the men probably went together. Indeed, everyone, the nurses included, thought that women had a special touch in healing and that that special touch required harbouring. More likely, what was being papered over with gender and justified by war was the difference between military time and motherly time. Military time organized the soldiers into automatons; motherly time remembered the person. Military time took soldiers "over the top" with a second's precision; motherly time listened for the resulting horror story. And if a soldier's ailment was ultimately an overdose of military time, his repair was a hefty infusion of motherly time. Even before they came into a nurse's presence, the soldiers recognized this when they disobeyed orders and broke ranks to tend to their fallen comrades. All the more, then, should they make it to hospital, did they expect and cherish the attention, the sensitivity, the very presence of the nurses. "You're doing the very best work of the war," Victor Lapp wrote to Clare Gass after he left the McGill unit. She returned the compliment and confirmed the gendered notion of it in a poem of praise she wrote in 1917 "To the Men of the CAMC": they had abandoned "the glamour of musket and sword" that was their due as men in order to take up "secrets supposedly women's" of comfort and healing. In fact, the nurses' task was to combine, in a military setting, their scientific knowledge, professional training, and those characteristics assumed to be theirs by nature. By all accounts they succeeded in their task. A formal acknowledgment in the official record of No.3 Canadian General Hospital (McGill) states: "They have been indefatigable in their efforts to make the wounded as comfortable as possible during their stay in Hospital, and their skill has been of the highest order." A more effusive matron delivered the same message: "In the opinion of Surgeons and those best qualified to judge no male nurse or orderly can take the place of a trained woman. Besides exercising the technical knowledge of her profession she exerts a wholesome and uplifting influence on the soldier and her ministrations help to give him confidence – the assurance that he is being brought back to the normal conditions of life."[33]

Clare Gass returned from war, her values and person intact. Like many women's travel diaries, hers ends abruptly with her arrival in Halifax in December 1918. In fact she spent another year in the army before general demobilization late in 1919. During that year she did "transport duty," accompanying wounded soldiers across the Atlantic and across Canada, with her last posting at the military hospital at Ste-Anne-de-Bellevue. Along with the army she discarded the one thing that had allowed her, as a woman, to go to war at all: her nursing profession. Perhaps private duty nursing was too tame after her war experience; certainly the field was becoming overcrowded and therefore increasingly underpaid. It seems also that former military nurses did not make an easy transition to the few executive jobs available for trained nurses in civilian hospitals. Whether Clare Gass considered either of these options is unknown. But the rapidity with which she turned to social work – a budding new profession for women – suggests that she had had enough of repairing maimed bodies. The war may in fact have given her a wider social context for considering health and transport duty may have given her the time to reflect upon the social integration of disabled soldiers.[34]

Certainly social work could represent one more adventure for someone who combined a strong sense of responsibility with enthusiasm for anything new. It also meant a decisive break with the contemporary feminine ideal of marriage and motherhood, an ideal frayed, of course, by the dearth of men but also perhaps by the experience of overseas military nursing itself. Whatever the impetus, she was among the first to take classes at McGill's newly formed School of Social Work in 1920 and she subsequently studied medical social work at Simmons College in Boston. As a pioneer of medical social work in Montreal she headed the Department of Social Work at the Western Division of the Montreal General Hospital and was active in the Canadian forerunner of the American Association of Medical Social Workers.[35] With a great capacity for fun and friendship, she gathered around her other single professional women, in Montreal and elsewhere; they visited her in the city and joined her for summer vacations in Nova Scotia. There, from a cabin on Martinique Beach, they impressed, entertained, and educated Clare's many nieces and nephews. Over many a summer Aunt Clare would organize her young relatives into treasure hunts, "toothbrush brigades," painting contests, plays, readings aloud of books of her choosing, and regular outdoor Sunday church services in which she would play the minister. The children reciprocated her fondness for them, treated her with the respect that both she and her brothers (their fathers) demanded of them, surmised that she was somehow special and knew it when she beat one of them at poker. Only once did she return to France, a commemorative trip in 1923 aboard the same ship sailing on the same day as it had in 1915. Among her effects on her death in 1968 was a memento of that trip: a tiny box marked "Forget-me-nots from Vimy Ridge." They had turned to dust.

During all that time Clare had tucked her diary away, close enough to slip in loose press clippings and poems and drawings but far enough away to keep the experience distant, from herself and her relatives. According to those relatives, Clare seldom spoke about the war. She could not be enticed to tell war stories. Nor did she ever keep another diary. Like most other nurses, and many soldiers too, silence seemed the appropriate balm.

This silence helps explain why we do not yet have a history of Canada's First World War nursing sisters. The silence affected the first attempt at such a history shortly after the war; Matron-in-Chief Margaret Macdonald spent a few years before her retirement from the Department of Militia and Defence in 1923 trying to put together an official history of the Nursing Services. In part she ran into the same overwhelming task that kept even the first volume of Canada's official history of the war from appearing before 1938. When a history of the medical services appeared in 1925, its author, Andrew Macphail, skimmed over the nursing contribution, perhaps on the assumption that the Macdonald project would fill in the gaps in his account. But Macdonald was unable to break the nurses' silence. Her plan had been to have different aspects of the history written by different people and she solicited information and memories from all nursing sisters. The response was minimal and the few sketchy results form the tiny collection of her papers at the National Archives. One contribution, by Clare Gass's matron at No. 3, which found its way into print in *The Canadian Nurse*, is included here as Appendix 6. The Historical Section of the Defence Ministry tried to continue the project, but it too ran up against the silence. Even by limiting the range of contacts to senior nurses, those who had been matrons or had achieved military recognition (notably the Royal Red Cross) or had had unusually varied war-time experience, section head Colonel Duguid was no more successful than Matron Macdonald. His appeal to patriotism fell on deaf ears or raised a hoot of laughter. When he quoted the official purpose of the history – that it "be read by every Canadian girl before leaving high school" in order to "bring out the characteristics of devotion and fearlessness as exemplified by Canadian nurses" – his correspondent, a personal friend and former military nurse, pleaded "On behalf of the present day school girl may I make so bold as to say 'Have a Heart.'" It seems that few others bothered to reply at all and the history never happened.[36]

And yet, all of Canada's military nurses wrote letters home and most of them seem to have kept diaries. Few of these documents have reached public archives, much less publication. The National Archives of Canada has a minuscule collection of the papers (small in themselves) of six CAMC nurses. The National War Museum has mementos of a few nurses, including those of the first Canadian nurse to be killed in the bombing of a hospital, but only one diary, that of a volunteer ambulance driver. The Canadian Nurses' Association has one diary, that of American Alice Isaacson who served with Canadian hospitals overseas. Like much of women's history, the nurses' personal records seem to have succumbed to public indifference, family protectiveness, and the nurses' own reticence.

That same reticence affected the nurses' publication of their stories. Towards the end of the war, Constance Bruce produced an illustrated, light-hearted account designed to show the adventure and good humour of the nurses. In the 1930s Mabel Clint penned *Our Bit*, a more serious and patriotic memoir that reveals something of the bitterness of a nurse financially strapped after the war. Clint spent a few months of 1918 at No. 3 during the bombardment of the Boulogne area that summer and her outsider's view of the McGill unit is included as Appendix 7. Some letters of Muriel Grace Galt, a Canadian nurse serving with the British nursing reserve, are buried in a collection of *Letters from Armageddon* published by her sister Amy Gordon Grant in 1930. Until the 1980s, when Katherine Wilson-Simmie published her recollections in a thoughtful memoir, *Lights Out*, those were the only published first-person accounts in book form. An oral history project of the University of Toronto's School of Nursing, begun in 1977, tracked down a number of aging nurse veterans in Toronto but never did anything formal with the interviews. The transcripts, of uneven quality, are in the archives of the Canadian Nurses' Association. They reveal the project's equal emphasis on the nurses' family background, nursing training, military service and subsequent career. Their military nursing is therefore only a fragment of their recollections. One of those veterans, Maude Wilkinson, did publish a brief memoir in *The Canadian Nurse* in 1977. The first diary to appear in print, Ella Mae Bongard's *Nobody Ever Wins a War* in 1997, is that of a Canadian nurse who served with the American Nursing Service; her diary therefore only begins in August 1917.

Secondary sources are equally slim. The history of the hospital itself, Fetherstonhaugh's *No. 3 Canadian General Hospital (McGill)*

1914–1919, produced in 1928, is a celebratory project of and for McGill University. All its information is taken from the official War Diary of the unit and the focus is squarely on the McGill men and their medical and scientific achievements. The nurses are of minor interest. Just after the Second World War, when 4,400 Canadian military nurses displayed Colonel Duguid's "devotion and fearlessness," the subject finally caught a historian's eye. But, just like the commemorative tableau erected in 1926 near the entrance to the Parliamentary Library in Ottawa, John Gibbon's overview covers three centuries of Canadian nursing; only one chapter is devoted to the First World War. Almost thirty years later, historians were still silent and the Canadian Nurses' Association had to commission military historian Gerald Nicholson to write a more modern study. He too surveys all of Canadian history and the military nurses of the First War occupy only three chapters of *Canada's Nursing Sisters*. Twenty years on and much feminist scholarship later, Kathryn McPherson's brilliant *Bedside Matters* gives barely a sentence to the nurses of the First World War. Indeed, by then, Desmond Morton, Canada's best-known contemporary military historian, had given more spacethan that to these nurses. His interest is the soldier but the chapter he devotes to the sick and wounded in *When Your Number's Up* is evocative of, sensitive to, and informative about nursing work. Since his study in 1993, only two graduate students have tackled the topic. Geneviève Allard's MA thesis for Laval makes skilful use of the oral history interviews done twenty years earlier with nurse veterans in Toronto. And that part of Leslie Newell's MSc(N.) thesis for Ottawa that deals with the war focuses on a Canadian hospital in England as part of the author's larger interest in military nursing in the interwar period. In all, then, neither military historians nor women's historians have given much attention to military nursing.

Why these nurses have remained in the historiographic shadows is a puzzle in itself. In terms of numbers and action, they are of course insignificant compared to the male war effort. And the memory of that war effort, as Jonathan Vance has unintentionally reminded us in *Death so Noble*, is a profoundly masculine one. Perhaps a concentration on nursing would impose a recognition of the behind-the-lines reality of war: that the broken bodies of young men were under the supervision and care of strong, competent women. The fact that the young men themselves idealized the nurses and pictured them as angels suggests that, like others, they had difficulty with a female presence in a war zone. As for feminist historians, it may be the very gendered nature of nursing work in general and military nursing in particular that has them shying away from its study. To see women's traditional familial roles of tending to the sick professionalized and doubly subordinated, first to medical and then to military authority – both male – can be discouraging. And to have women actively and enthusiastically abetting a war effort can be equally distressing. What the military and feminist historians appear to share, in common indeed with the wounded soldiers, is the notion, gendered itself, that women and war don't go together. To that, Clare Gass and all the other nurses we have yet to hear from say, "Nonsense."

The Gass diary came to light in a small town in Nova Scotia. A ten year-old girl, dressed as a nursing sister, read from her great-grand-aunt's diary as part of Remembrance Day ceremonies at her school in 1997. A Halifax paper caught the story and it came to the attention of the National Film Board, which was having a documentary made about John McCrae, the doctor-soldier-poet and colleague of Clare Gass at No. 3 CGH. Because Clare quoted McCrae's poem "In Flanders' Fields" almost six weeks before its publication in *Punch* in December 1915, her diary gets a footnote in history. It warrants more.[37]

Since the 1980s feminist historians have been scrutinizing women's diaries as documents of social history and women's culture. Literary scholars have added yet another interpretive layer by arguing for women's diaries as a literary form, the female version of autobiography. In that light diaries merit all the critical attention traditionally reserved for autobiographies by men. Helen Buss's *Mapping Our Selves* is an elegant and persuasive Canadian example of the trend in literary studies. Such studies remind us that there is more to diaries than meets the eye, more to the Gass story, for example, than a major historical event seen through a woman's eyes. Where historians may balk, however, is the literary emphasis on "self" and "identity," two concepts that would be puzzling, perhaps even distasteful, to the self-possessed but not self-conscious, much less self-absorbed, military nurses of Clare Gass' generation.[38]

Clare Gass nonetheless intended to record her war-time adventure. While still in Montreal she obtained a substantial daily journal for 1915 (8"x7"x1") and began it on the eve of her departure for Quebec City and military training. Following contemporary conventions of women's domestic and travel diaries, she records events and sights more than emotions. She is circumspect about any physical hardship she experiences and only twice while overseas does she mention weeping. One can only guess at her level of anxiety as she reads daily lists of casualties for names of friends and relatives. Sustaining her spiritually are religion, poetry, and female friendships. Religious services draw her as a believer; the frequent insertion of poetry reveals her state of mind; and some of the friends – Granty and Ruth of the diary – predate the war and last a lifetime. Clare has an eye for landscape and a Canadian's sensitivity to European dirt. Writing the diary seems to have been a late-night occupation, the punctuation alone – periods and dashes galore, often in the oddest of places – suggesting speed, interruptions, or particular remembrances that, once stated, evoke additional detail. The busier Clare became, the less she recorded. The more routine her days, the less she commented. Her diary is a verbal photograph album. As such it matches her penchant for photography, one she pursued for the rest of her life and which emboldened her during the war to disobey army rules. Cameras were forbidden but Clare Gass went on snapping merrily away. Her photograph album covers the same years as the diary but seems to have been constructed well after the war. With the exception of one drawing from her autograph book, that album provided all the illustrations for the diary text presented here; pictures in the introduction and notes come from other sources, both public and private.[39]

As the war progressed, the diary entries become more concise. Even at the beginning of the war, however, Clare usually only filled half of each day's allotted page; so in 1916 she simply began the same book again, usually altering the day (1916 was a leap year) until she caught up with herself in March, and continuing the record of 1916 on the bottom half of the pages. As she was doing so, she likely reread the top part of the page and this may explain some of the marginal notes that context and handwriting suggest she added later. I have chosen not to impose her practical but idiosyncratic and occasionally confusing format on the readers of this publication; I have also checked her sign-posts to ensure that the two years are distinct. Where there has been any doubt – particularly when she copies a poem into her account – I have raised the question in a note.

For some months I thought the diary ended after Christmas 1916. That required some explanation. Was she bored, tired, overworked, ill, cold? Had she, as many of the nurses did, changed units and gone off to places like St Petersburg, Lemnos, Alexandria, Salonika, or, more prosaically, to an elegant convalescent hospital for officers in England? Might she have gone home, as other nursing sisters did, to care for an ailing parent, usually a mother? Might she have resigned to be married, as did still other sisters, perhaps to that Montreal cousin?

Historians' questions both lead to and bump up against the evidence. Official military records in the National Archives of Canada show that Clare Gass, besides being a 5′5″, 128 lb., blue-eyed redhead, did none of the above. But nor did she stay put. She was not, for example, among the nursing sisters who were shipped off to England in "batches" in 1919 as a consequence of the McGill unit's being turned into a venereal hospital. By combing the Nominal Roll of Nursing Sisters for No. 3 CGH I spotted her leaving Boulogne at the beginning of November 1917 for action closer to the front with No. 2 Canadian Casualty Clearing Station (the CCS of her diary) at Remy Siding on the Belgian border. From there I was able to track her weekly duties in the nominal roll of that unit, a much more precise accounting of the whereabouts of the far fewer nurses there.

The roll also recorded her return to Boulogne at the end of June 1918; from there she left for her final months of overseas duty in England in September. At that point the answer to my question about the diary ending in 1916 seemed to be that she was either too cold (the winter of 1916–17 was the worst in thirty-five years) or too busy to sustain the diary.[40]

But no. If historians are loath to give chance a role in their writings, they do rather appreciate chance's personal call, which it made to me during a visit to the Nova Scotia roots and relatives of Clare Gass in the spring of 1999. Shubenacadie, Hilden, Porter's Lake, Martinique Beach, Halifax, Bedford: each revealed mementos and memories of Clare. And among them, the continuation of the diary for 1917 and 1918. A historian's dream come true.

I was still right, nonetheless, that Clare was busy. The diary books for the last two years of the war are tiny, the kind to slip into a pocket, the one for 1917 $31/2''$x$3''$x$3/4''$; the one for 1918 smaller still, $4''$x$3''$x$1/2''$. Her writing becomes even more condensed and the gaps longer. Indeed, the closer she is to the front, the less she recounts, almost as if the experience was beginning to be too much for language. Instead she records people and places and unusual events; she continues to do so at nightfall, jotting down the highlights of the day. This tends to happen on her days on leave, when she clearly has more time and more variety to record. That in itself may explain the many empty pages of 1918, for she seems to have had no leave at all from September 1917 to at least December 1918. By then she may have looked as "wretchedly" as the colleague she was replacing at the Casualty Clearing Station in 1917. Photos in her own album reveal – across the years of the war – a woman thinner, more drawn, and, with all due acknowledgment of contemporary photographic poses, more sombre. She was intact but clearly the war had taken its toll.

The diary as presented here is an unaltered transcript of the original. As editor, I have wished to be as unobtrusive as possible. Except for the notation "No Entry" and the translation of nursing script into regular numbers (1,2,3,4), all is as Clare wrote it, including spelling and punctuation. The latter are a charming reminder that diaries are fundamentally private documents; they are not classroom exercises. The punctuation reveals the rhythm and style of her language, perhaps also of her day, even of her personality ("lively, outspoken but friendly and understanding," remarked the *Montreal Star* on her retirement).[41] The spelling emphasizes the strangeness of her new landscape. On the maps, which show the locations of most of the European places mentioned in the diary, and at the first occasion in the text I have provided, in square brackets [], the standard place-name spellings (as well as filling out the acronyms she uses); thereafter, unless comprehension is an issue, her spelling prevails. What to make of her consistent grade school misspelling of bicycle is another matter, for she is obviously familiar with this means of transport and recreation. In terms of content, a series of numbered notes seemed the most discreet way to provide identification, explanation, and commentary. Even here one runs into the hazards of women's history: men are more easily identifiable than women. In some cases, however, neither can be traced and I have left such individuals unidentified in their passing appearance on the stage of Clare Gass's wartime adventure. I hope her adventure will inspire readers to comb attics and basements for similar accounts, in diary or letter form, and to bring them to the attention of public archives throughout Canada.

SUSAN MANN
Montreal
January 2000

The Western Front, 1914–18

⊞ Clare Gass nursed here

···—·— Furthest German Advance, Aug. - Sept. 1914

▬▬▬ Trench Line, Dec. 1914

·········· German Withdrawal, Mars. 1917

– – – – German Advance, Mar. - July 1918

▬ ▬ Armistice Line, Nov. 11, 1918

Ambleteuse

Marquise

Offrethun

Wimereux

Wierre - Effroy

Olincthun

Souverain-Moulin

Le Waast

Colembert

Rupembert

Boulogne

St-Martin

Le Portel

Montlambert

Baincthun

Outreau

Pont-de-briques

Wirwignes

Desvres

Hardelot Ch.

Carly

Samer

Wierre-au-Bois

Hardelot - Plage

Tingry

Neufchâtel

Halinghen

Dannes

Widehem

Hubersent

Camiers

Frencq

Paris - Plage
(Le Touquet)

Étaples

Trépied

Cucq

Montreuil

Canche River

Merlimont

Berck - Plage

Berck

HOLLAND

BELGIUM

FRANCE

N

0   5 km

⊞ Clare Gass nursed here

xlv

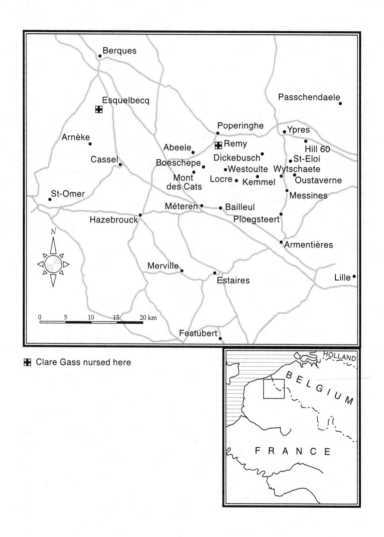

⊞ Clare Gass nursed here

⊞ Clare Gass nursed here

The War Diary of Clare Gass
1915–1918

We accomplished a great deal in
our supply room today. We are
quite warm & cosy at our work. Miss
Duncan sent an old stove from London
which we are using.

                   Sunday 22nd.

A couple of nights ago with the
convoy came a very young New Zealand
lad, a shell shock case — Edney —. His
talk in his sleep was all of "Reg" — & "We'll
get there yet Reg" the most frequent cry. Tonight
he told me his story — poor laddie — a gentle
sweet faced boy. from whom this war has
claimed its own.

He & Reg came out from New Zealand a year
ago & as Regimental stretcher bearers have been
together ever since — Reg apparently the stronger
lad of the two, but the last action while
carrying out a stretcher together Reg was hit
& had to give up his place & another. When
Edney returned to his friend after getting his
patient to a safe place Reg was so weak he
was unable to walk & no help was at hand
so Edney with all his strength managed to
carry him almost three miles when a great
shell burst near him & when consciousness returned
he found Reg still beside him but the poor lad's head.
had been severed from his body. Edney wishing to die
also was found by other stretcher bearers & compelled to go to the
dressing station & so down to us. He can't sleep poor laddie
& I sat beside him for a long time tonight & he unspelled the long
sad tale to me while the others slept around us. Then when we
had both wept as little over it he became quiet again & I gave him a
sleeping draught & he had a dreamless sleep till daylight

1915

MARCH 4

Report that second contingent of the nurses for Magill [McGill]
Hospital is to depart for Quebec [City] at very short notice.

MARCH 5

Heard at 12 AM. we were to go to Quebec to Military Hospital by
special train at 1.30. Cannot get away today but are told we can
go tomorrow by 1.30 train. I spend afternoon with the
McFadzens, but go home to tea & pack my things in the evening
under Granty's watchful eye. Granty gave me my birthday gift
early as I am going to be in Quebec on the 18th. A dear little
wrist watch which is going to prove a great convenience & which
I love already.[1]

MARCH 6

Left Montreal 1.30 P.M.
Slept & played cards on train journey not too trying.
Found Miss Cooper, Miss Tate Mrs Giffin & several more of our
friends to meet us when we arrived in Quebec at 6.30. Decided to
take up our abode with Miss Cooper's party at Dufferin Terrace
House 5 Genevieve Ave. Walked up the many hills & arrived finally
at a high stone house of ancient aspect. Molly [MacDermot] & Gray
& myself share the room with Miss Cooper's party. The room originally must have been either a ballroom or a huge drawing room.
The great mirrors from floor to ceiling in their heavy gilt frames, the
marbel mantels & stuccoed ceiling all speak of a different & older

period of Quebec's history. Everything looks quite cosy & comfortable in the dormitory like arrangements made here for us.[2]

MARCH 7

We had breakfast at 8 AM this morning & have reported for duty at 9.30. Were dismissed by [Matron] Miss [Katherine] M[a]cLatchy, (who seems a very charming woman) within the hour.

Too late for church so Molly & I walked far on Grande Allée & finally went into the Ursuline Convent, where the white-robed nuns never leave the altar deserted. Came back in time for dinner, after which we had music – a young celloist & a lieutenant Creacy Miss Tate at the piano.

Wrote letters afterwards to Granty & Mother. then had tea. Church in the evening.

MARCH 8

Nothing of note has happened today. We ordered our uniforms & coat at Holt & Renfrew's on speculation this afternoon. I wish someone would arrange a new system of political economy in this old world. Molly is mad as a March hare this evening We played Five Hundred & she lost everything in sight.

MARCH 9

Lecture with Miss McLatchy today. She has a sweet face & is most dignified. I am sure we shall like her. Spent the evening with our friends at Mount Carmel St. Under Whitneys management, an impromptu entertainment was produced. We played a few rounds of Bridge.

Martial Law in our house so we must be in early. Miss Cooper is a stern moniter. Granty says as a tonic she has too much iron in her constitution for my especial needs. Granty is right though she little knows the circumstances. Cooper was so rude to me today. I am depressed, yet she is a most excellent woman.[3]

MARCH 10

Typ.[hoid] Vaccine given in PM. – A dear letter from Granty. Great excitement when the first pilgrim returned from the bathroom this morning. A notice posted in that room probably the work of Lieutenant Creacy & his friend the only other boarders on this flat. They evidently have been inconvenienced by our monopoly of bathroom.

NOTICE:
Operation Order No 1
By Capt. X
Co. Barricade No 5
St Genevieve St

Parade	<u>Reference to AM parade</u>
	1. The Commander wishes to call your attention to the fact that abuses have been signaled in connection with morning parades to the bathroom.
Advance Guard	2. In future the AG. i.e. the officers of the Guard Medical Corps will please parade from 6–7 AM
Rear Guard	The Rear Guard, that is to say the shaving party, must parade from 7–7.45.
Flank Guard	These Flank Guards will parade as circumstances permit
Penalties	Any person not obeying these orders will be court-marshalled.
	The minimum penalty will be $100 fine; the maximum two days CB [confined to barracks]

Signed
Adjutant in Charge of 2nd Floor

In evening an indignation meeting held in our room over M.A's appearance in our midst.[4]

MARCH 11

Sore arms this morning.

Wrote letters & posted them before supper. No excitement today. A quiet evening.

I feel more cheerful today but Cooper's uncharitableness is decidedly depressing – & they talk – talk – talk till I am weary

MARCH 12

This afternoon went out for a walk with Mollie in search of Notre Dame Church but could not find it. Went on the Terrace instead. Quebec is beautiful – the view this afternoom from the terrace was wonderful.

MARCH 13

Played Bridge this evening. Miss McLeod & Whitney came over for the game. Whitney and I won.

Great talking all day today in the ward about M.A. A cutting letter in the Quebec Telegraph on the subject.5

MARCH 14

We went to Mrs Ritchies this afternoom to tea (just Molly & I). Mrs Ritchie is rather like Miss Young her baby is a little doll Tonight I went alone to St. Matthews. Walked both ways. Am going to write to Granty.

We sang hymns again today after dinner

MARCH 15

Nothing worthy of note today.

A list at last from England regarding our outfit, read to us by the Matron.

10.30 Such foolish dancing tonight downstairs.

MARCH 16

Played Bridge at Miss McLeod's room. Whitney and I won.

MARCH 17

Molly went to dinner with Martha Allen [Allan] tonight. We changed to afternoon duty today.6

Birthday wishes from home today.

MARCH 18

My birthday. A dear letter with birthday wishes from Granty before breakfast. I went off by myself for a walk this morning to an old church in the lower town (Notre Dame de[s] Victoires) built in 1688 & afterwards for a walk on the terrace. An uneventful afternoon on the ward. Birthday wishes from [brothers] Rob and Reggie in the PM.

MARCH 19
Lecture in P.M.
Gray & Tate went to a room upstairs. It is better so, there are too
many of us here

MARCH 20
I had my second dose of Typhoid Serum & also vaccinated for
Small pox today.
We went to Moving Pictures tonight.
Mrs Hall called today. I was on duty.

MARCH 21
I went to early service this AM.
It snowed during morning so we stayed in our room. I wrote
letters.

MARCH 22
Molly went out to dinner
Nothing else of note today

MARCH 23
Had a long letter from Father today in which he says he spent a
day with [brother] Cyril recently. He thinks Cyril's battalion will
be sailing on the 28th.
Ruth Loggie & I went for a long walk round by the Citidal &
Plains of Abraham to Ursuline Church where we stayed for the
five o'clock Service.7

MARCH 24
Lecture 3 PM.

MARCH 25
Father writes Cyril is in Hospital with mumps & terribly disappointed as he fears his battalion may sail without him.
Also a long letter from Granty telling me her brother Greggie is
very ill. Poor Granty has surely had enough to bear already & is
so dear and good

MARCH 26
Lecture 3 PM.

March 27

Lecture 3 PM.

Third dose of Typhoid Vaccine

March 28

Spent all the afternoon with Mrs Hall. Went to church with Molly in evening. Mrs Hall talked of the babies & Forsythe. She looks remarkably well. Leslie has asked Molly & me for dinner Tuesday Eve.

March 29

Examination today. A long paper. I wrote only fairly well but know I will pass.

March 30

Edith Engelke took snapshots of us in the Operating room this morning.

Went through the Hotel Dieu afterwar[d]s with Miss Gray & Tate to the service in the Ursuline Church at five PM. Molly & I went to dinner to the Halls. Had such a nice evening. Molly thoroughly enjoyed it.

March 31

Tomorrow we leave for Montreal. Am thankful in many ways. Although I have liked Quebec very much & in some ways have enjoyed the month – many things have happened which took the heart out of things. I don't know what is the matter with me but I have wept on several occassions of late. I must be growing thin skinned, or foolish to say the least of it.

Government cheques this afternoon.

Holt Renfrews also for fittings

Tonight Mrs Giffin Molly & Miss Cooper have gone out for supper at the Frontenac so I am alone. By this time tomorrow I will be at home with my dear Granty – one person at least who always wants me & can forgive my foolishnesses.

April 1 – May 5

NO ENTRIES

May 6

We left Montreal at 10.30 AM on the RMS Metagama. Such a wonderful leave taking & so many people on the pier & such beautiful sunshine. The morning on the river was perfect & at night as we neared Quebec the lights of the city & the last lights in the sky made a scene like fairyland.

Bands on deck. Wrote Mother & Granty for post at Quebec.

> I would be true for there are those who trust me
> I would be pure for there are those who care
> I would be strong for there is much to <suffer/conquer
> I would be brave for there is much to dare.
> I would be friend alike to foe to stranger
> I would be giving & forget the gift
> I would be humble, for I know my weakness
> I would look up & love, & laugh & lift.[8]

MAY 7

We have kept near the south shore all day. The weather very fine & warm. We watched the men on the lower deck with much interest. There are twelve hundred of the 21st Battalion and all full of life.

The Hospital (French Canadian) No 4 Stationary Hospital & Queens University No 5 Stationary Hospital are with us. Col Hughes a very nice man apparently Sir Sam's brother – is OC [Officer Commanding] of the 21st.[9]

MAY 8

Dinner parade – 1st No 3. Colonial [Colonel H.S. Birkett] first then officers then sisters – Dress uniform, then other hospitals & units as they pleased

We wakened this morning with no land in sight but soon after breakfast we neared the east coast of Newfoundland.

Inspection at 9.30 on deck.

We are all in uniform.

After rounding Cape Ray we lost sight of land again & only about 5 PM saw Cape Race in the distance. New & stricter rules appear daily.

An operation (appendectomy) this afternoon One of the men of the

21st. Dr. Elder operated. Minnie Engelke is on duty for the night. This morning a mock court martial held by officers of the 21st The Guard for prisoners made up of nurses the crime being rules broken with regard to gambling The prisoner having won $20.00 at Pool. After the usual routine – many funny remarks – the prisoner found guilty & condemned to buy chocolates for nurses with the money. Jones the prisoner very funny & something of an actor.

These men of the 21st seem a splendid all round lot.

MAY 9

Communion Service 6.30 AM

Much colder this morning with small pieces of floating ice. Later in the day many large ice bergs in sight as many as ten at one time two of them within two miles of our ship. Photograph Service at 10.30 AM for the men. Such well trained troops these of the 21st. We sang "O God Our Help in Ages Past & Stand Up for Jesus" & the men sang lustily.

The boat has pitched & rolled all day though the sea is very calm. (Report says because of ground swell in Banks of Newfoundland) So many Storm Petrels about with the ice, such singular birds which half fly and half swim on the surface of the water.

A few faithful Roman Catholics had a song service in the afternoon.

Boat rolling & pitching all day.

Sick tonight

MAY 10

An officer of 21st started drilling sisters in fun but Colonial disapproved – when Sgt Major reported the matter, & sent Col Yates out to stop the performance. After this regular drill by Sgt. Major.

The ship not rolling so much this morning & all ice seems left behind. Saw a large boat on the horizon at 7 AM. Inspection at 9.30. Drill from 9.45-10.30 by Sergeant Major. A passenger ship with French flag passed near us about 10.30 Report says she sent

Aboard the Metagama watching the sports of the men below

messages & tried to find out our identity but the Captain says he
is both deaf & dumb on this trip so our course was changed &
she was soon out of sight.
Sports among men of 21st Batt. Raining heavily towards night
Wind also very strong
Broke crystal of my little watch.

MAY 11

Raining all day today & very windy but ship is remarkably free
from rolling
Bridge tournament tonight.

MAY 12

Very stormy all day – with very heavy seas. Ship rolled & pitched
to great extent. Many very sick people. I spent practically all day
in my raincoat on deck & really enjoyed the wonderful sight –
waves dashing against the boat & the great boat, a toy, pitching
down into the hollows between.
The sea gulls have appeared again today.

When the cabin port holes are dark & green
Because of the seas outside
And the ship goes 'whop' with a wiggle between
And the steward falls into the soup toureen
And the trunks begin to slide
And Nursie lies on the floor in a heap
And Mother says to let her sleep
And you're never waked nor washed nor dressed
Then you may know if you havn't guessed
That its fifty North by forty West.

MAY 13

Rain has stopped but wind still high.
Concert posted for tonight. Sky cleared late in day. Report says
we have gone south into the Bay of Biscay today because we have
not picked up our convoy as we should have done by wireless, &
that we are just marking time outside the danger zone till our
captain is able to communicate with them.

MAY 14

We have seen several ships today on the horizon & in the afternoon several large sail boats quite near.
No land in sight. The sea is very calm today.
About 5.30 PM cruisers appeared at regular intervals on the horizon & later a torpedo boat destroyer came in sight.
With dusk five Destroyers closed in around us. The night has
been wonderful. The water still as a pond & such lovely phospe-
rus lights with the swell of the boat. About 9.30 PM a cruiser in
the distance began to flash signals which lasted about five minutes & the "destroyers" seemed to creep closer. We feel so safe
but if the tale of the Lusitania is true I know how anxious the
dear ones at home are about us. We are surely "in the Hollow of
his hand".[10]

And I smiled to see Gods Greatness
Round about our incompleteness
Round our restlessness his rest.

We will surely come into safe harbour before morning.

MAY 15

At four-twenty AM I was wakened by the fact that the engines had
stopped. I took out my flash light & looked at my watch, then
moved a tiny corner of my port hole covering to find that day
had dawned & that our boat was near shore – a beautiful wooded hill. Dressed quickly & went on deck. Such a beautiful scene.
We were entering Plymouth Sound. The shores on our left hills
& dales, huge old oak trees & beautiful green fields, here &
there old homes among the trees. All knowledge of last night's
darkness & caution gone – beautiful sunshine & our first
glimpse of England.
Such a winding route to our dock through this land locked harbour. Past the Tunisian being loaded with troops for the
Darde[a]nelles: still being towed by our little tug. Quiet waters
once more & dry land at last.[11]
An Admiralty officer came on board soon after breakfast
Lunch on board, then the shrill whistle of the little English
trains summoned us & we were packed on board the special
through train to London. Devonshire the most perfect landscape as a whole that I have ever seen beautiful green green
fields & dark red earth – every square inch apparently under cultivation. Old oaks & copper birch trees distinctive among the
other lovely trees. Ivy covered walls & such well kept villages.
Stopped at Exeter for ten minutes. Seed farms growing most
gorgeous flowers in all colours. Sheep & lambs in the fields: the
hedges the most wonderful of all the sights in this countryside.
Arrived in London 7.30 PM. Miss Cooper Mrs Giffin & I went out
after dinner at the Premier Hotel where we are to stay to see a
little of the London streets near our Hotel.
Col[onel] Elder Major Howard & Capt[ain] Hutchison came to

In Kensington Gardens

London with us. Remainder of our unit & 21st Batt to go to
Shorncliff[e] later on in day
Sent cable home.

MAY 16

Up fairly early & went to ten oclock service at Westminster Abbey.
The Abbey too wonderful for words. Afterwards walked across
Westminster Bridge, to see the Parliament buildings from the
other side. Past St Thomas' Hospital along the Thames embankment & back to the Hotel for lunch by the Underground Railway.
After lunch started out on the top of a bus, past Trafalgar Square
with its lions past the Whitehall Guards, past Westminster Abbey
& the Parliament buildings again & finally to the Marble Arch
entrance to Hyde Park from Hyde Park into Kensington Gardens
which are beautiful; the old trees, the Serpentine, & the chairs
for which one pays a penny. Peter Pan's statue Kensington Palace

Mrs Giffin, Miss Cooper

& on by another gate to see the Albert Memorial. I liked its four
corner's statuary immensely. back into the Gardens for tea under
the trees near a small pavilion where the waiters in their pale
blue coats & white straw hats look very picturesque.
Walked along Rotten Row & up Park Lane to the bus for the
hotel supper. Being too late we could not go to church so Ruth
Loggie & I went on the top of a bus for a long ride (quite two
hours) to Tooting in order to see London by night. The search
lights from the bridge towers at work. The streets look so shiny.
Got back to the Hotel about 10.30. By chance we had been sepa-
rated from the rest of our party.[12]

MAY 17
Sent short notes home
Went out shopping this morning with Mrs Giffin and Miss Cooper
(just to see the shops & streets myself) Oxford St. the Strand,

Regent St. & Old Bond St. Had lunch on Oxford St. & afterwards took the bus for the Tate Gallery. Spent the whole
afternoon there among its wonderful pictures. I liked Millais so
much better that I thought I would. Bought post cards of as
many of the pictures as possible. On arriving at the Hotel found
the order had been given to the effect that 35 of our number
were to leave for France in the morning. Luggage went off at
8 PM. Miss Cooper & I went to see Potash & Pearlmutter at the
Queen Theatre. Very amusing & a very excellent company.
About twelve of our girls are to go to Clievedon[Cliveden]
tomorrow the rest to remain in London till further notice.
Watch mended & money changed.

MAY 18

Raining

Sent cards with new address home

Left the Premier hotel at 7.30 for station for the Folk[e]stone
train. An uneventful journey through the hop districts of Kent.
The hops showing green & three feet from the ground at present. Went on board a small steamer at Folkstone. Captain Wal-
ters appeared unexpectedly to see his fiancé off. It was both
foggy & rainy.. the boat rolled badly, but the passage not rough.
I stayed on deck, we went at full speed. Near the entrance to
Boulogne we passed two hospital ships leaving the port. We were
conveyed by the Ambulance Waggons to our hotel the Hotel
Louvre. Such a funny place. Blue lights in the sitting room
which are ghastly. A wide tiled hall. Close smelling rooms. Curtains of beautiful French embroidery palms & plants in abundance – old tapistry on the walls & no ventilation. We room on
the 4th floor (Ruth Loggie, Louise McGreer, Miss Waters & I)
three windows (which we opened wide on entering) over looking the docks & & square in front of the station, This road is one
continual stream of ambulance wagons with the wounded. In
fact this seems to be to all practical purposes, an English town,
there are so many British soldiers about its streets. The visitors of
the Hotel are practically all English Military. We were very tired

today so are going to bed early. Saw [Frances] Upton. She is at
No 1 Canadian Stationary near No [?] Imperial Stationary

MAY 19

Slept very little as there was such a continual traffic outside &
such a traffic! I watched for hours from the window. British
troops disembarking in the darkness – thousands – forming
fours & marching away in the darkness. – Engines shunting &
apparently whistling signals & the continual stream of ambulances down to the wharf. It is awful. We are only about 37 miles
from the nearest part of the fireing line here & a[t] times &[a]
low distant rumble of the guns can be heard. Went out about the
lower village in the morning & did a little shopping – Tea at No
1 Stationary Hospital Host: Colonel McKee – Walked back from
Wimereau [Wimereux]. Roll call after dinner. Town in darkness
so we all went to bed early.

Mrs Austin & Miss Archibald of McGill arrived at the Hotel on
their way through to Rouen.

A most tangible proof of Molly's desertion today!

Heard that the Strathcona Horse went through to the front a
week ago without their horses.

Majolica is in so many of the shop windows here – called
Boulognaise china.[13]

MAY 20

The same course of events to be seen & heard from our window
last night. I heard the order form fours in a most distinguishable
Canadian accent. I am sure they were Canadian troops last
night. Ruth & I went up to see the old town, battlements &
Cathedral. It is all a wonderful sight. This morning, with the
exception of Miss McLatchey Miss Duncan Miss Parks & Seaborn
Robinson the rest of our McGill sisters arrived on their way to
Rouen. (Saw Dr. Owen in AM. Told him about his young sons)
Miss Mann & Miss Starke of our party sent to a hospital in
Boulogne Went to tea with the Matron of No 1 Stationary in
Nurses Mess tent. Met Col Finlay, Capt Shanks & Capt
Ramsa[e]y Cecily Galt & little Pel[le]tier.[14]

"the large anti room in our Mess tent"

MAY 21

Orders to stay in the Hotel in force all day till 4 PM. when we went out & bought a few things preparatory to our leaving for No 1 General Hospital at Etaples in the AM. Our Matron is to be Matron [Violet E.] Nesbit[t].

MAY 22

Left Boulogne by Ambulances at eleven o'clock. Came at a fairly rapid rate about twenty miles in a southerly direction through picturesque villages & up & down hill on long straight white roads & finally to a very sandy hilly district near Etaples where our tents are pitched No 1 Canadian General Hospital – Nothing is ready yet for work but the actual tents – After lunch which we brought with us from Boulogne we arranged our sleeping tents & the large anti room in our Mess tent. Our tents are very comfortable Ruth & I are together in one of the larger ones.

After supper went for a long walk by the river shore to outskirts
of Etaples. A wind tonight has made it quite cool again though
the day has been hot.

Soon after taking possession of our tent saw young Dixon of the
Royal Bank Shubenacadie cutting grass outside. A great surprise
as I did not know he had enlisted. Dr McKenzie Forbes, Robson
Kenneth Cameron here to welcome us[15]

A small grove of pine trees forms the only shelter near our
encampment – Otherwise old sea bottom

MAY 23

Did not sleep very well on account of the wind which at times
threatened to blow everything in the hut away as we had the
ends open. The larks wakened us in the morning. Such wonderful little birds. A beautiful day. Military Service at 10.30 – no
Church of England Chaplain – After dinner wrote – A few of the
officers came into tea. After supper we went for a long walk up
among the sand dunes: they are very interesting but frightfully
barren. – A comprehensive view of the river & sea beyond from
the topmost hill. Saw [Dr] Earnest MacDermot & gave him the
snaps I had of his Mother & the girls

MAY 24

Walked to Paris Plage in the morning. A very isolated spot. The
walk near the town very beautiful. Several Hotels on the way
have been converted into red cross hospitals. The town itself a
summer resort with a beautiful beach. The whole town is new &
not like Etaples through which we passed on our way out In the
latter place there is a very old church into which we looked (but
I hope to explore that more carefully later) & the houses are old
& very quaint but from all appearances very dirty also. We saw a
funeral procession wending its way to the church here. Quite a
different procession to one we would see at home.

Came home by Motor quite hot & tired. It must have been a
four mile walk & it is very hot today.

Several of the sisters have been allotted to wards & are busy
unpacking equipment. We made dressings this afternoon. After

supper we went for a long walk among the dunes nearest the shore – small oasis at intervals in which we found forgetmenots & a wild flox also the small pink daisies. Nettles grow in abundance in this district. – We saw an aeroplane to the northwest.

We heard a cuckoo tonight & the other birds in these few low bushes have such sweet clear notes. A dear little brook flows through this park

MAY 25

Walked to Etaples this morning with Ruth – made a few purchases in the village, tacks, creton, water jug etc – then went on to see the church. It is most interesting. Built in 1004 by the English – Visited by Charles VIII & Henry VII also Napoleon I on different occasions. Its history written up on a tablet inside – the wood carving above the altar & on some of the Confessionals is very beautiful. Very old paintings some remarkably fine especially one of Christ & St Peter on the sea. Some old legends of Miracles illustrated & explained – The same style of chairs for kneeling on which we saw in Boulogne. Walked home by the River shore & discovered the three graves among the sand dunes. [Marginal Notation:] 1st graves at Etaples Soldiers' Cemetry. Made dressings after dinner & made beds in one of the wards after supper till dark. The building & tent pitching is progressing rapidly.

MAY 26

Five of our number including Pearl Babbit went to the "Duchess of Westminster's Hospital" near Paris Plage today to help out there till the end of the week.

The Queen's nurses arrived today, hot & dusty. Their Matron Douglas is with them.

I was informed this morning I am to have charge of Ward N. but it is not ready for occupation so I worked at the Surgical supplies all morning & made beds in one of the other wards in the afternoon.

It is very cold today & such a change from yesterday's intense heat is felt greatly by all the workers in the camp.

After supper walked out the Lower Boulogne Road with Louise MacGreer to see the sunset. The sunsets are gorgeous every night. Tonight it went down in the shape of a Japanese Lantern. Last night it looked like a huge teacup. & in the east there has been a full moon to add to the glory of the evening.

Ruth & I got tea for the family today. Each day two of our nurses are detailed for this duty to spare the batmen the extra work.

MAY 27

The usual routine of Surgical Supplies & bed making for me today as my ward is not ready yet.

After supper Ruth & I walked out the Upper Boulogne Road to which we came after exploring a Pine Ridge just beyond our encampment to the North. After walking some distance on this road we went south again through a pretty woods of pines & hawthorn with a few elms at intervals & came suddenly upon open fields beyond which was a huge Mansion evidently modern & apparently uninhabited at present. In the fields, without exaggeration hundreds of Bunnies turned up their heels & ran at our approach. We crossed the fields near the house & saw three children playing on one side (probably the children of a keeper). Beyond the house were other barren fields also literally full of Rabbits. & then we came once more to these relentless Sand Dunes (the higher hills) which lie on the North West of our encampment. In many ways these sand dunes give the impression of cruelty & power like the sea, & it would be so easy to lose one's way among them – there is such a monotony of outline about them. But they are fascinating to me. Ruth says she is afraid of them & always wants to get out of them as quickly as possible.

MAY 28

Rations are scarce & very unappeticing.

Made surgical supplies & beds all day. Our work is progressing but it is so enormous that a days work does not show for much. We have about 400 beds ready now.

Went through an Ambulance train on the siding after supper. It

In the sand dunes

is well equipped & very comfortable. So many trains of the kind go through in a day. Later in the evening went for a walk with Ruth, DeCou & Ross around by No 18 General Hospital. Played a game of Double Canfield before going to bed.

It is frightfully cold tonight.

A letter from Granty came this morning & it was oh so welcome the first news from my dear ones at home.

MAY 29

Made beds & surgical supplies all day. Went for a long walk with Ruth out in the upper Boulogne Road. This road is very pretty & the fields around show more sign of cultivation than anything I have seen amid these sand dunes. Passed the drive to the Mansion that we saw two nights ago.

John James Ower came over from La[Le] Touquet today & called me from work during the morning for a conversation on

the one subject of importance – "the twins". [Marginal notation:] His newborn babies at home

MAY 30

Spent morning Bed making in Ward L. A beautiful sunshiny day
but still cold. Off duty in afternoon. Tidied my posessions &
wrote letters.

A "Standard" from Granty came this morning.

Service at 10 AM. in an empty tent. Five letters after supper, one
from Father, one from Rob one from Daisy B. & two from
Granty dated May 11th & May 13 & 14th.

MAY 31

Walked to Paris Plage after tea. Purchased two handkerchiefs
(French embroidery) & two small bits of china – one little
Copenhagen vase. Had supper at "Le Chat Bleu. Walked home.
When we arrived went on duty & received Fifty one patients,
some badly, some only slightly wounded. Only two or three
Canadians among them.

The prevalence of Majolica called Boulognaise china as decoration for shop windows is a very distinctive feature of both Etaples
& Paris Plage shops.

Our work has really progressed speadily. There is wonderful
management & system somewhere at the head of things & it is
certainly not the OC. I think the NCOs [non-commissioned
officers] & most of the men here are splendid.

JUNE 1

Troops go through on the trains (& such long trains) almost
daily, with guns & gun carriages in sight. When we are able we
always wave strenously & they also. They seem so happy & full of
life. Poor lads. There is a difference when they come back on
the Ambulance trains: then it is usually night & they are silent
& we are too.

JUNE 2

Supplies in AM. My ward is not ready yet.

We were asked to tea at No 2 Stationary Hospital at La Touquet
this afternoon. Walked the four miles in the heat & came back

in the Ambulance. Saw several caravaners & their families as we walked. The Boulevard of Etaples is very picturesque & interesting. With its village pump, its small court yards full of chickens & dirty children, Its sail boats at rest on the beach waiting for the next tide – & its big Cross & figures. For unsanitary conditions it is equalled only by other streets of Etaples.

In the evening Louise MacGreer & Ruth & I sat out on the sands near the shore till dark.

Played Double Canfield for a little while.

JUNE 3

Letter to Mother.

Supplies in AM.

Half Day off in PM.

Letter from [brother]Gerald written May 30th. He has been in the trenches but is unharmed & very well.

Such a long Canadian Casualty list today. Several Strathcona Horse officers among the number.

Finished a letter to Mother & sent it with a handkerchief French Embroidary one also to Mrs Laughton.

Walked in to Etaples this evening to get cigarettes for Gerald. The children followed us all the way in begging for pennies Gathered beautiful scarlet poppies in the field on our way. The few fields now in the neighbourhood are wonderful with their light new green covering literally glowing with scarlet blossoms. Our bathtubs ready for use today. Had my first bath in France & bubbled over with excitement. Result got in with my watch on. Water is as hard as a rock but that is a minor detail.

JUNE 4

At 10 PM. a few of us were called to augment the night staff as an Ambulance train was expected. The patients did not come till 2.30 AM. 88 in all. Poor lads. & so uncomplaining.

JUNE 5

Slept all day.

Several of the Toronto University Hospital arrived here today accompanied by their Matron.

In the poppy fields

JUNE 6
   Slept in & had a little breakfast in our tent with Ruth & Lilly Gray. On duty in P.M. A sacred concert at 7.30 & hymn singing in our Assembly tent with the men & patients able to come. Officers particularly requested not to attend.
   An Ambulance train arrived about 9 PM. 118 patients admitted. The others went on to No 18.

"Rank & File"
O Undistinguished Dead!
Whom the bent covers, on the rock strewn steep
Shows to the stars, for you I mourn I weep
O Undistinguished Dead.
None knows your name.
Blackened & blurred in the wild battle's brunt

Hotly you fell – with all your wounds in front: –
This is your fame!

Austin Dolson

JUNE 7

Some of these new patients have dreadful dreadful wounds. One
young boy with part of his face shot away both arms gone &
great wounds in both legs. Surely Death were merciful. Many
head cases which are heartbreaking, & many many others. The
men are all so good & patient. & so grateful for even the small-
est attention. These are the horrors of war. but they are too horrible. Can it be God's will or only man's devilishness. It is too
awful. Our boy with both his arms gone is only twenty years old.
Two dear letters tonight from Granty – & one from Miss Davidson & one from Edith Goossens. Also Montreal papers. Took
them down on the shore to read them. This is Dorothy's
birthday & I have not written her. She has been in my thoughts
all day.

JUNE 8

Sent Letters to Granty & to Gerald.

Very hot.

Saw an aeroplane in the distance this morning

The management in this Hospital is an abomination. Everyone is
disgusted with it. [Marginal – later notation:] Something has
changed

Had my half day today.

Great heat this morning & a thunder storm with rain in the
afternoon.

An Ambulance train came in at 9 PM. I went to Ward K to
receive patients there as the [my] ward had not yet received
patients. Came off duty at 3 AM when the regular night nurse
came on.

Earlier in the evening Miss Hoerner & I had a long conversation
with three patients nice Englishmen who had walked over to our
hill to see the sun set. One young lad of 1st London Reg[iment]
a stretcher bearer told us very interesting tale of life in the

trenches & also of the camp in this place to which he had been sent here on our site in January when they were sent on from the camp in Malta. He also let me read parts of his diary.[16]

JUNE 9

Slept in this morning till 9 AM.

Trotted around with Miss Hoerner most of morning trying to make arrangements for serving tea & biscuits for sisters second breakfast. No results, as all the usual stupidity connected with giving out supplies prevails. I have been spared a great deal of these annoyances as my ward is not yet ready for furnishings & I have been going about from ward to ward when needed with no actual worries of responsibility & only the supply room stock to look after at other times. But the management here is a fearful & wonderful thing. The OC is a doting old idiot & the Matron is surely mentally unbalanced. The good men are disgusted & the poor men are lazy & won't do their work. Some of the notices signed by the Matron & appearing in our Assembly tent are supposed, by their origination to be clever, but in the opinion of most of the McGill sisters are nothing more or less than impertinent foolishness. I have copied some of them.

I walked to Etaples with Annette Tate this evening. Bought flowers in an old French garden for a Nova Scotia boy in the ward & some cakes & other dainties for Dixon. The little French lady of the garden behind the shop with the green vases, tells us her husband is a prisoner in Germany She dresses in black & has such a sweet face

JUNE 10

Another convoy of patients came in last night so I was wakened at 11.30 sent to Ward "L" & did not get back to my tent till after 3 AM. Slept this morning & worked at supplies this afternoon. Saw an aeroplane quite near today but very high above our heads. It circled around near our camp then disappeared to the North west. We now make supplies in one of the tents far up in the field of poppies & the view is most beautiful. In front of us the field glowing with scarlet & beyond the sand dunes & higher sand hills, with their white sand shining in places where the sun falls & dark & barren looking in the shadows.

Walked with Ruth to Paris Plage this evening. It is 5 miles. Bought a beautiful (Flanders lace) tea cloth for Mother & two small pieces of French embroidary. The patterns of lace here are called Dentelle & Fuseaux Flanders patterns The lace shop people tell me there are about 20 to 40 patterns of the Dentelle & 400 Fuseaux. Had supper at "Le Chat Bleu" Found a note from Gerald on my return. He is well but expects soon to go back to the trenches. It is dated the 7th.

JUNE 11

Worked at supplies all day.

Went for a long walk North East over the dunes with Ruth tonight. Such a strenuous walk, but such a wonderful country. Unexpected signs of vegitation are continually surprising us with their presence on these walks among the dunes. We crossed the Upper Boulogne Road (built by the Romans BC) tonight & went up into the dunes beyond. The Rabbits at dusk running in hundreds from us as we approach.

A letter from Father saying that Cyril left on May 20th by the Saxonia Mosher, also (as supernumery lieutenant) for England.

JUNE 12

I found three interesting Canadians in Ward L tonight. Lent them my Kipling & gave them my Montreal papers. One of them a Montreal man Dahlman of Goodwin's (small ware) under the dock he said.

Walked out Lower Boulogne Road with Ruth till dark.

From what I can gather from conversations with different men who have come from the district the Strathconas have been in the trenches at Festubert about a mile to the North west of La Basée [La Bassée][17]

Mrs Giffin went to Boulogne today on an ambulance. so I sent a cable home to Mother with her kind help.

JUNE 13

A note from Gerald today saying he is once more out of the
trenches for a rest & is well. After supper Ruth & I went for a
long walk. We crossed the Upper Boulogne Road & went far
back into a farming country on the hills – quite different from
the dunes. Large properties, lovely hedges & trees & many
horses (all white) with foals feeding in the fields Picked lovely
dark dark red clover, about three times the size of our clover at
home: the blossom long in shape. French boys as usual begging
for pennies. We returned home by same route, down terraced
hills to Boulogne Road, then through the pine wood by an old
road & back to camp through the dunes at dusk. Rabbits scut-
tling away from us as we walked

JUNE 14

Wrote Cyril & sent book to Gerald
Had my half day & went to Paris Plage with Mrs Giffin Miss Gray
Louise McGreer Hallie Carmen & Watters. From there went in
the motor to Montreuil. Such beautiful roads through a farming
country & along the banks of the River Canche. Passed Chateau
de la Calotterie, surrounded by beautiful woods – (swans in the
river here) then on through picturesque little red roofed villages
along the winding white road till we came in sight of the old
walled town standing high on the hills with green sward stretch-
ing from its walls down to the river. The town is quaint & has a
history of having withstood many a siege in the old days. Its walls
now are ivy grown & crumbling in parts. We went to see the old
L'Eglise Saint Saulve which has a wonderful entrance
& is fascinating, then across the square, went into the chapel of
Hotel Dieu also with a beautiful entrance (carved figures, fewer
in number than at St Saulve and inside most wonderful of all –
the wood carving. Dark wood panals (figures) & the pulpit a
marvelous piece of work. A huge painting of the Descent from
the Cross on one side. Bought postcards. Saw a number of Hindous from Hindou Hospital.[18] Back to Paris Plage. Supper "Chat
Bleu" Bought little silver box with Reproduction of Leonardi di

Vinci's "Prodigal's Return" on cover. Back to camp. Sat on sand on shore till dark. Such a nice day.

JUNE 15

Found out that Miss Hoerner is Mrs J McKay's niece
An Ambulance train came in at 5.30 PM. We received about 80 patients. In the evening Miss Hoerner & I went for a long walk to the North over the sand dunes. The dunes are ever revealing new & distinctive attributes & are always surprising me. We walked home by the Upper Boulogne Road.
A letter from Granty dated May 25th

"I & you"
Knowing you love me
I can do
All that we dream of
I & you.

Knowing you love me
I can go
Singing to trials
I do not know.

Knowing you love me
I can be
All that you wish
And hope for me.

Mary C. Davies

[Marginal notation:] Send this to Laurie[19]

JUNE 16

Letters to Granty & Father.
A letter today from Montreal dated June 4th An ambulance train came in at 7.30 tonight. Only 50 patients came to us.
Capt Johnson has been singing for us lately. He has a wonderful voice.

To love someone more dearly every day
To help a wondering child to find his way
To ponder o'er a noble thought & pray
And smile when evening falls.
This is my task.
To follow truth as blind men long for light
To do my best from dawn of day till night
To keep my heart fit for His Holy Sight
And answer when He calls.
This is my task.

Maude Louise Ray

Dusk & the shadows falling
O'er land & sea
Somewhere a voice is calling
Calling for me.
Night & the Stars are gleaming
Tender & true
Dearest my heart is dreaming
Dreaming of you.[20]

JUNE 17

Walked to Paris Plage with Mrs Giffin after tea.

A convoy of 180 patients came in tonight. Very few Canadians.
Letter from Cyril tonight. He is in England at Sandling Camp.
He had not had my letter as his is dated 9th of June. He thinks I
am in England & hopes to see me. He is a dear boy His letter
says "I suppose you are a lieutenant & a private is not allowed to
speak to you but when I see you I guess I will take a chance on
it" He evidently loves beautiful England. & their entrance into
Plymouth Harbour after a dangerous voyage made a great
impression on him apparently as it did on me.

We have received over 800 patients here in the last two weeks
& we are only a tiny part of this great sea of hospital tents.

JUNE 18

Walked with Ruth after supper three miles on lower Boulogne Road to Camiers where it is rumoured our hospital (McGill) is to be situated. Camiers is a most picturesque little village & not nearly so dirty as Etaples. I will probably know more of it later.

JUNE 19

Heard today that Colonel Birkett & his party have arrived at Camiers.

A convoy of patients arrived this morning. some terrible cases, oh so much better dead (one young lad with eyes & nose all gone – one blur of mangled flesh – & body whole & sound.) heads shattered to pieces or limbs hanging by a thread of tendons. Oh why must such things be All are so brave, & yet those who are not badly wounded are so tired of the war, at least those who have been long in the trenches – tired in such a hopeless way.

[Marginal later notation:] No steel helmets at this time

I lay me down to sleep
With little thought or care
Whether the waking finds me
Here or there.

A bowing burdened head
That only asks to rest
Unquestioning, upon
A loving breast.

My good right hand forgets
Its cunning now
To march the weary march
I know not how.

I am not bold or brave
All that is past
I am ready not to do
At last, at last.[21]

JUNE 20

Letter & lace to Maam –

Walked today in afternoon hours off, by upper Boulogne Road
west & south to Camiers (about seven miles I should think) with
Ruth & Jessie Sedgewick – through beautiful & very extensive
farming country, along the hard white road which winds, around
& in & out on the sides of the hills. Finally got a jug of sour
French wine at a farm house & ate our tea on the top of the
chalk cliff above Camiers. These farm buildings along the road
are most picturesque – (& most unsanitary) built either with
mud walls or stone walls the buildings enclose a court yard –
each with its own pond of stagnant water – inhabited by pigs (all
sizes) hens dogs horses ducks & children. Over the arched gate-
ways ivy or climbing roses grow luxuriantly & white thorn trees
blossom in many cases in a hedge screening the whole from the
highways. After careful search we at last discover which part of
the line of buildings is the house. It usually has beautiful Flanders lace edged curtains in the windows otherwise there is little
difference in its outward appearance, to the buildings occupied
by the animals. The view of the village of Camiers from the chalk
cliff above is a delightful one. We started on our way home only
to be overtaken by Col Birkett & Col Yates & Major Archibald in
the ambulance on their way to No 1 for dinner. They were very
pleased apparently to see us, so we rode back to Camp.

JUNE 21

Went tonight to the rose garden in Etaples. Such a dear is our
little lady of the Garden with such a sweet face & such pretty
manners I could talk to her for hours, she is so patient with my
French. The roses are still beautiful & the garden will have many
wonders to show before the summer is over. Tonight there is an

abundance of pansies & sweet peas, also zinnias & Delphenias & Canterbury Bells. [Marginal notation:] The Campanula Les roses noires

Ruth came with me & loved the Rabbits (there are about 12 large ones & a Belgian Hare with little ones) & the flight of stone steps (ivy covered) to the roof. She also loved the green vases. I wish I could get a large one to send home but they are too cumbersome, but so pretty & artistic.

Discovered my flash light battery is worn out, tonight. I have used it continually & it has lasted well. Thanks to my dear Granty's thoughtfulness, I have two extra refills by post.

JUNE 22

A letter from Granty written June 9th

> Hart[d]elot Castle Built 811 AD Restored in
> 1223 by Philippe le Hurepel, Count of Boulogne.
> Inhabited by Henry VIII of England in 1688.

Such a nice day.

In the morning I helped with the dressings in Ward Q. In the pm (Ruth & I had our half day off) we went to Paris Plage on the car, had our hair washed & engaged the Gray Motor to go to Hartelot Castle. Such a pretty drive through Camiers Dannes, Neuve Cha-tel[Neufchâtel] & Hartelot village to arrive at the Castle Gates. The Lodge is a pretty little old stone cottage with the usual court-yard wall over which the roses climb & its pretty garden filled with a profusion of bright blossoms of all kinds. At the top of the drive we come to the entrance gate which in ancient times was also the main gate of the Castle, possessing its draw bridge & port cullis. These have long since disappeared, the gate is covered with ivy & the moat is filled in. Inside the gate is the little enclo-sure in the wall which formed the guards room in the olden days & in which through several apertures, he was able to command the entrance to this sronghold of an ancient family. Next we ascended old stone stairs, ivy grown to the top of the wall built in 811 A.D. which at a certain later date has been reinforced by five towers, four only of which remain. Here a shiny leafed ivy falls over the parapets in abundance & creeps along the top of the wall. Some of the watch towers on the walls are in ruin. After walking some distance on the wall & enjoying the view of the river & Hartelow woods below, we came down to the outside of the wall to see the old ivy trunks grown through the centuries to the size of a mans arm & also grown into the wall. After walking around the back of the Castle we came to the dungeons which were used in more recent years by Napoleon I for his prisoners. We explored the dungeons, then returned by the front of the castle to another incline of steps to another part of the wall, where the view is very lovely.

The Castle itself, built on the ancient foundations at a much later date we were not able to see as it is being prepared as a hospital, by some English Duchess.

Stopped at Vetenary Hospital on the way home.

JUNE 23

Walked to Paris Plage & La Touquet with Hallie Carman after hours Called at the Hospital first to see her cousin Stewart Molson then went on to the town.

Bought little silver Box with Teniers "Kermess" engraved on top. for Granty.

The Campanula growing in all the gardens at present is wonderful. Such lovely pale shades of pink & blue The little French children are selling them on the road & we have huge bunches in our mess tent & the wards.

We gave pennies to two such beautiful urchins in Paris Plage this afternoon. Little boys ragged & dirty but not a bit bold. They all think we are made of money, a fact due to the prevalance of brass buttons on our uniforms.

JUNE 24

Saw a photograph of the Matron today. – A unique & wonderful occasion – Also had several bouquets from her. She is certainly a most singular woman. "A wee bittie daft" as Mrs Cantlie would say.

After supper Ruth & I went down to the cemetary. Such a pathetic row of small double crosses – one or two Canadians among them. Everything is arranged with decency & in order – the mounds of the white sand marked with a cross of the small yellow "Everlasting" blossoms of the country around.

Two dear letters from Granty tonight one registered on the 6th & the other written of the 11th.

Sent seeds to [brother] Athel & cards to [brother] Reg tonight.

JUNE 25

Went to Etaples after supper with Ruth. Went to the 8 o'clock service in the old church. The white caps of the old women & the sweetness of some of the little children appealed to me. Two little ragged girls brought us small bunches of crushed flowers on that dirtiest of all streets leading to the tower. Poor lambs! Some of them have wonderful little faces. Read all the way home by the shore "Peeps into Picardy"[22]

The daylight lasts here till after nine oclock. It is a wonderful climate. The air is so clear & though some days may be frightfully hot, the evenings are always cool. We have only had two or three days of rain since we have been here altogether.

Started furnishing Ward N today. It has been so long in getting ready that I had almost despaired of it's ever being completed.

JUNE 26

We went to Paris Plage today after tea, got my boots which were being half soled – also a little silver box for Granty's rings.

Arrived in camp at 8 PM just in time for the Concert given by an English entertainer who was very good indeed. All patients able to walk were present & a few who were able to be carried on stretchers to our Mess tent where the concert was held

A letter dated May 30th from Father tonight.

JUNE 27

Let[ter] to G. with Hartelot snaps & cards

Spent my hours off on sands by the shore. A quiet day.

JUNE 28

Wrote Mother

Worked on Ward N furnishing all day. The Wards are gradually emptying. Evacuating to England daily & no Convoy from the front recently. The Motor bycicle dispatch riders interest me – they have such intent earnest faces as they fly past on the bycicles & their pockets & pack are so bulky with papers.

It has been rainy all day & is very cold tonight. About 9 PM Ruth & I had a race among the dunes on the shore to get warm before going to bed.

JUNE 29

My furnishing of Ward N is practically finished. I have worked all alone with the help of Lake the orderly & I could receive patients now at a moment's notice.

There was a convoy of 81 patients came to us last night before twelve & afterward an Army Service Corps unloaded all night long & far into the day Although I was in bed shortly after twelve I could not sleep & could interpret every sound of the unloading. Finally a pair of horse got stuck in the sand & it took hours to get out. I keep wondering where Gerald is. Had a long talk with Dixon today –. This afternoon the Princess Victoria Party gave a concert for the patients. After supper Miss Bliss & I walked into Etaples to the rose garden & our little French lady. She was sweet as always.

A letter from Father tonight. He says [brother] Blanchard is eager to enlist. I hope & pray they will not allow it.

Did not sleep all last night

My lungs are full of sand.

JUNE 30

Went to Etaples with Miss Hoerner in the evening. We stayed to the evening service. Then had strawberries & coffee at Ioos – the Artists' Hotel. The dining Room walls covered with paintings the pay which poor artists have left behind to recompense the proprieter for the services he has given them.

Another convoy last night of 130 patients

JULY 1

Half day off duty. Mrs Giffin Ruth & I went to Boulogne by the
2 PM train & returned by the 8.30 PM. Bought a little ivory
St. Anthony
Another
Another interesting day. Boulogne seemed quite different
& much gayer than when we were last there

JULY 2

L to G with Etaples cards
A convoy again last night

JULY 3

A big Convoy came last night I got twenty-five patients, all
surgical – Some bad hand & arm cases.
Only one Canadian

JULY 4

Fairly busy as I am alone on the ward & have only the one orderly. Three cases went for operation this morning.
Ruth was sick all night & is not on duty today. I was tired so went
to bed in my hours off. Went down on the shore with Ruth to
see the sunset Read aloud "The Long land [road?] that had no
turning"
Capt Mallone was here to tea & played for about an hour. He
plays beautifully[23]

JULY 5

Ruth is going on night duty. I am sorry. Am all alone in my hut
tonight.
Must write some letters. Miss Mobray went M to the Clearing
hospital at Aire today
A convoy at 6 PM.

JULY 6

I got fifteen new patients last night & sent out twelve of my old
ones today to the Hospital ship & home to England.
Such a storm of rain & wind today & tonight, my hut is swaying
& creaking. I should not be surprised to waken up under the
ruins in the AM.

Clare Gass, nurses' quarters, Etaples

Letters from Granty.

I shall never forget the sound of the Motor Ambulances as they bring in the Convoys The continual burr as they pass our huts, as one follows the other from the siding up to the highway, some slower than others according to the severity of the wounds of the patients they carry. Sometimes they seem to continue all night long. & when I waken with them I cannot go to sleep for hours listening & thinking what it all means & of the condition of these poor lads, tired in body & spirit, sick of the war, sick of France, aching for their homes & their dear ones. As Whalen with only a slight wound told me, "If I could only see the Missus & the children I could go back satisfied". He has six children – so I spoke to Capt Creighton & Whalen went home to England with his pin prick of a wound!

JULY 7

I miss Ruth in the evenings.
Went to bed early tonight & wrote Granty in bed.

The Winds
By the mother of a Midshipman
She of her want did cast in all she had.

"Oh! winds who seek, & seek the whole world over
Changing from South to North from heat to cold
Many & strange the things that you discover
Changing from West to East from new to old.

Seek out & say, My sailor is he living?
Oh! foolish Mother dreaming winds would tell!
The winds are deaf with thunder dumb with grieving
Who heeds a boy, when all the world is Hell?

You seek a boy! For all the millions dying
Who drown at sea or landward fighting fall,
The winds have heard the voice of women crying
Where is my love, who dying takes my all?

When kings & captains die the world regrets them;
My boy is proud to serve the self same State,
Proud though he die, & all but I forget him,
I will not grudge him for the cause is great.[24]

JULY 8

Went to bed early again tonight Am very tired at the end of the
day just now. My ward is a busy one just now.

JULY 9

Walked into Etaples to see Mrs Giffin & Miss Gray off in the
train to Boulogne. Then went into the old church for a little
while & walked home by the shore. Just away an hour.

The Exodus across the hill has begun. The Mess tent & Anti tent disappeared from our side this afternoon.

I wonder if we will have to move.

JULY 10

Ruth & I have permission to buy bycicles.

Have been nervous all day. Went to Paris Plage in evening to bargain with a mean Frenchman over bycicles. Miss Christie & Miss Harrington came with me.

Mrs Giffin is coming to sleep in my tent tonight. I am lonely & tired.

JULY 11

Walked into Etaples during my hours off with Jessie Sedgewick.

Slept after dinner: then went on duty. My ward is lighter today.

JULY 12

Went with Ruth to Paris Plage & rode our bycicles home. A letter from Gerald tonight dated July 9th. Moved over the hill today to a hut with Miss Flint & Mrs Giffin. Ruth is in with the night nurses. Miss Flint is sweet, when we arrived bag & baggage into her tent, she said by way of welcome "This castle is yours & I mean it"

JULY 13

Rode round the beautiful Upper Boulogne Road with Mrs Giffin after supper. Such a lovely landscape on all sides. About halfway to Camier we met on the white winding road, a flock of such docile quiet sheep, driven by a French peasant & his wife. Camiers looked so pretty from the cliff with the sun setting over the sea beyond. We were home at 8.30. Such a nice evening

JULY 14

Beautifully fine this morning & very rainy in the afternoon.

Had such an interesting talk with my men in Ward N this afternoon about conditions in the trenches.

Wrote letters tonight with the music of the rain on the canvas for an accompaniement. There is a most facinating lizard about four inches long who has his home under my end of the hut. I'm very fond of him in the day, but hope he will not grow too friendly at night

JULY 15

Bycicled tonight with Margaret Parks out a country road beyond Etaples & enjoyed the ride

Col Birkett was up to tea this afternoon He has sent for us so we expect to go to Camiers in a few days. Miss Flint is expecting a bunch of "hens & hair pins" to arrive when we leave.

JULY 16

Miss Hartley the Toronto University Matron left today for Shorncliff England to start the work in their hospital there. Violent wind all day with rain storm in pm. The tents rock & sway with the wind & the ropes creak & strain. The day orderlies stayed on the wards tonight & will sleep there in case of an accident, from the wind.

JULY 17

Very windy all day with rain at times. Walked into Etaples with Miss Parks & Jean Bell tonight.

Matron MacLatchey arrived tonight & will proceed to No 3 on Monday. She is if possible more helpless than ever.

JULY 18

Ruth's birthday.

I took morning hours & we bycicled around to Camiers, & back by the Upper Boulogne Road. Such a nice ride through beautiful grain & wheat fields to which the harvest has come. We sat for a long time on the top of our favourite hill (no human being in sight) & feasted our eyes on the glory of sky & earth – the view unspoiled by any human habitation. We had a second breakfast on our return & I gave Ruth the little blue jug vase for a birthday gift.

JULY 19

Miss Flint's hens & hairpins have come. Quite a number of the French Canadians among them. They are the "hairpins" I think I was sent off my ward at 7.30 to pack for No 3. I hated leaving my patients – they are so good – & so sorry apparently to have me go. The orderly "Lake" was almost in tears when I announced the fact. We (18 sisters in all) left in a large motor at

10 AM. Ruth did not come. Col Birkett met us at No 3 & escorted us to our tents which are bell tents & are pitched at the foot of these most beautiful plaster or gypsum hills above Camiers. In the pm I walked back alone to No 1 with messages for the Matron – Came back in an ambulance. Our dinner dishes at No 3 were such a treat – no one but those who have been using the iron spoons & forks & the tin cups & bare oil cloths at No 1 can understand how great a pleasure this dinner was – the clean blue edged dishes – the silver cruets the table linen & specially the smoothness of the spoons. The Durbar tents for the patients are very imposing & I think will prove very convenient. No water at all yet in camp.

Sat with Miss Steele on the hillside for a long time this evening to watch the dying day after the sun had set. Molly came also with us today.

Nurses' quarters, Camiers

JULY 20

Slept well last night alone in my tent – Such wonderful moonlight & such a wonderful skyline. Wakened this morning to the
singing of the larks & the sunlight upon the hills. "Unto the hills
around do I lift up my longing eyes" might have been written in
this place. For on the hillsides are flocks of sheep feeding – also
cows & three white horses, I can see from my tent door. I do
hope we can get to work & will have patients soon. Dickie & Miss
Duncan & the other girls from Cliveden came this pm. Ruth &
Stephie rode over from No 1 & Ruth & I had a ride out to
Dannes & back.

In the evening Dickie & Watters & I went for a long climb to the
top of the hills. to see the sunset A wonderful panorama lay
beneath us.

Came back to camp rather tired & ready for sleep.

The ear wigs – spiders & beetles which frequent our tents are
legion. There are no sand dunes in sight except down by the sea
which is about a mile & a half from us.

JULY 21

Went to No 1 with Dick Mrs Giffin, Sammy & Starke by Ambulance in the AM as we had nothing to do. From there we went to
Etaples (Mrs G & I on the bycicles) where we had a very nice
dinner at Ioos from there in the pm to Paris Plage where the
girls did some shopping. Then back to Camiers in time for supper. Ruth & Stephie joined us in Paris Plage. They are not busy
at No 1. Eight more of our sisters came on today.

Mrs Giffin scraped her cheek on the stones of the bridge as she
passed it in Etaples & when we arrived in Paris Plage we went
into an old Chemists to get some alcohol to wash it off. Such a
nice old bear of a Frenchman. When Mrs G. made a fuss
because the alcohol smarted he treated her as if she were a baby
& when afterwards she would not let him put the plaster on as
he wished, he pretended he would slap her cheek & insisted, so
she gave in. It was all in a kind fatherly way not a bit rude.

JULY 22

Very rainy all day with a high wind. In the pm a party of six walked down to the beach which is about a mile & a half from her[e] & had a delightful bathe. The tide was coming in & the surf fine.

No work yet. I wish things could be hurried up.

Two letters from Granty tonight

JULY 23

This morning Dickie Handcock & I walked to Dannes & into the little church there. A Gallo-Roman font is the only thing of interest in the church – although the church itself is quite old & very quaint. At two p.m. tired hungry & dishevelled our 21 sisters from Rouen turned up unexpectedly. Also Ruth, Stephen[ie] & one other from No 1.

Violet E. Nesbitt was invited for tea & came late but stayed to supper. Also Miss Flint & Marjorie Ross We sent Violet E. the odd Matron from No 1 home in our car. She was tickled pink & most charming. Her rouge also was not quite so pronounced as usual. Ruth & Dickie have the tent next to mine. I am still alone. Letter from Father tonight.

JULY 24

A tiresome day. We went in to Paris Plage to show the Rouen girls the way & to help them with their shopping Ruth & I bycicled & the ride was nice We stopped at No 1 to see our old patients on the way back.

Bought a bathing suit for myself.

JULY 25

L to Gerald   BVG

                              cards

        Cyril   Athel

Such nice church services. Mr Allan P Shatford is a man in earnest & I feel sure he will do good work here.[25] And he is alive which is more than can be said of the Chaplains at No 1 Tonight wc walked through Dannes accompanied by all the

children of the village. I love them & they are so bright & clever
– they marched up & down for us & sang the Marc[s]ellaise"
with such vim, especially the boys, that they looked quite fierce.

JULY 26

We are allotted to wards today I am in charge of Ward F 2 & we
began the furnishing. These big Durbar tents are lovely to look
at I hope they prove as good in rainy & stormy weather.[26] It is so
windy in this part of the country & storms come up so suddenly
that the tents need to be very secure. Last night we went to bed
with a beautiful cloudless moonlit sky & at twelve oclock it was
pouring the heaviest rain I have ever seen & blowing a hurri-
cane; I had to get up & hammer some of the tent pegs in & tie
down my flap securely & of course got my pyjama legs soaking.
No water in camp at all & no hope of getting it soon. We went
down to the sea early this morning for our bath. After tea Ruth &
I bycicled out through Dannes to Neuve Chatel – a pretty village
with several beautiful estates with huge houses near the village

JULY 27

Worked in Ward F most of day.
After tea Ruth & I bycicled up beyond the hills through Widehem & another village Hubersent on to the Samer road then
returned home by Neuve Chatel. This farming country beyond
the hills is now in the full glory of harvest time & the cultivation
is marvellous Such great stretches of wheat & oats. Looking at
this peaceful land it does not seem possible that forty or sixty
miles away the land is blackened by this horrible war fare.
Capt Herringer & Capt. Creighton came up from No 1 this
evening

JULY 28

Ward F furnishing today again
Went with Ruth after supper, bycicling around by the upper
Boulogne Road to Frencq – such a picturesque dirty little
Picardy village with its winding streets running up the sides of
the hills. Came back again by Widehem & down to camp by the
Chalk Cliff just at dusk – the tiny twinkling lights of the camp &

"An exhausted pupil of the art of bycicle riding"
(quotation from album)

the full moon rising over the hills made the place look like fairy
land.

Last Post is just sounding. They are such sad notes, & have such
a lonely sound.

JULY 29

Ruth & I had a half day off so decided to go to Wirwignes to see
the little church, built by the hands of one man, the Curé of the
Parish We went through Neuve Chatel, on to Samer, out through
Wierre aux Bois & Carly: then at the sign post turned into a narrow stony unfrequented road which took us out to the Montreuil
road in sight of the spire of our little church. Nearer the church
on the road side we passed such a curious monument, with a sor-
rowing figure of a woman life sized, in the forground. On the
flat stone an automobile evidently in a wrecked condition. We

were quite puzzled but the lettering on the upper part of the monument told us the whole was in memory of one who had been killed in a motor accident at that part of the road. Our church was even more wonderful than the description in Peeps into Picardy led us to believe. It surely does not carry out all the laws of architecture, but love is the sign that is written all over its workman ship, & the cleverness of the detail & of the whole construction is wonderful. We sat in the church for a long time thinking of the single minded ness & the earnestness of the soul of the builder. As our road to Wirwignes had all been downhill, we decided we must find another way home – the dozen & dozens of white roads are most intricate but the sign post system is so complete & perfect that travelling even for absolute strangers is easy but dusk came upon us before we reached familiar roads so we had a bit of excitement for a time & were tired as we had gone over thirty miles since we started. Finally however we reached familiar ground & came out in the dark on the cliff & crept down to our lines unobserved

JULY 30

I worked all day in the ward. It is almost ready now. Capt Hunt & Theo Lomer came up from No 1 this evening. I have never seen Dr. Lomer look better.

Took my letters up on the hills after supper. A beautiful sunset, but it gets dark soon after eight oclock now. The demon of unrest & loneliness is upon me tonight. We are really not busy enough these days for my good health's sake & the beetles & earwigs in my tent are thicker than is convenient

JULY 31

Rumours of reverses among our troops in France & Belgium. I hope they are not true. It is also said tonight that the Russians have been defeated also.[27] Our camp is growing steadily. The whole encampment from the top of the hill looks like a town with its streets laid out in even rows – a city of tents – Really a wonderful scene. – the buzz from the camp itself: the railway with its shrill whistling trains beyond – beyond that the road with its busy traffic of ambulances & trucks to & from Boulogne then the village with its red roofs then the sand dunes then the sea sparkling in the sunshine. A wonderful never to be forgotten scene.

AUGUST 1

A quiet day.

I spent most of my time off lying on my bed.

Holy Week 1915

On the Rue du Bois   Ypres

By George F. Scott

O pallid Christ, within this broken shrine
Not those torn hands & not that Heart of Thine
Have given the Nations blood to drink like wine
Through weary years, & neath the changing skies
Men turn their backs on those appealing eyes
And scorned as vain Thine awful Sacrifice.
Kings with their armies, children in their play
Have passed unheeding down this shell-ploughed way,
The great world knew not where its true strength lay.
In pomp & luxury, in lust of gold,
In selfish ease, in pleasures manifold
Evil is good, good evil, we were told.
Yet here, where nightly the great flare-lights gleam
And murder stalks triumphant in their beam,
The world has wakened from its empty dream.
At last, O Christ in this strange darkened land,
Where ruined homes lie round on every hand,
Life's deeper truths men come to understand.
For lonely graves along the country side,
Where sleep those brave hearts who for others died
Tell of life's union with the Crucified.
And new light kindles in the mourner's eyes
Like day-dawn breaking through the rifted skies
For Life is born of life's Self sacrifice.[28]

August 2

Princess Victoria Concert party entertained in the YMCA this evening. Such good voices & attractive personalities. A dreadful rainstorm during the performance – such heavy rain that the wooden hut leaked & the rain came pouring in in places & made such a noise that the whole audience were obliged to join in a chorus till the worst was over.

No 1 played base ball with our men this pm. but the rain spoiled the game.

Violet E. Nesbitt came to tea also.

August 3

The YMCA held "Sports" today for the men, the four Hospitals 25 – 20 – & Harvard & McGill taking part. McGill came out far ahead – 93 points as compared with 35 & 8 & 10.

The Princess Victoria concert party entertained again at 6 & the prize giving followed.

The Sea Gulls are all in on the hills today – I wonder if that means a storm out at sea.

Choir practice in the evening during which the rain poured down in torrents.

August 4

An early service this morning the anniversary of the declaration of war.

Today Ruth & I rode around through Frencq, & Etaples to Paris Plage. Ruth bought some pretty lingerie for a wedding present. Stopped at No 1 for a few minutes on the way back to camp.

A service at 6 oclock.

August 5

On duty in AM.

Hon. Sam Hughes & Sir Max Ai[t]ken came to inspect the hospital this afternoon. I was in the ward. Sam held my hand for about five minutes & talked about my family history with all the British aristocrasy of the surrounding Military Base standing around, to say nothing of our own officers. Afterwards he spoke to the sisters again in the Anti tent – which looks so pretty this

afternoon decorated with the season's flowers. the yellows of
August —
Went for a bathe at 4.30 PM.[29]

AUGUST 6

Got up very early this morning to go to Market at Etaples with
Mrs Giffin & Mrs Austin. Too early for market so Mrs Austin & I
went down to the church for a little while to look at its old furnishings. The Market is most facinating. Went into the wine
shop for soda water & saw such a beautiful type of French
woman. Back in camp at 9.30. on duty for rest of morning.
Our ward looks well. We have had the inner curtains put up on
account of the leaking. In the P.M. I went in on the ambulance
to Boulogne to get some things for the Ward. I wish we could
get some patients. It seems so dreadful to be idling when there is
so much to be done, but apparently the ADMS [assistant director medical services] does not want us to get patients till the
water supply is ready.

AUGUST 7

Spent most of the morning putting up the nice golden brown
sateen hanging I got yesterday for the ward. It looks very pretty
against the tan walls of the Durbar tents.
A base ball game between the Harvard Officers & McGill men at
5 PM. McGill winning 6–4. Such a good game. I was sitting
watching the game when a convoy was announced for 8 PM. & I
have been detailed for Night Duty Ruth & Dickie also. We went
on at 7.30 & the wounded began to arrive about 8.15.

AUGUST 8

I slept well today. Got up for church at 6 PM. Went up on the
hills for a short walk with Ruth before going on duty at 8. Such a
beautiful sunset. Capt H C Burgess & Capt Robertson (Miss
Jack's fiancé) are our MO's in Ward F. Capt Robertson is very
nice & I hope H C Burgess will make good – so far he has
worked well. We have heard lately that No 1 Stationary hospital
under Col McKee has gone to the Dardenelles. Miss Upton &
Cecily Galt have gone with them.

AUGUST 9

Did not sleep all day. Was relieved for a couple of hours in the evening to recite at the concert given by No 3 in the YMCA. We are expecting a convoy after midnight.

This morning Ruth & I bycicled down to the shore where a pier & a beautiful modern hotel have been destroyed by the sea. We sat among the ruins for a long time & watched the spray dashing up over the stones of the ruined pier. This hotel had been built among the dunes & was five stories high commanding I am sure a wonderful view. The central part still stands, but the ends are gone. Although it has lain in this condition for two years or more, no attempt has apparently been made to clear up the debris.

AUGUST 10

We had a big convoy of wounded at 12.45. The fighting alone[g] the lines near Ypres has been heavy lately & the men say very successful but so many wounded & such tired men. They are all so pleased to get into bed. [Marginal notation:] These men came from Hooge.[30]

Our Canadian Womens' Comfort bags please to such an extent & they really are very nice.[31]

I slept well today after a dip in the sea when I came off this morning. Frances McKeen & I rode down on the bycicles & were all alone on the beach.

There was another convoy this morning at 9 AM. but our ward only got six cases.

Martha Allen arrived in camp today.

AUGUST 11

Had a delightful ride to Montreuil this morning before we went to bed P Babbit Nell Handcock Miss Steel[e]& myself in the OC's car. Came back by the Berke[Berck] road.

Am glad I am out of the confusion of settling down to routine of the day work. We have too much efficient help in this unit – but things will ajust themselves in time I hope.

August 12

We Miss Steele Ruth & I bycicled by Widehem through Neuve
Chatel & back to our camp this morning before going to bed.
Our lines were so noisy today. I slept only about one hour.
Such internal unrest in our unit at present. – these medical stu-
dents nice boys, as orderlies are a great disappointment. I have
come to the conclusion that there is too much efficency in this
McGill Hospital for practical purposes.

August 13

Miss Steele & I bycicled down to the shore for a bathe before we
went to bed. Three English sisters who went out beyond their
depth gave us a scare.
Martha Allen is doing duty in the Dairy & food distribution tent
work which she will do very well I should think if she is content
to stay there.

August 14

Bycicled into Paris Plage to pay laundry & other bills before we
went to bed. Very windy this morning especially near the shore.
It is not daylight now in the morning till 4 oclock – but the
notes of the first birds are very sweet & the Revaillé [Reveillé] at
6 is such a pretty bugle call – & such a welcome sound for then
we know the long night is nearly over.
It is quite dark now at 8 PM. – there is only a very short twilight.
Most of my patients are now on the road to recovery so I have
no worry at present – These medical student orderlies are a
problem, with no idea of how to accomplish a day of practical
work & of course they want to see everything in the way of dressings & operations no matter what other work lies & waits
Have had no letters since Sunday last.

August 15

Nice church services. I stayed up for the one at 10.30 & got up
in time for one at 6 PM. Sleep so badly in the day, as usual.
Today four of us moved into one of the dark canvas tents (our
little white bell tents are so bright) but it did not help me very
materially.

AUGUST 16

Had a fright at 2.10 this morning when my precious little watch stopped but it started again about six so I came to the conclusion that I must have wound it up too tightly. My patients are being evacuated in threes daily, so my work is diminishing in quantity.

Rode into Paris Plage again this morning to settle her [on?] purchase of a bycicle.

AUGUST 17

Went for a ride around the back road with Ruth & Whitney Such a beautiful summer morning after the bitterly cold night. We ate biscuits & the remains of some candy on the top of our little knoll. Whit loved this our favorite ride

Captain Shatford is sick on Ward E

AUGUST 18

Started for a bathe after breakfast but the clouds opened & torrents of rain came down upon us so we were obliged to turn back.

The seven last sisters came from No 1 yesterday.

Our orderlies seem to be improving. They are beginning to realize – that though a scientific outlook on life may be a necessity yet "the trivial round" (the sweeping of floors, & other household duties & small attentions to patients) is at present more conducive to the happiness of the general public.

AUGUST 19

A convoy again tonight

Broke my spectacles

AUGUST 20

Very disappointed this morning when after being promised the car for an hour or two to run in to Boulogne to have my glasses mended, the OC took it himself into Etaples.

Slept only about one hour today though I went to bed early & tried all day long to settle down to sleeping. Today a spy was arrested in our camp. A French woman apparently selling fruit from a panier (there are several of these women who come daily to the camp) was discovered to have a basket with a false bottom under which two carrier pigeons were concealed. The day has been an exciting one for later tonight about 9.30 a drunk man, one of the RAMC privates was discovered asleep in our sisters lines. Great consternation among the nurses. Capt Dixon went over & sent him away.

AUGUST 21

Bycicled in to Paris Plage with Miss Steele & Miss Brand & left my spectacles with the little old "Antique" man. I don't know what sort of work he may do on them. Had a short walk with Dick & Ruth before going on duty.

Harvard played Base Ball against our men again today — our men won easily.

The war news is not good. The progress is so slow[32]

AUGUST 22

Went out with Dickie & Ruth this AM back on the Upper Boulogne Road. Took some photographs for Mrs Giffin who is going on leave to England tomorrow. Poor Dickie is the funniest thing on the bycicle. She can't ride at all well, but is a brick about learning.

AUGUST 23

A Report today says eleven of the German fleet have been sunken in the Baltic Sea. & the war news from different parts seems good the first good news for many days.[33]

An airoplane flew over our camp this afternoon.

Sound of guns presumably from the sea heard again this morning.

I bycicled down for a bathe before going to bed & slept well afterwards

Boots & veils came from Granty this PM. Magazines also.

A convoy again last night.

AUGUST 24

A big convoy tonight.

Princess Victoria Concert party entertained the men this pm.

Ruth & I rode to Paris Plage this morning but had to leave our

Ruth Loggie

bycicles behind for repair. Came home on the train to Etaples &
were lucky enough to catch the bus to Camier. Otherwise we had
intended to walk.

AUGUST 25

Went for a bathe this morning & slept well today, so well that I
was late tonight for dinner

An uneventful night.

Des Brisay – a fourth year student was operated on today & we
have the care of him in our Ward – He is a regular boy.

AUGUST 26

Walked with Ruth into Etaples this morning. Found there that
the train did not leave for Paris Plage till 11.15 so bought some
fruit & waited. This car ride in through the pine woods is such a
nice one. I always want Granty here to enjoy it with me. – such
sweet scents from the pine & wild flowers. We rode our bycicles

home to camp. Really I know no two other women who have as much endurance as Ruth & I. We both had a fairly busy night & though we did not get home till one oclock we were not nearly so tired as we were really entitled to be.

I slept very badly this afternoon. The day staff was invited to a picnic on the hills by the Harvard people. It was a great success from what I hear.

AUGUST 27

Bycicled down to the beach this morning with Ruth & Dickie for a bathe. The tide very low.

Had a convoy last night. Two nice Canadian lads of the 13th Batt[alion] came to me among others Clifford Johnston & Victor OHara, both from Montreal.

An air ship that looked like a Zeppalin flew over our camp today. We suppose it was a French "dirigible."34

All letters are censored most severely at present in our unit. Tonight after some discussion on the subject a student announced that in tomorrow's orders it would be posted that in future all prayers in this unit must be said aloud so that they might be censored.

These students are a constant source of amusement & are fine fellows but for practical work babes in arms would be just as helpful at present, but of course they will improve.

AUGUST 28

Got up early & watched a base ball game between the officers of our unit & the men. Needless to say the men won.

AUGUST 29

Walked up the hills with Miss Cooper for a little while before coming on duty. Truly this is a peaceful valley & the little valleys running in among the hills are very lovely

AUGUST 30

Ruth brushed my hair this morning while I read sitting in the sunshine at my tent door. then we all went to bed early. We expect a convoy tonight.

Wrote Mother & sent her set of collar & cuffs, French embroidery.

AUGUST 31

Went to the Dentists this AM

At 1.30 AM when I went over to our lines for a few minutes
Martha Allen still up & about with her light on. She is a very
poor influence among some of our girls. Cigarettes – money
bridge & disregard of rules. She is still giving out milk in the
Dairy tent in the day.

A Zeppelin raid scare today but nothing materilized.

SEPTEMBER 1

Another trip to the dentists this morning. He has a well
equipped little tent & is a good conscientious man & is doing
good work here.

Such a storm of wind & rain today from the south – the fulfill-
ment of the early morning sky. Our Night duty tents almost blew
down – none of us slept.

The days are growing so short too it is quite dark at seven
o'clock & the sun does not come up over the hills now until
after five oclock in the mornings.

SEPTEMBER 2

In spite of dark clouds in the South west, Ruth & I went to Paris
Plage this morning. Going through Etaples we saw a quaint picture. A sailor lad evidently returned from a long voyage – the
people called from one house to the other & all rushed out in
the street to greet him. Finally he reached his own door where
an excited group awaited him. He kissed each of the parted
[party?], both men & women in turn on both cheeks – (no
embarrassment no self consciousness, just wholesome affection-
ate natures.) he seized the babies (of which there were several)
& devoured them & threw them up in the air with a shout. Finally these ceremonies over he was finally almost carried into the
house by the little crowd.

The rain started again shortly after we reached our lines.

A letter from Father today saying Blanchard has enlisted in NS
[Nova Scotia] 64 Batt. Highlanders. I am very sorry, the lad
won't be seventeen until Oct 15th[35]

SEPTEMBER 3

Such a down pour of rain all night & very cold & damp. It continued all day with the result that the whole camp ground is very dirty – this clay soil is so sticky & nasty when wet.

Did not sleep today & feel sick tonight from lack of it.

SEPTEMBER 4

It rained torrents, pitch forks & shovel handles all last night & the greater part of the day.

I slept badly.

Rumours afloat that we are to be moved away from our present situation before many weeks.

SEPTEMBER 5

Went this morning through Neuve Chatel & around by the Vetinary Camp to Hardelot Plage. Such a beautiful beach with a pretty boulevard & terrace. An ideal summer resort. Not spoiled by too much pretention –. There is a hospital here for the Hindoos, a couple of houses annexed to the rows of tents. We passed several black faces in the street, they all saluted. Returned past the lake & golf links to the Chateau & home by the Boulogne Road. Past the Head Quarters car & staff as we entered Neuve Chatel.

Went right to bed after we reached camp, but did not sleep well. It has been beautifully fine all day, but cool.

SEPTEMBER 6

This morning Ruth & I rode into Etaples to buy some French bread & pastry & other dainties for the patients. Saw such a funny old donkey with panniers. Halfway to Etaples, there is a new camp established apparently a training camp – there are hundreds of men who when we passed were going through manoevers. Etaples spirits seemed at a low ebb this morning. We passed a funeral in the village & the atmosphere in the cake shop was heavy with trouble. The old man there had been crying & the younger woman usually so bright was very worried.

We gave a little tea in our Anti tent today for Harvard, Hosp (No 22). I did not get up for it.

SEPTEMBER 7

Last night we had a big convoy of patients so my last night of night duty was a busy one. After breakfast Ruth & I started out on our bycicles in the direction of Berke. We passed the Army Service Camp with its long lines of carts. through Cucq & Merlimont until we came to the Guards outside the little town of Berke. This is the Paris road so the guards are very strict but after some persuasion in my bad French they let us pass. We went on then to the road to Rue where another four sentries saluted with great courteousness & let us pass. It was then about 10.30 & we had come 17 kilometres. At eleven we stopped at the turn of the road to Le Temple after coming through Groffliers & Weben, & ate some biscuits & read up the history of Rue in "Peeps into Picardy" After that we crossed the river D'Authie (such a pretty little bridge, then through Quend on to Rue. Such a pretty mill stream at the entrance to the town. We went to a little café for lunch. Had an egg omelet & French rolls & butter & coffee. Such a dear little Refugee boy of ten in the Café. Ruth gave him a button. After lunch we went to a bookshop & got some maps & postcards – then went to see the church & chapel: the chapel is the only remnant of the Cathedral (see P into P) & very wonderful. On our home journey we went to Berke Plage where I bought a little collar for Granty. We reached Camp at 6 PM tired but well content with a lovely day.

SEPTEMBER 8

Sat up on the hills during my hours off today. Intended to write but gossiped & watched the sunset instead. No 18 General Hospital recently moved with a twenty four hours notice to our midst from Etaples where it has been stationed for some time.

SEPTEMBER 9

Matron[-in-Chief Margaret] McDonald[Macdonald] came to our camp today. Also Lady Perry. [36]
Sir William Osler also came all made rounds in Wards & were charmed with everything.[37]
It is a beautiful sunshiny day. Had they visited at midnight on a

Heading for a sea bathe

cold night conditions would not have appeared so favourable.

SEPTEMBER 10

Went for a bathe during my hours off this p.m. Very windy today. Bridge for officers & sisters of our unit arranged for this evening. Sir William to be there. I played with Capt MacMillan & Col McCrae most of the evening by chance.[38]

SEPTEMBER 11

The day returns & brings us the petty rounds of irritating concerns & duties –

Help us to play the Man – help us to perform them with laughter & kind faces – let cheerfulness abound with industry – Give us to go blithly on our business all this day – bring us to our resting beds, weary & content & undishonoured & grant us in the end the gift of sleep. [Marginal notation:] R.L.S.

Early this morning when I first came back to life & thought,

these words were put into my head, by an unseen power. It is the
pettiness of the individuals in our ward that is wearying unto
death. Surely I can rise above them & not let my real work
deteriorate in consequence. I am so weak & get angry inside
so quickly these days about paltry things. "Help me to play
the Man"!

SEPTEMBER 12

Ruth & I went up over the hills today in our hours off. Such a
pretty walk. From the top of the highest hill, the distance down
into the valley seems immense We came out to a road near
Widehem – The peasants are putting in their crops – & the
sheep grazing on the pasture land.

We have named these hills the Bluebird Hills. They are so happy
& peaceful & their lines so restful. Later we will give each separate hill a name suited to it.[39]

SEPTEMBER 13

Father writes tonight that Blanchard has joined the 64th Batt
Scottish & is in Camp at Sussex N.B. [New Brunswick]. The lad
is too young but it evidently was wisest to let him go as his heart
was set upon it.

SEPTEMBER 14

Had last hours today & rode to Paris Plage with Ruth to pay bycicle rent.

Princess Louise – Duchess of Argyle visited the hospital earlier in
the day & passed us in the Motor as we rode

SEPTEMBER 15

NO ENTRY

SEPTEMBER 16

We have one frightfully sick man today. Sarj Read has developed
Bacilli Aeroq. Caps. in his wound.[40] A convoy of 180 patients last
night. Very foggy all day with the mists rolling in from the sea &
up over the hills. These mists are wonderful to watch they move
so slowly but so decidedly up to the hills. In spite of the damp
Ruth & I decided to go to Desvres as we had our half day, trust-
ing to luck that it would not develope to rain. Had such a nice

ride through Widehem, Halinghen & the Tingry Forest – Samer Wierre aux Bois to Desvres. Such a pretty forest outside Desvres & the Forest of Tingry is lovely. Came back by the road across the hills from Widehem to Dannes just at dusk.

Ruth gave me a vase of the Desvres pottery. Such a quaint old lady with a black Boulonaise bonnet talked to us outside the pottery shop.

SEPTEMBER 17

Poor Read our gas gangrene case died today. Such a fine young man. The wound was a schrapnel one in the buttocks so nothing could have saved him.

I spent practically the whole day with him away from the other patients in the back tent. He was unmarried but leaves a mother in England.

Ruth darned my socks & I read aloud in my hour off.

Col McCrae lectured on Battle of Ypres tonight. I have a bad cold so went to bed early instead of hearing the lecture.[41]

SEPTEMBER 18

News of Miss Geegan's sudden death came tonight in Granty's letter.

SEPTEMBER 19

Things in general are much happier in our ward now. We three foolish women understand one another better.

Went to the early service this morning The church tent looks so well. Mr. Shatford has spared no pains in this setting up of an Altar in the Wilderness – A red cross flag serves as the altar cloth & the hangings are of red, & we got white flowers yesterday for the vases.

SEPTEMBER 20

Queen Amelia of Portugal visited the Hospital today.

SEPTEMBER 21

Surg[eon] General Sir George Markins [Makins] came today & later General Jones visited the Hospital.[42]

SEPTEMBER 22

Ruth & I had our half day today so bycicled into Montreuil. Such

a pretty ride passed the upper courses of the Canche, through
Neuville across the tracks & up the hill to the town: At the crossing we saw a French troop train – the men cheered lustily. We
were hungry but decided to go first to the Hotel Dieu for a bath
– disappointed in that we went to the Hotel de France – my bycicle tire puncturing on the way. We gave it to an automobile
place for repair. The Hotel de France Court yard where we had
our meal is most picturesque with its dormer windows high up
on the older wing & the long French windows opening into the
dining rooms. We were served artichokes in the court yard
where the vines hanging from their trellise over head are turned
quite red & yellow. Afterward we went out on the Ramparts near
the Hindoo hospital – there saw & spoke to several wounded
hindoos – they spoke both French & English: Came down from
Ramparts by another path & went into a shop to buy material for
bed socks for Ruth. Rather unsuccessful purchase. Home by the
hill road, through Me[a]delaine, in time for second dinner.
Episode of the butter at dinner.

SEPTEMBER 23
Rumours of a bombardment of Ostende today from the sea

SEPTEMBER 24
Orders from headquarters to send every patient out of the hospital who can be moved.
Rumours of heavy fighting going on at the front & of great casualty expected.[43]

SEPTEMBER 25
We have only two patients left in our Ward. One MacDermott &
the other will go in the morning.
We heard guns several times this morning – they were probably
from the sea.
Sometimes it is said we can hear the land guns here – but I
would not know the sounds it is so distant

SEPTEMBER 26
In our hours off this afternoon Ruth & I walked in to Dannes.
Went into the Church for a little while, then walked around by

the Mill Stream. Were followed as usual by the children & distributed MacIntosh's toffee among them. Later walked along a pretty bridal path for some distance in the Hardelot direction then came back in time for 2nd dinner. Such a big convoy came in to us & to 25 about ten o'clock. I went with Whitney down near the admission tents in the shade of Ward A to watch the ambulances arrive. – Such a pathetic stream of them, alternating one to us & one to 25. A great many head wounds – three lads died before they reached the wards. All the time the stretchers were passing I watched for my curly headed boy – & all these lads have someone waiting just as anxiously for news of them. It is dreadful.44

Our McGill students worked so well & are so good to the patients. Enough cannot be said in their praise. With one or two exceptions they are behaving splendidly.

Several aeroplanes flew over our camp today.

SEPTEMBER 27

The men who came last night bring confused accounts of the action, but all speak of success around Lille & at hill 60 but each says that the slaughter is terrible. The Germans losing infinitely more men than the Allies.

Rumours of an advance by the French in other districts while German guns are centred on Hooge & the English. Also rumours of Kitchener being in the fighting going on at present. Two "dirigibles" flew over our camp at noon today – going in a North westerly direction.

220 patients came to us last night A great many Gordon Highlanders among them who tell a tale of their regiment being practically wiped out.

The rain has come down in torrents all day today. We are very busy

SEPTEMBER 28

Another big convoy of patients came in last night. Miss Jack went on night duty, so Miss Eastwood & I are alone in the ward.

A great many highlanders came in again last night.

Another rainy day & very cold.

War news from the front very good but the losses are dreadful. – and such terrible wounds. Harold Begbie's talk of wounds as "scratches & pink marks" is a trifle out of place in the face of these shattered limbs & great areas of lacerated flesh.[45] One of our men such a nice lad of 21 has the whole of his lower jaw, tongue included – gone. Another boy next him in almost the same condition. I feed them with a rubber tube. Fortunately they cannot see their disfigurement – & in the ordinary course of events they will get well

A card from Gerald dated 26th saying he is quite well.

SEPTEMBER 29

Another convoy last night again.

The War news is still good but the cost is great.

Still another rainy day. The camp ground is one mass of sticky clayey mud.

One of our head cases, a piece of schrapnel lodged in the brain, has been having convulsions all day.

Miss Duncan & Miss Cotton have left us, Miss Duncan for her old post in the Wilmington Hosp. & Miss Cotton to represent Canada in the Allies Hospital which is being sent to Russia where I believe work of the sort is badly needed. Miss Hoerner is assistant [matron] in Miss Duncan's place.

SEPTEMBER 30

We are very busy in the ward. Such enormous dressings. Capt Burgess sends the patients home to England as soon as they are fit for travelling – but their places are soon filled again.

I am feeling sick – a regular influenza I think. Came off for my half day at noon & went straight to bed & stayed there shivering the rest of the day. Temp 102.

It is still raining

Another convoy of patients last night. Our stretcher bearers are very tired: they have been working night & day lately.

OCTOBER 1

We are very very busy. I cannot get half done of all that should
be done. We are now doing just the necessities & those things
for the comfort of the patients. Sweeping dusting & keeping the
place tidy we are entirely neglecting. I still feel frightfully sick.
Temp 101 tonight but too busy all day to bother with myself.
These lads are so much worse.

A letter from Gerald written on the 28th he says he is going to
try to see Cyril.

I wonder if we will ever see the sun again. Another rainy day
today. I have lived all this last week in rubber apron & old brown
sweater.

OCTOBER 2

Still very busy.

Our patient "Plant" shot in the head seems to be a little better,
but another man Newbury, shot through the lungs is in a very
serious condition

We sent eighteen cases home to England today. Very short
notice, so we had to hustle to get them dressed & ready. I am
still feeling very sick shivery dizzy with pains in every limb. Think
I had better stay in bed in the morning as my temp is still 101.
They will have to send some one else in my place.

OCTOBER 3

Stayed in bed all day today

Everyone is very kind. Temp still over 100 at night. I have had a
regular Grip.

A beautiful sunshiny day all day today.

OCTOBER 4

Another convoy last night. Two lads Miss Eastwood tells me back
cases paralyzed below their arms. Mere lads. One boy of the 25th
Humes from Sydney Mines. I am better today but stayed in bed.

OCTOBER 5

Got up this morning but the Matron would not let me go on duty
till noon. Miss Rodd is on in my place so after tea Miss Eastwood
sent me off again & I went up the hills for a walk with the Matron.

OCTOBER 6

Ruth & I had last hours off today so had a very hurried dinner & went to the Service in the quaint little church in Dannes. Such a pathetic service. the congregation few in number, & women all in black The church only lighted by the candles. It was very dark bycicling back to camp.

We heard today Mrs Jalgard & another nurse who went to the Dardenelles are dead with dysentry, & that Col McKee is very ill. I hope Miss Upton will be alright. She is such a delicate looking girl.

OCTOBER 7

We have sent so many patients home to England that our ward is almost empty again.

Our bad head case Plant went home vastly improved. Also the two boys paralized – but with very little improvement there. Newbury is much better & very happy with us.

Miss Steele & I rode to the beach in our hours off today Part of the trenches taken last week by the British have been recaptured by the Germans: – todays paper says.

OCTOBER 8

Ruth & I went up on the hills in our time off duty. We read Ben Hur. Ruth read while I started Granty's new jacket. Went to the Canteen after four oclock & got some things for the boys. Parcelled them up after dark.

OCTOBER 9

Miss Steele & I went for a short ride through Neuve Chatel in our hours off today. through the pretty lane which runs back of the village to the Station. Went into the church in the village then came back to camp at dusk.

OCTOBER 10

Went to the Early Service this morning. In our hours off Ruth & I walked up on the hills & took "Potash & Perlmutter" with us & sat on the highest peak for a time & read, then moved down near the "shingly bed" out of the draft. It is very windy today. Lorin & Hersey took our bycicles to Hardelot for the afternoon.

Went to the six oclock service.

Heard this morning that part of the trenches occupied by the
2nd Division Canadians have been undermined & blown up
& that a convoy of wounded was brought into Etaples last night.
The attitude of Greece at present & Bulgarias going over to Germany makes things look a bit gloomy – & surely will prolong the
war to a certain extent.

OCTOBER 11

A convoy came in to us last night. Many Canadians & quite a
number of the 25th Batt men. the trenches of B & C company of
the 25th were practically blown to pieces by the mine on Saturday.[46] Two men on A Ward know Cyril but have not seen him
lately. Patrick Brogan in C knows him, & thinks he was not hurt
but does not know for sure.

Todays report says that Col McKee has been invalided home to
England & will not be fit for work for some time so is going
home to Canada.

Thanksgiving Day today.

An early Service this morning. Capt. Shatford lectured on "The
flag" tonight

We were given mattresses today

OCTOBER 12

I did not sleep well on my mattress last night. It was too soft after
nearly three months on the Wolsey Kit.[47] In our hours off today
Ruth & I bycicled to Neuve Chatel – around the village by the
lane back of the large estates there. The leaves have fallen yellow
on the ground & we rode over them. All or nearly all the song
birds have gone now.

Mr Shatford came to us today to say good bye as he leaves
tomorrow to join the 5th Brigade of the 2nd Division. I spoke to
him about Cyril. Mr. Hepburn has come in his place.

No 2 Stationary Hospital, it is reported is to go to Greece in the
near future.

Heard tonight that Lily Carter has come to No 1

OCTOBER 13

Todays report says that No 2 Stationary is to be situated near Boulogne & is not to go to the East.

Miss Eastwood went with the Matron to Boulogne for the two new sisters who are to replace Miss Duncan & Miss Cotton. Edith Stuart & Miss Lamont came.

A foot ball game this PM our men versus the men of No 1, No 1 won.

Captain Tidmarch operated on for appendecitis & admitted to our ward at 9 PM

OCTOBER 14

Ruth & I bycicled in to Boulogne this aftenoon as we had our half days. Did a little shopping & started for camp at 5.15. – A heavy fog settled down before sunset & the road was almost thick darkness before sunset. We rode hard as we wanted to get in for 6.30 dinner – (the distance is over ten miles). I had too many parcels dangling for comfort but we were home in time but very wet our hair & blue dresses very bedraggled. After a hasty hot dinner we undressed for bed, By this time the fog had lifted & the new moon shone out

The ride in the fog was an experience not easily forgotten – the motor lights coming towards us – lighting up the fog but not actually in sight till they were almost upon us, the dark object we passed might be either men horses or trees as far as I with my near sighted eyes could see – my only object being to avoid them. We had bought new bycicle lamps so were safe enough & were only a little more than an hour & a quarter on the road.

OCTOBER 15

A convoy at 8.30 this morning. Heavy fighting at Loos. Only eight patients admitted to Ward F. a couple of bad leg cases among them. Some of them came from the region of La Bassée – where the Germans are keeping the civilian population as a protection although the English have warned all civilians to leave the city the English have been using gas & the objective of this latest struggle is La Bassée.

Letters from the boys tonight acknowledging recent parcels.

OCTOBER 16

I arrived off duty for my hours today to find our lines in an uproar tents being pulled down while sisters sat upon their posessions till they were moved farther up the hill preparatory to building our winter huts on the old site. My tent was moved quickly & I soon had my things in order.

OCTOBER 17

Ruth & I went for a bycicle ride during the morning up over the hills & down a shorter rough road to Frencq. Read Ben Hur for a little while before going on duty.

Our Ward is light again as they have sent many home to England. The two bad leg cases are still with us & are very sick

OCTOBER 18

Rode with Ruth to No 1 after four o'clock, She to see Kerr Loggie who is wounded at St John Ambulance Hospital I to see Lily Carter at No 1. Lily was away from Camp so I had a bath – the first in a tub since I left in July. Princess Victoria Concert party entertained in the YMCA here at 8 PM I went with Miss Bliss & Miss Eastwood

OCTOBER 19

Cyril sent me his watch this morning so I went in to Paris Plage during my hours off to have it mended.

Extract from "McGill Weekly"

Ward Orderly on Guard – "Here comes the Royal Family"
First Sister –   "Away with the coffee & cake"
Charge Sister –   "Good morning Colonel"

At 10.30 AM. if we have time, the staff in the Wards have tinned cafe au lait & Hospital biscuits

OCTOBER 20

This morning they moved our last three patients into Ward G in order to re-pitch our tents one of which the recent winds have damaged.

OCTOBER 21

I go to the front tent of Ward E (which has also been emptied with a contract for making & having sterilized as many dressings & other supplies as possible. Six other workers with me.

OCTOBER 22

We accomplished a great deal in our supply room today. We are quite warm & cosy at our work Miss Duncan sent an oil stove from London which we are using.

OCTOBER 23

Early this morning we heard of the sudden death of one of the Chicago nurses at Etaples – Menengitis – She had been on duty the night before last. Ruth & I bycicled down this afternoon to

Soldiers' cemetery, Etaples

the little cemetary where she was laid. It was such an impressive service, this military funeral. The little cemetary lies in the hollow between two sand dunes, that on the left is covered with pine trees and under the pine trees today there was a wonderful assembly gathered to pay its last token of respect to one whose life, lost for the "cause," had proved "she had done what she could". In the clear cold autumn afternoon the crowd under the trees waited – among them were khaki clad men of our own forces – Etaple fisher men with ruddy faces & red kerchiefs – the white veils of nurses. Etaple peasant women with their babies, blue uniformed patients from the nearby hospitals – Etaple fisher girls & the scarlet trousers & blue coats of the french soldiers.

Soldiers' cemetery, Etaples

When the procession entered the gates the whole earth seemed
still, till the voice of the chaplain broke the silence – the flag
covered carriage was followed by a long procession of nurses
from the different units – also officers – & a company of the
RAMC soldiers of No 23 Hospital, the dead girls own unit. The
last Post sounded & somehere in Indiana a mother probably
& many friends are looking forward to the homecoming of
this girl.

OCTOBER 24

Went to the early service this morning It was bitterly cold & very
windy & the flowers on the altar had blown down during the
night. We rearranged them before the service. Our new chaplain
has a very handsome & a good face – I hope he will be a worker
among the men.

OCTOBER 25

Our work is progressing in the supply room – Very windy & cold
today

OCTOBER 26

All day long a terrific storm of wind & rain put the camp into a
great state of unrest – Many wards proved unsafe & patients had
to be moved – the men being kept busy retieing & fixing those
which were safe – the clay mud is inches deep.– nothing but rubber boots is possible – Last night the rain beat into my tent with
such force that only the part behind the post was dry. I moved
my bed today. – Everything in the camp is sodden with rain – I
hammered for nearly an hour making my tent secure for the
night tonight.
In spite of the rain Miss Glendenning Capt Peary[Pirie] & I went
to the Convalescent Camp for the concert – I recited "The
Revenge"

OCTOBER 27

As Miss Watling got permission for us to have a shopping expedi-
tion to Boulogne today Dickie Ruth, Beatrice Armitage & I started off with her in the 8.30 train – After many troubles about
passes tickets etc. we had a very nice day. I had very little to do

but helped the others. Ruth after much search got woolen underwear (of a sort) & paid an exorbitant price for it. We went to the Folkstone for lunch & had tea in town. The traffic on the streets of Boulogne is a most wonderful sight in itself. All Nations seem represented. & the colouring of the different uniformed men & the picturesqueness of the peasant women & the motly collection of nurses – together with the continuous processions of ambulances make the whole seem, when one is first plunged into it, unreal. Unfortunately it is too real! Saw the little lady of the rose garden in a shop. She was in deepest mo[u]rning – her brother has been killed. Captains Dixon & McKim came home with us in the 9 PM train. Strange to say the day was fine.

Letters from home tonight, such welcome welcome visitors. Sir Montagu Allen, Martha & Col Yates turned up at the Folkstone to lunch. Col Elder operated on a persistant haemorrhage case today. A transfusion of blood. Major Howard gave the blood.

OCTOBER 28

Rain all day today. We are still working steadily at our supplies but the news that our Ward tents have been condemned & that we must move is current today. How true it is no one knows.

OCTOBER 29

More rain today.

Sent Mother's Christmas parcel.

For weeks our men for various reasons have been not in their usual good spirits. so we asked Col Birkett if we might not give them a party for Hallow e'en, as they get no entertainment of any sort; but he does not approve of the idea on principals of Military etiquette but says we may have one with the officers which of course is not what we wanted.

OCTOBER 30

There was a big convoy of patients came in last night. Capt Burgess opened up a new line of Hubert Neilson tents to serve for his ward for the present.[48] Miss Eastwood & I went there this morning. Another rainy day with bright half hours at intervals.

We are still able to get lab roses for our dining tables. It has been a wonderful summer of Poppies & Roses

In Flanders Fields
by Col McCrea

In Flanders Fields the Poppies blow
Between the crosses, row on row,
That mark our place; & in the sky
The larks, still bravely singing, fly;
Scarce heard amid the guns below.

We are the Dead: short days ago
We lived, felt dawn saw sunset glow.
Loved & were loved, & now we lie
In Flanders Fields.

Take up our quarrel with the foe:
To you, from failing hands we throw
The torch: be yours to hold it high:
If ye break faith with us, who die,
We shall not sleep, though Poppies grow
In Flanders Fields.[49]

OCTOBER 31

Went to the new Ward F this morning. Such nice patients – one or two bad cases among them.
Freeman the transfusion case in G had another haemorrhage last night. He is having every care it is possible to give. Ruth is specialling the case.

NOVEMBER 1

Our hallow'een party tonight. Sheets & Pillow cases with red masks serving for fancy dress. I did a tall ghost. A fairly nice evening. Not enough music but the decorations were very pretty in both tents. (We used the rain sodden Ward J & our own anti

tent) A delicious supper. Officers & sisters from the American
Hospital & some officers from No 1 & the Engineers Camp on
the hill. One of the officers from Harvard was done up as the
Camiers Village Priest (a quaint figure with long unkempt black
hair & big angular face & frame) & was splendid. Our Captain
Piery as a witch was also very very good. The girls with their clas-
sical drapery of sheets looked very pretty. The rain streamed
down in torrents & the mud is inches deep.

NOVEMBER 2

Col Birkett surprised us today by agreeing to our party for the
NCO's & men so invitations were issued at noon for a fancy
dress dance for this evening. The costumes were marvels of inge-
nuity as all material was procured in our own camp. Perhaps
Gallighar [Gallagher] as His Satanic Majesty & Kinsman as a girl
were the best but there were other wonderful costumes. Some of
the younger lads as nursing sisters were almost unrecognizable.
Boysie Woods & Rankin were the best of these. Cooper was
awfully good as Bluebeard but early in the evening met with an
accident which might have been a trajedy. Her beard caught fire
& burned her face: only her usual presence of mind saved the
situation. I went as Sir Hopkins with Boeuf Mrs Austin's little
dog on a ribbon with a white (bandage) bow. The party was a
great success & the enthusiasm of the boys a wonderful thing to
see. they also did complete justice to our supper table. The Rain
streamed down as usual, but no one seems to mind it now. it is
part of the day.

NOVEMBER 3

Our hospital tents have been condemned as unfit for winter work.
– these last rains & heavy winds have made them look the part.

NOVEMBER 4

In my hours off Ruth & I went down to the Hotel du Lac to
order cooked chickens for the boys in the trenches & afterwards
walked around the lake & down into the dunes.
A lovely autumn day today.

NOVEMBER 5

Many rumours afloat about our future situation but no one knows anything authentic.

Walked into Camiers during my hours off Such a wonderful colouring of the lake as the sun set red behind the pine trees

NOVEMBER 6

Bycicled to Paris Plage with Ruth & Miss Steele. Ruth got such a dear little rose enamel locket for her sister Rays [Rachel/Rae] birthday. Had chocolate at the corner Patisserie. Miss Steele ran into a man on our way home which was our only excitement

NOVEMBER 7

The Sunday Observer has changed its name to the "McGillican" [McGilliken]– Its editing staff consists of Capt McDonald[Macdonald], Bielor[Bieler], Gallighar[Gallagher], Jenks & Beveridge[50]

A very cold night. I slept in this AM. Later went out for a short bycicle ride with Ruth –

Absolutely no news of a movement of any sort from the front.

NOVEMBER 8

Sarj Wilson has come to our Ward in Church's place.

The flowers in our Anti tent are still lovely. Now the predominating decorations are asters (lovely shades) white chrysanthimums & Holly & yellow berries. Miss Parks Miss Car[r]–Harris & Lilly Carter were to come up to tea but failed to do so

NOVEMBER 9

Rain & wind in the night last night & tonight it is bitterly cold & the rain & wind still keep up.

The huge durbar tents each day show new rents & become unsafe & uninhabitable & one by one are coming down.

The Tent Question   by Captain Piery

Ten little tents all standing in a line
The wind blew a hole in one & then there were nine
Nine little tents & rather out of date

The rain washed away one & then there were eight
Eight little tents as luxurious as Heaven
The Sister burnt a hole in one & then there were seven
Seven little tents with poles that wouldn't fix
One broke its back & then there were six.
Six little tents as busy as a hive
The Quarter Master wanted one & then there were five.
Five little tents & one without a floor
It was condemned & then there were four.
Four little tents as cosy as could be
A Primus went & busted & then there were three.
Three little tents & one that wouldn't do
A gramaphone had played too hard & snapped it in two
Two little tents & one was nearly done
We ripped it up for Fancy dress & then there was one
One little tent so fragile & so dear
We'll take it back to Canada to be a souvenir.

NOVEMBER 10

Posted Grantys Christmas parcel
Very cold & windy all day. Rain in torrents at night.

Extract from the McGilliken:

We wandered up Happy Valley this evening. How unlike the
good old days it was! No strolling, no music – nothing save
rain & a jack rabbit or two. Will this old world ever right itself!

NOVEMBER 11

Another rainy, cold windy day. It is officially stated today that our
unit is to move. Started to walk in the wind to Etaples this PM.
But the rain became too heavy so we came back in the ambulance with Boysie Woods.

NOVEMBER 12

A wild night last night. Today's rain was in showers fast & furious. Col Yates admitted to our ward. Three of our girls were sent down to No 1 to help out. they had a convoy of 400 last night.

NOVEMBER 13

Frightfully windy & cold tonight & all day. The dismantling & packing up of the wards has begun & the patients left put all together. The ADMS was here on important business but no news of our destination. Ruth & I walked down to the sea just at dusk to see this great wind in its battle with the waves. It was a wonderful sight.

A foot ball game with No 20 this PM resulted in a tie.

Col Yates is very miserable – His condition looks a serious one – Heart & Kidneys

NOVEMBER 14

Stephie & I bycicled down through Trepied [Le Trépied] in our hours off this morning. Was on duty with Col Yates this afternoon. Miss Parks & Miss Carr-Harris came from No 1 to dinner. We walked about half way back with them after eight. It is a beautiful night. We like our new chaplain Capt Hepburn very much.

A boat wrecked off this coast yesterday & a great deal of army service stores cast up on the shore.

The browns & yellows in this dune country are wonderful these November days. All the birds have left & crows take their places hundreds of them flying over the dunes with their harsh noises.

NOVEMBER 15

I dismantled what was left of old Ward F this morning & turned in the equipment. Late in the afternoon Miss Steele & I rode to Chateau D'Hardelot. Such a clear cold November day. We had tea at "the Pre Catelan" & came home just at dusk.

Our patients have practically all gone home to England, Convalescent Camp or the Base

NOVEMBER 16

A strange unfamiliar Picardy met our gaze this morning for three inches of snow fell in the night. It does not suit these landscapes. It is very cold.

A concert by the Princess Victoria party tonight a wonderful young girl violinist & such a clever funny ventriliquist

NOVEMBER 17

We took our bycicles back to their owners today as we have definite news that we are to go to a Convent near Boulogne very soon. Leaving the bycicles felt like parting from old friends.

We still have Col Yates in the ward. All the other patients have gone.

NOVEMBER 18

The NCO's & men gave a party tonight for the sisters. Two of the empty tents were used. It was a great success, the pleasure of the evening however was spoiled by the news that yesterdays hospital ship from Boulogne was sunk by a floating mine 85 lives, mostly patients, lost.

These poor lads leave for home in such good spirits & so thankful to be going back to Blighty[51]

NOVEMBER 19

Worked at packing in the ward this morning & in the PM Ruth Dick & I walked into Etaples stopping on our way at the little cemetary: All our lads are laid here two together. but today I noticed a new grave with one alone. He was a German! Another new grave is marked "Unknown"!

Dick wanted to get fruit in Etaples for a patient in No 1, so we walked from the cemetary by the shore & had some tea at Ioos' before returning to No 1. Twelve of our girls went to No 1 to help out there. Cooper, Molly, & Sara McNaughton were among those sent

NOVEMBER 20

Everything that the nursing sisters can do towards the packing has been done. Col Yates is to leave for England tomorrow. We walked to Hardelot this morning as Dick had never been there

Had lunch at the 'Pre Catelan' & walked back early in the afternoon. It is bitterly cold & in walking is the only hope of keeping
warm.

NOVEMBER 21

After lunch we walked to Frenq & back to camp by the Boulogne
road & Widehem a distance of about ten miles At Frenq we
stayed to the 2.30 service a children's service in the little old
church. A very cold gray day.

Preparations in the old Monastery in Boulogne are being made
for our occupation.

NOVEMBER 22

Col Yates left for England today. He is still far from well. I walked
out the Etaples road with Peggy Parks & Miss Woods this afternoon & back by a path by the brook which runs out of the Lake.
Ruth & Dick went to Paris Plage today.

A beautiful sunshiny day

NOVEMBER 23

A gray day with a dense fog towards night. I hope soon we will
be given work to do. All along this line at present however things
are very quiet. Moved our anti tent down to the Operating
Room where it is warmer.

Watling & I walked around the lake this P.M.

NOVEMBER 24

Walked this afternoon through Neuve Chatel. had some tea at
"Preudecoeur's" [Prèdecoeur?] & got back to camp soon after
dark.

NOVEMBER 25

Had Louise McGreer & Sally Watters in to my tent to tea this
afternoon. Mother's cake & Grantys cookies serving as material
for the party. Ruth Dickie & Watling having arrived in camp
after a drive to Montreuil in the "ford" in time to partake. Also
Cooper up from No 1. They are busy at No 1 just now & can well
do with our extra nurses. I wish we were busy at our new quarters but they are not ready yet.

November 26

Walked into Paris Plage today to get my glasses which I have broken. Louise McLeod came with me. Lily Carter came up from No 1 to see us this morning.

It is very cold with snow falling tonight. At the Chaplain's Capt Hepburn's instigation we are learning a couple of little plays for our patients' amusement later on. Had our first rehearsal tonight In "Ici on parle française" the one in which I am taking part. Capt Little Capt Hepburn Capt Dixon, B. Armitage, Jackie, & little McKay are the personelle.

November 27

The "Fifth Year" students of our unit have had orders today to leave for home in order to finish their course at old McGill. We asked them & their friends to our Anti tent this evening for a little farewell party.

November 28

Advent Sunday.

I went to the early service this morning & later for a long walk with Ruth.

It is bitterly cold.

November 29

Rained steadily all day. Had a rehearsal of our little play this evening. The ADMS who was here today has decreed that we are to be billeted in Boulogne to wait for our hospital's opening there. This is the latest rumour.

November 30

Miss Brand Ruth & I started reading The Queen's Mairies" aloud. Ruth & I are reading Les Miserables also –

December 1

Walked with Ruth up over the hills & down by the Plaster Cliff at Dannes.

December 2

NO ENTRY

December 3

Posted Grantys knitted jacket today.

DECEMBER 4

In spite of a heavy rain Ruth & I walked down to No 1 & had tea
with Miss Cooper in the club there.

No further move about our going on ahead to Boulogne so we
have concluded that the authorities have given up that idea
Besides these huts here are nearly finished[52]

DECEMBER 5

We had very nice services today. I read with Whitney & Morewood in the pm. as it was wet & very muddy. It rains now during
some part of every day practically. Last night our mess tent blew
down with the storm & many of our dishes were broken. Today
we were obliged to move into the new hut for our mess –
although the carpenters have not yet finished there.

DECEMBER 6

This morning at breakfast like a 'bolt from the blue' came the
orders that thirty of our sisters were to proceed to England for
service at Cliveden & at Shorncliff. I am to go with the fifteen to
Cliveden Wednesday morning In the PM. I went into Paris Plage
with Ruth to do a couple of final errands there. This evening No
20 Hospital gave a concert in the YMCA an excellent programme. As usual it rained all the time we were in Paris Plage.
The sea gulls came in to the hills today which they say means a
storm out at sea.

DECEMBER 7

A rainy day. – Everyone is slightly depressed at our approaching
separation, though the Colonel declares it will only be for a time
& our help is needed in the Canadian Hospitals in England. We
invited the officers into our anti room for the evening. The party
was a successful one – I came to my tent & went to bed early as I
have a pain in my back tonight from packing here in the damp
today. Ruth & I conversed at length today – on the subject of our
life in France.

DECEMBER 8

A beautiful morning to see us off – the sunny land of France
once again. We left our lovely hills with regrets. A large party of

sisters, officers & men gathered to see us off in Char a-bancs –
Ruth & I in the last of the two followed the lines of the hills with
our eyes & said good bye to the little roads & quaint villages on
our route as to old friends. The truck with the luggage broke
down in the mud outside Neuve chatel so we proceeded without
it. Although the sun shone, it was very windy on the Channel &
we were all frightfully sea sick – crossing – arrived in London at
3.30 P.M. sea sick still & faint from hunger. Went to the
Kin[g]sley Hotel & were sufficiently recovered by dinner time to
make a pretence of eating & afterwards went to see Jalta Neilson
& Fred Terry in the Scarlet Pimpernel. Wonderful old London
again & civilization – Little things impressed me tonight: the
unlocking of a door to get to our room. Switching on of electric
lights & going to bed under a roof seem unnatural conditions &
the ascent in the elevator was almost a sensation.

DECEMBER 9

Had a hair wash this morning to remove the salt water water of
the Channel, then went with Miss Brand to do a bit of shopping
on the way to the station. An uneventful journey to Taplow.

Some of us are big ships & some of us are small;
Graceful yachts & rusty tramps but one thing over all:
We've got the same wide sea to sail, the same last port to
make;
So here's to you & here's to me tho' waves & wavelets break.

DECEMBER 10

Went on duty in our mess uniforms as our baggage has not
come. I to the convalescent ward & Dental clinic
Taplow Lodge the Nurses' quarters is a picturesque old house.
The large drawing rooms & sitting room have been converted
into sleeping apartments 8 or 10 beds in each. The room
reserved for a sitting room has wonderful old tapestries on its
walls – with a large oil portrait of Queen Elizabeth above the
dark wood mantel under which is a huge fireplace. The other

rooms are done in white & gold the elaborate finishings of the old days with gay wallpapers. Fine old fir & pine trees, with holly & shrubery edge the drive. The Hospital Wards which are on the opposite side of the highway are high & light & well-equipped, but very cold at present. They have about eight hundred patients. We seem aliens & strangers here, the atmosphere of the whole is not that of McGill yet Ruskin says Sojourn in every place as if you meant to spend your life there, never omitting an opportunity of doing a kindness or speaking a true word or making a friend.

DECEMBER 11

> Oh to be a turtle, a slow lethargic turtle,
> With nothing in the world to do
> But roam around the long day through
> To sun oneself upon a log, To idly gossip with a frog

Nurses' quarters, Taplow Lodge

To wallow in a marshy pool
Among the reeds & rushes cool
To feel no matter what befell, one need
but crawl within ones shell
And let the whole world go to —

We took a taxi into Maidenhead this evening Ruth & Dick & I to calm our feelings & to get away from this Duchess of Connaught's atmosphere Went into a book Shop & got Christmas cards & read Christmas quotations & felt the better of it. I have come to the conclusion with Miss Drake that this hospital has "A Queen Anne front & a Mary Ann back – A gray day, but there were some dear letters from home waiting when we returned from Maidenhead.

DECEMBER 12

Very cold this morning with snow. The wards are bitterly cold & the only fires in the Lodge are the grates & they must not be lighted till 5 PM. Ruth & I went for a long walk in our hours off to keep warm, through Burnham & back to the Lodge by another road. There seem to be a good many Canadians among the patients here.

There is no Service for the Sisters on Sundays. I suppose we will have to find the nearest church which I believe is at Taplow village two miles away.

DECEMBER 13

A convoy of over one hundred came in this afternoon.

DECEMBER 14

We had our half-day & went up to London chiefly to get a few things to send to the boys in the trenches. Went to His Majesty's to see "Mavourneen" in the evening & back by the late train. Had dinner in the Winter garden at Frescalis on Oxford St.

DECEMBER 15

Went to Ward F today to special the two serious cases there. Ran into Maidenhead with Miss Stewart tonight as she could not go alone. Am very tired tonight with rheumatism in my wrists & ankles.

DECEMBER 16

Poor Price one of my patients a lad of twenty fine looking & big,
is dying far away from home. His people are in India. He gave me
a little bunch of violets & maidenhair fern which his mother sent
in her letter today. Poor lad, He is so ready & anxious to go.[53]

DECEMBER 17

Jane Rodd & I were alone on this big Ward this afternoon. She
came here a stranger at noon

DECEMBER 18

Walked into Maidenhead this afternoon in hours off to post our
parcels to the boys at the front. It is a pretty walk along a narrow
hedge road round pretty curves past thatched cottages & beautiful homes to a very clean little town with good shops..
Price died this morning – a merciful relief from pain & suffering

DECEMBER 19

Went around the golf course this afternoon – My first game.

DECEMBER 20

I have such a bad cold today.
We have begun the ward decorations for Christmas.

DECEMBER 21

We are quite busy in the mornings especially. the doctors here
leave all the dressings to us. I don't approve of the method.

DECEMBER 22

Our ward looks very pretty & Christmassy I hope the men will
have a happy time. We three nurses on the ward are giving them
cigarettes.

DECEMBER 23

Busy as usual on the ward – the weather is most uncertain here.

DECEMBER 24

Off duty at noon & up to London on the afternoon train. Went
shopping with Dickie & Ruth. then back to the Kingsley (where
we are staying) for dinner & to see Stop Thief at Prince of Wales
theatre in the evening
Christmas Eve in London. London so dark that in some streets a
country lane could be no darker – the shop windows even have

only one small light & the street lamps only throw a small circle
of light downwards

DECEMBER 25

> "A little child with heart so wide
> it takes the whole world in"

Christmas Greetings, speed ye forth, even as a flight of birds – &
alight one by one where dwell our thoughts – then sing ye there
glad songs to show – that friends are guarded & held fast – by
memories kind & wishes true, like friendship's flowers unfading
round the door

I got up early & went to the early service at St. George's, an old
church next door to the Kingsley. It rained later in the morning
& we took a taxi to St. Pauls, where we had the most beautiful
service I have ever heard. Met Boysie Woods & Dr. Enright coming out of church. Later met Des Brisay & later still the two
Hunter boys. Went to lunch at the Strand Corner House &
explored the city on tops of buses & in a long walk in afternoon.
Went to dinner to Frascati with Dr. Enright

DECEMBER 26

Dick & Ruth went to Bramshot[t] camp to see Ruth's brother so
I had the day to myself. Went with Jane Rodd & Krolick to the
morning service at Westminster Cathedral walked home with
them. Had lunch at the hotel, & spent the whole afternoon in
the Wallace Collection Art Gallery. Walked back to the Hotel &
had a fire in our room for the evening. read & wrote letters till
my friends returned.

DECEMBER 27

Ruth & Dick went to see friends so I spent the morning between
the National Gallery & the Abbey.
Westminster Abbey is surely a wonderful old place. [Marginal
notation:] The wax figures are most curious & fascinating.
Ruth & Dick found me there about 1.30. Kingsley to lunch – to

the Zoo & to the Tower of London with Dr. Enright in the afternoon. Also to dinner with him at Frescales Afterwards to see
Peter Pan at the New Theatre & back to Paddington station by
underground & to Cliveden by the late train

DECEMBER 28

Back to work this morning.
Miss Ramsey went to Shorncliff yesterday. Had last hours off
today & sat before the fire & opened my parcels & letters.
Granty's box contained a copy of Peter Pan. Had several dear
letters from home too & one from Cyril

DECEMBER 29

Went around the Golf course with Jenkins & Freeman, two of
our patients in my hours off.
We heard today that Col Yates is still very ill & that Miss Lindsay
& Miss Steele have gone to Ramsgate to nurse him.

DECEMBER 30

Went around the Golf course with Freeman today again for fresh
air & exercise.

DECEMBER 31

The last day of a sad year. In spite of worries we have tried to
make the best of things at most times. Surely this terrible war
will soon be over – though nothing definite seems to be going
on at present towards an early ending.

1916

JANUARY 1

Taplow.

I came off duty today preparatory to going on night duty tonight. After lunch started to go around the golf course with Jenkins and Freeman two of our convalescent patients but it began to rain & we had to return before we reached the second green. Later I joined a party who were going to Ockwells Manor to tea. Lady Barry – the owner visits the hospital quite a lot & had asked all sisters who cared to go for tea today. Such an interesting old place dating back to Henry VI's time & well preserved. From the entrance we came into the old banquetting Hall with its long table, its musicians gallery its armour & its arms & spears & fireplace. Here are wonderful old stained glass windows put in when the house was built by its owner & bearing the arms of his different friends at the Court of Henry VI. The beams and walls of rough hewn oak are so beautiful in their simplicity. – Built with wooden pegs instead of nails – this old wooden house has stood through the years. Lady Barry showed us about the house. All the rooms are furnished absolutely to suit the period of its building & there are many wonderful carved oak chests & other furniture. The four post carved & canopied beds in all the bedrooms most fascinating – old tapestries & old paintings on many of the walls.

One room in which Elizabeth of England slept boasts a ghost.

JANUARY 2

Night duty tonight. My patients not very sick so I had a quiet night.

JANUARY 3

Moved my goods and chatels to Night Sisters Quarters – had a bath & retired this morning.

JANUARY 4

Last night our poor lad Bunker had two haemorrhages from the lungs. I am so worried about him.

A beautiful day. – so I went out after breakfast & played golf after which I explored the paths to the river & returned by Cliveden House & back by the drive to the Lodge. Parts of the estate are very beautiful & the river & river banks must be lovely in summer. The house of course is immense, the fountain & statuary very fine.

Rudyard Kipling came this afternoon to see the hospital & spoke to the men in the Recreation room afterwards.[1]

JANUARY 5

Very rainy all day.

Bunker is better though very weak.

Marie Lohr entertained the patients in the recreation room in the afternoon.[2]

JANUARY 6

Walked into Maidenhead this morning with Dick & Miss Drake. Got my watch & did a few other errands for other people.

JANUARY 7

It rained this morning, so I went to bed early. Davies Armitage & Louise McLeod on leave in London from Camiers came down to see us this afternoon. Letters from Camiers this morning say that the male personnel of the camp has gone on to Boulogne to our new quarters there.

Moved with the rest of the night sisters to a cottage in the grounds. I go to a room with Ruth and I think will be very comfortable – This cottage was originally a gardener's abode.

Bunker "had a head wound with fractured skull was
shot in two places through the lungs & had one leg
amputated" (quotation from album)

JANUARY 8

Walked with Miss Drake around by Hedsor Lord Boston's estate
& by path on River's shore to the Cliveden Ferry. There the boat-
man took us across – the river here is beautiful & today very full
with a swift current – & we walked by a path up to Cookham Village. Such a pretty little English village with an old ivy clad tow-
ered church. We went into the church & wandered for a little
while in the church yard afterwards. Then returned to the Ferry.
The view of the Cliveden woods from the opposite side of the
river is most beautiful.

JANUARY 9

Walked with Miss Drake to the eleven o'clock service at the little
chapel at Hedsor. Such a complete & beautiful little chapel – a
beautiful 16th century altar here & everything so well ordered
& well kept. The congregation consisted of the retainers on the
estate Lord Boston & ourselves – 9 boys & four men formed the

choir & the congregation sang heartily. Church lighted by candles only. Lord Boston read the Lessons. The old clergyman dignified & sincere – the sermon – the simple Epiphany story. A good organ & a lovely old font also very fine stained glass windows & very sweet sounding bells. The churchyard, which surrounds the building, is very quaint – all stones flat on the ground & the grass green & perfectly kept. – some of the tombstones dated as far back as 1606. Some very quaint epitaphs. The church is situated on the top of a hill & the panorama around is a wonderful one – on an opposite hill there is the ruin of an old castle, the Towers of which date back to the Roman period so we were told.

JANUARY 10

A beautiful sunshiny morning. I went around the golf links before going to bed – Also through the Maze near the Japanese Gardens.

Epitaph in Hedsor Church yard
Near this place are interred the remains of Susanna Lycester late wife of the Rev Ralph Lyster late Rector of Hedsor who departed this life 18th of Dec 1658. Her maiden name was Hammer. She was descended from the ancient & honourable family of Hammer in the County of Flintshire. How she acquitted herself in the different characters of daughter wife & mother is by her particular desire left in silence (being an enemy to all Monumental Eulogism) until the great day when the secrets of all hearts shall be revealed – on which awful day she humbly hopes, through the merits of our Blessed Saviour & Redeemer, to rise to a happy Immortality

JANUARY 11

Went up to London this morning by the early train to do some shopping – ordered a new uniform at Shoolbreds, got a navy blue sweater coat at Evans; boots & other necessities elsewhere. Went to a late Matinée when we had finished in afternoon. "The

Pedlar of Dreams" at the Vaudeville Theatre. Met Colonel Hughes as we came out. He looks much older than he did on the Metagama. He is in London on a three days leave. His regiment has recently been in action.

JANUARY 12

Went to bed early as I had no sleep yesterday – & stayed in bed all day.

JANUARY 13

Played golf in AM. with Ruth & my two patients. After the game went with Ruth to see the little chapel on this estate. Built on the side of the River Bank the tower which forms the chapel is ivy covered. A flight of stone steps leads down to the entrance which faces river. In the interior nothing short of millions could produce this result. The walls for the first 4 ft are of a dark green marble. Above this both walls & ceilings of wonderful mosaics. The Altar too is mosaic & the Rurdos of hammered brass depicting scenes from the life of Christ & studded with jewels – the Cross on the Altar is of platinum set with huge rubies – the prayer desk wood carving is beautiful & the chairs are of light inlaid wood: the different coloured & shaped marble tiles of the floor are from all parts of the globe: India, Arabia, Africa Ireland – and represent a fortune in themselves. The Chapel was built by the present owners father about 20 yrs ago.

JANUARY 14

We got up early this afternoon & went to the Taplow station to meet Ruth's cousin who came down from London for the afternoon. From the station we went in a taxi to visit the little church at Stoke Poges, & from there through Eton to Windsor.

JANUARY 15

I cannot sleep well these days & am tired.

Sleep, Sleep, come to me, Sleep,
Come to my blankets & come to my bed,
Come to my legs & my arms & my head,
Over me, under me, into me, creep.

Sleep, Sleep, come to me, Sleep,
Blow on my face like a soft breath of air,
Lay your cool hand on my forehead & hair,
Carry me down through the dream-waters deep.

Sleep, Sleep, come to me, Sleep,
Tell me the secrets that you alone know,
Show me the wonders none others can show,
Open the box where your treasures you keep.

Sleep, Sleep come to me, Sleep,
Softly I call you: as soft & as slow
Come to me, cuddle me stay with me so,
Stay till the dawn is beginning to peep.

Henry Johnstone.

JANUARY 16

I went for a solitary walk this morning in the direction of Bourne
End. Returned by the little Hedsor Church & the Hedsor Drive
– I met no one till I reached the Hedsor Road – there two small
boys on their way to Sunday School talked to me for a little
while. The birds in the wood had such sweet notes this morning
– & the pheasants & wood pigeons were out in numbers & flew
across the road at the sound of my approach.

JANUARY 17

Went with a party in to Maidenhead this morning to do some
shopping. I bought some things for Roy Mitchell Miss Eastwood's
friend, just a lad in Ward G 1. His right leg has been amputated
at the hip. Also left my spectacles to be mended & my films at
Eastmans

JANUARY 18

Marie Lohr & party entertained the patients this pm.

JANUARY 19

Played golf this morning. Prince Arthur of Connaught & the Princess visited the hospital today. The Matron in Chief is also here.

JANUARY 20

Went to bed early this morning. Read Peter Pan during my wakeful hours but stayed in bed till 6.30 pm.

Edith Stuart one of our thirteen developed pneumonia suddenly yesterday & is very ill.

JANUARY 21

Colder today. We really have been having wonderful weather for England at this time of year. We have had very little rain for the last two weeks.

JANUARY 22

Walked this morning with Ruth & Dick down to the Ferrymans cottage to return a lantern which Miss Nichols borrowed last night.

JANUARY 23

We heard today that our poor old friend Col Yates died yesterday. He will be greatly missed in our unit. He was liked by everyone & I can't think of any one who will fill his possition of Co[mmanding] Officer so acceptably to everybody.3

Edith Stuart is better.

JANUARY 24

Walked into Maidenhead by the river road. A beautiful sunshiny morning. The road for the greater part of is covered with fallen leaves & the old knarled trunks of the trees are fascinating – like Rackhams illustrations of the old trees in Kensington Gardens.4

We were back to the cottage & in bed by 12.30.

JANUARY 25

Lady Strathcona came to visit the hospital today

JANUARY 26

Played gold before going to bed this AM.

JANUARY 27

Walked by River Road to Maidenhead with Miss Drake Miss Moore & Miss Ladeux. Had a fitting of my new blue uniform at Martin's.

JANUARY 28

Made my toilet with great care & took the 10.25 train from
Taplow to Oxford. Miss Lefroy met me at the station – A prim
old coach man in livery & a fat old horse took us over the cob-
blestones to Christ Church where Miss Lefroy acted as guide &
I saw something of the wonders of the Old Oxford University. In
the Christ Church Chapel the Norman & old English architecture mingle, & the whole is most interesting. One part of the
Wall dates back to Saxon days. The old tombs, some of them
defaced in Cromwell's days the beautiful old wood carving
& old windows & the lovely modern Burn[e-]Jones windows.
Then we walked to Queens College, in which Miss Lefroy lives
with her Uncle, who is Provost there I met the uncle a dignified
learned old gentleman with a lovely old face – After lunch Miss
Lefroy & I talked of old days in her sitting room. & later went
with a few messages to one of the big university building which
has been turned into a hospital & to which Miss Lefroy is Canadian visitor. Then we went to Magdalen & saw the river walk &
the black swans & the wonderful old cloisters. & the old Oxford
city walls. then back to the Provost's to tea. My uniform was
much admired & I was the centre of attraction in many ways.
Such a wonderful view from the front windows of the spires
& roofs of the other colleges. Miss Lefroy showed me some
lovely recent photographs which she has taken. Back to Taplow
by the 5.45 train.[5]

JANUARY 29

A long days sleep to make up for 36 hours of wakefulness.

JANUARY 30

Walked with Miss Drake to Burnham Beeches this morning – the
old knarled trees were lovely & the roads very pretty even at this
time of year. We returned by Burnham.

JANUARY 31

Walked into Maidenhead by river road this AM with Dickie &
Ruth & Miss Veits. Miss Veits is a sister of Gerald Veits of Kings
College days.[6] An older brother has been wounded in the face

in France & she is now waiting here till he is ready to travel
back to Canada with her as he has one eye out & the other so
mutilated that he is stone blind. Miss Veits has been in the CAMC
at La Touquet all summer.

FEBRUARY 1

NO ENTRY

FEBRUARY 2

The patients gave a concert this afternoon in the Recreation
Room. Princess Arthur of Connaught was present. Several of the
lads of F 1 helped.

FEBRUARY 3

Read in "Canada" that Helen McMurrich had brought over a
party of nurses from Toronto to work with the French Government Hospitals.

FEBRUARY 4

News reached us tonight that the Parliament buildings at Ottawa
have been blown up. Where is this World War to end?[7]
I took a few pictures this AM of the Taplow Lodge trees.
Heard also by letter from Miss Tuck who is in London.

FEBRUARY 5

Sir Henry James Vansittart Neale
Kitty & Helen Arnoldi arrived here tonight
Walked this AM with Miss Drake, Jane Rodd & Ruby Graham
(after crossing the river on the Ferry boat) through Cookham,
Cookham Dean, the Bisham Woods, & along by a river path to
the village – & to the Bisham Abbey gates – then up the long
drive & to the old 12th Century Porch of the Abby. Sir Henry
James Vansittart Neale a courtly old gentleman, the owner
received us & showed us first the great Hall (12th century) with
its wonderful old tapestry illustrating the Life of Tobit[8] – & its
Gallery & Great fireplace & old world furniture.
The tapestries here date back to Henry VII's reign when the
house was redecorated by the King & given as a present to Anne
of Cleves. A tiny window high up on the r[igh]t & opening on a
flight of steps served Elizabeth when she wished to show herself

to her courtiers assembled in the Hall below. A stately dining room 16th century with rows of beautiful portraits, a bright pretty old time drawing room & many quaint bed rooms with four post beds with lovely old hangings. In one the motto over the grate carved in old oak —

Then we went up a long winding flight of stairs (the original stairs used by the old 12th century monks) to the top of the tower, from which there is a wonderful view of the Thames & surrounding country, & the site of the old church in which Warwick the King Maker & Henry Plantagenet were buried. We said good by to Sir Henry under the old arch of the doorway beside the heavy studded old door with its old bolt. Walked back to Cookham & had lunch there – then back by the ferry to bed.

FEBRUARY 6

Tuckie came from London to see us & we had such a nice afternoon. I went to the Taplow station to see her off. Coming back my taxi broke down in Back Lane & I had to wait there in the dark while the taxi driver went to a near by house to telephone for another conveyance. After a very long half hour a tiny pony & trap driven by a very English youth appeared – & we fairly flew back to the Lodge – The Pony, Polly was small & the youth said thirty years old but she went at full speed & I was on duty in time after all.

FEBRUARY 7

Off night duty.

Ruth & Dick & I went up to London by the noon train. did a couple of errands at the Army & Navy Stores – then went to the Drury Lane Pantomime,"Puss in Boots." back to Taplow for dinner.

Mrs B's trial began.9

FEBRUARY 8

On day duty in F 1.

After a good night's sleep I feel a different person.

Settled in my new room which is very cosy with Jane Rodd & Edith Leslie. Six more of the Laval sisters came to Taplow today.

FEBRUARY 9

Bycicled alone into Maidenhead for my snaps at Eastmans but they were not finished. Came back by Taplow. Enjoyed the ride though I was alone & on a borrowed bycicle

FEBRUARY 10

Wrote a couple of letters in my hours off. The Matron says we may have leave so I have asked for mine for next week.

FEBRUARY 11

My half day today but it rained heavily so Ruth & I sat in front of my grate fire & wrote letters.

FEBRUARY 12

NO ENTRY

FEBRUARY 13

Trajedy in Alex 1 this AM. We are a sad world today.[10] Edith Leslie went of duty today with very sore hands.

FEBRUARY 14

Walked in to Maidenhead alone & came back in an Ambulance with Ruth and Dick.

Edith Leslie's hands have been diagnosed as Iodoform poisoning in her hands. Frightfully sore hands they are

Miss Drake is ill with a bad cold

FEBRUARY 15

First a rumour then Authentic Notice that we are to leave for France on Friday.

Miss Drake better today

So happy at the thought of our return to France.

FEBRUARY 16

Spent hours off today reading to Miss Drake.

FEBRUARY 17

I am so sorry to leave my nice lads in the ward & they are sorry to have me go.

Packed my things tonight while Miss Phipps entertained the girls with her banjo & southern songs in the drawing room. I did not feel like going down.

FEBRUARY 17 [repeat]

Packed my things this evening

FEBRUARY 18

On duty till 11.30.

Ambulance to station.

Spent afternoon shopping, then looked Nell Tuck up. Had dinner with her at the Kingsley & the evening in my room after having quite a long walk down Oxford St.

FEBRUARY 19

Off at 9.15 to Victoria Station through the Kent hop districts. The Crossing was an easy calm one & we arrived at the dock of Quaint old Boulogne with the feeling of a home coming. The Ambulance to meet us was late so we walked up to the funny old Louvre to lunch. A typical lunch. Ruth & I sat at a little table alone & compared notes with our first arrival in Boulogne. We are so glad to be here.

The Char a' banc took us up the hill to our new quarters later on & we arrived in great excitement at our new mess hut where the girls were waiting to greet us.

The new huts are very nice. Cooper & I are to room together Miss Hoerner took Ruth, Dick & I through Hospital.

FEBRUARY 20

Ruth & I went for such a nice walk in the AM. to Napoleons monument: Such a fine outlook over the Wimereux district. On duty in afternoon fitting up M 2 Ward. Walked with Cooper down the hill to Wimereux with Miss Harkin who came up to see us today. She tells us Aunt Emma is dead.

FEBRUARY 21

Such a beautiful situation.

We have the old Jesuit College, which when the monks were driven out of France ten years ago they distroyed, rather than leave a valuable property for the use of the Government. Two large buildings still stand – one is in use as men quarters, the other as hospital building; the rest is in ruin but the ruined walls are being utalized in the erection of the hut wards, which are

Approaching No. 3 CGH, Boulogne

under the trees in the grounds, & in among the ruins – the old trees are lovely & will be beautiful in summer & the paths & little knolls & rockeries are already covered with primroses & snow drops. A high wall surrounds the place but the hospital huts overflow at the back into the field beyond – If possible all surgical wards are to be inside the walls. There are 450 patients in the hospital. Our quarters (across the road, on the north of the medical huts in the field) are very comfortable. Miss Cooper & I room together. It is a very cold night tonight.

FEBRUARY 22

Such a cold miserable day. Snowing this evening. Col Birkett came back yesterday. I am quite busy hammering & making our room cosy in the evenings. Miss Drake across the partition wants to know if we are building a grand piano.

Pte. Victor Lapp

FEBRUARY 23

Another cold day with rain.

A convoy of 85 last night. Some bad cases.

FEBRUARY 24

Another bitterly cold day.

FEBRUARY 25

A regular Canadian snow storm. A convoy last night.

FEBRUARY 26

Snow enough for sleighing but no sleigh of course used here. Over 900 beds are ready now.

I went to Ward N 1 today & with a busy afternoons work equipped, & had ready 25 beds by evening. Eighteen patients admitted before I went off. Lapp is Ward Master. & is of course "pure gold"

FEBRUARY 27

Miss Cooper is off sick this morning. We are to take in local cases in my ward.[11]

FEBRUARY 28

Miss McNaughton was transferred to No 14 General Hospital at Wimereux for an operation for appendicitis. This is the provision made for sick nurses in this district

A convoy of 87 last night.

FEBRUARY 29

NO ENTRY

MARCH 1

We miss the sight of the English sisters with whom we were surrounded at Camiers. Of course in Boulogne & Wimereux there are many English Hospitals but none near us on the hill.

I often think of the verses written of the Sisters by a British "Tommy" after being in Hospital at Etaples

> Women of Britain, garbed in gray
> Untiring cheerful, through the long day,.
> How can we tell you just how much
> We feel in our hearts your gentle touch;
> Angels of Mercy we find you are such
> And you'll live in our Memories, Aye!
>
> Women of Britain, garbed in gray,
> Christ when on earth showed you the way.
> And now in his footsteps you follow here
> No task too humble your help so near,
> With an arm to guide & a voice to cheer
> And we thank the good God for you, Aye!
>
> Women of Britain, garbed in gray
> How can we thank you, who can say,
> All that our hearts are feeling tonight
> When wearied & battered we rest from the fight

And we catch a gleam of Heavenly light
In your smile that we dream of for Aye!

Women of Britain, garbed in gray
May the Scarlet bands in your capes so gay
Like the blood stained portal in Jewish lore
Be a passover sign above your door,
That sickness & sorrow will pass you o'er
Is our hope & our prayer for aye!

Women of Britain, garbed in gray
Wives, mothers, & sweethearts nightly pray
God bless you always & keep you strong
Unwearied by toils though the day be so long
For your brave sacrifices are Britains proud song
And will sing loud your praises, for Aye.

MARCH 2
A fine day in spots only.
My ward is filled & I am very busy but enjoy my work if it were
only possible to forget its cause.

MARCH 3
A convoy of 96 last night.
Latest sensation Miss Lamont is resigning from CAMC to be married

MARCH 4
Ruth & I went out into the fields at the back at 4 PM to a lane &
little brook – such a spring atmosphere in a typical French landscape. It will be lovely here in summer. A convoy of 100 last
night.
My Grantys birthday – & I have been thinking all day of her wonderful unselfishness. Down in the lane it seemed possible that
before another year is over we may be together again & this
dreadful war over.

MARCH 5

I have bad chill blains & am very miserable with them.[12]

MARCH 6

NO ENTRY

MARCH 7

A convoy of 107 last night. The men bring stories that the Germans before vacating the trenches taken by us left quantities of salt petre in them with the result that our men have terrible trench feet – many of which will have to be removed[13]

MARCH 8

Ash Wednesday.
Ruth & I had our half days & went into Boulogne to the Club to do some shopping though we both have bad bad feet.

MARCH 9

Last night in the night a terrific explosion wakened us – an ammunition vessel we discovered later in the day has been blown up at the mouth of the harbour.

MARCH 10

NO ENTRY

MARCH 11

I planted some seeds in boxes. I hope they will do well as our ward front needs decoration. The larks have returned with their liquid beautiful notes – We hear them early in the mornings.

MARCH 12

Ruth & I in our hours off walked down to Wimereux to No 14 to see our sick nurses there. It is a beautiful day & though we both are cripples & the sentries as we passed persisted in saying – Mal aux pieds – we enjoyed the walk.

MARCH 13

Another beautiful day but I was very very busy all day.

MARCH 14

News in camp today that Capt Dixon & Amy were married before we left Canada.

MARCH 15

Ruth & I walked out in the moonlight after dinner on the football field & up the road talked & talked chiefly of people about us.

MARCH 16

A large convoy last night. Many French air ships about today

MARCH 17

NO ENTRY

MARCH 18

Had my half day today & such a wonderful birthday picnic with Ruth. We walked to Wimille by the Calais road, went into the Church, stayed in the cemetary till a shower stopped, then up the hill to a wonderful view of Boulogne & the vicinity back to the village by the main road & started down a lane on the out-skirts of the Village to find ourselves in a wonderful Valley "Vallé[e] du Denacre" with a stream with waterfalls, a beautiful woods, the path winding along by the river. past " Le premier Moulin" with its dam & waterfall, over little rustic bridges – past a chateau with a wall & garden & fountain & tiny moat then by a second mill with a café & tea garden, out to the back road near our camp. A Valley of Peace & quiet with the birds singing & the sunshine & the trees just beginning to put on their new leaves; the mauve lights of the dying day were beautiful as we came up the hill to camp.

Had a quiet party in my room in the evening.

MARCH 19

We are still having beautiful spring like days.

I sent Lapp to see "the Happy Valley" this afternoon. He too thinks it too beautiful to belong to a world in which war exists

MARCH 20

Ruth is very miserable with a bad throat, sore eyes & a cold & cough which she has had for a long time.

MARCH 21

Princess Victora Concert party tonight. We have had real treats in a musical line of late

MARCH 22

Had letters from Bunker & Eddy at Cliveden.

MARCH 23 – 26

NO ENTRIES

MARCH 27

Ruth went to supply room so that she might have lighter work till her cold is better.

Col McCrae went to Paris today.

Very windy & stormy this pm.

MARCH 28

A furious gale here today & very cold.

A convoy this afternoon

A cable came today saying that Allison Elder is dead.[14]

MARCH 29

Ran back to the ward about 9.00 PM to see if my seedlings were in. Found Lapp at work still in the "lab" so he brought them in. They are growing – though it seems a long time since I planted them. Col Elder has gone home on leave. Poor old man: he is completey unnerved by this, his latest calamity

Ruth went back to Ward K again

MARCH 30

Ruth & I had our half days & had planned a picnic to Le Portel. When – such a wonderful surprise – as we went out our gates Cyril, weary, lean, & dirty but still looking fairly well came in on his way for 9 days leave to England. – Such a war broken soldier & so tired & restless. I took him first up on the ramparts of the old town to a quiet seat & Ruth went for a walk while we had a long talk: after which we went down into the town & had a substantial chicken dinner for our lad, the first dinner of its kind for him for many months. then after doing a bit of shopping for him we went down to the barracks to see when the boat would sail – finding it would not go till 7.30 we walked back into town passed the Nurses Club & up to the quiet grounds of the Musée where we sat & talked till it was time for Cyril to leave. We left him at the Barracks – then walked back to camp

Pte. Cyril Gass

MARCH 31

Corporal Wilson from 1st Can[adian] Artillery Brigade came this AM to take Lapp's place in our Ward. Walked with Ruth in hours off up over the hills & by a new road to Wimille & back by the Vallé

APRIL 1

We were given identification tags this morning.

A year ago today we went from Quebec to Montreal after our Military training.

APRIL 2

Two boys from Geralds regiment, Scholey & Noble came up today, while waiting for the boat to tell me that Gerald is at present on leave in England.

APRIL 3

A beautiful sunshiny day.

Cpl Wilson came on the Ward at noon & Lapp had the half day off.

The Royal Artillery Band played in our grounds tonight – such beautiful music. I sat on the steps of Ward N[A?] with Ruth to listen – a wonderful evening.

APRIL 4

Lapp – "up the line with the best of luck" tonight No 5 Convalescent Camp entertained in the YMCA in a review "La Salle de Libertée." I sewed during my hours off

APRIL 5

The mists hang low over the Happy Valley in the early mornings of late & it is good to be alive on these clear spring mornings – If only this dreadful war were over & our boys in Safety once more!

Father writes that [brother] Athel has enlisted. Athel will not be fifteen till the 20th of this month. I am discouraged.

APRIL 6

Gardens are springing up in the night around our hut Wards. The convalescent patients are taking a great interest & doing most of the work. The days are so fine.

APRIL 7

Cyril came back from leave today & brought another NS boy up with him. Ruth & I both had our half days & went down town with the boys. Had a substantial meal the last they will have for some time: then saw them off on their train, "up the line" it is such a terrible term these day[s]. A convoy all Canadians came to us down the line this pm. A great many 27th men.

APRIL 8

Ten sisters of No 3 Can[adian] Stationary Hosp. came tonight to wait here till their hospital – which is to be opposite the Monument on the Calais road – is ready. the[y] have just arrived in France from Lemnos.

Some terrific explosions seemingly out at sea heard tonight. Ruth and I read "the Fleelands" tonight but as usual wandered away from the subject to a discussion of other things. Three of our girls returned from leave tonight

APRIL 9

We get a convoy almost every night lately.

Little Whitney & I went for a walk in the Vallé as we had

morning hours. It was almost summer heat at midday. We took a
few snaps. One with two of the Allies dirigables in the sky as we
went down over the fields to the Valley.

APRIL 10

A lovely day.

Miss Cooper Ruth & I went plant hunting to an old garden in
the suburb just above us. I want plants for my ward garden. we
succeeded in getting pansy forget me not & daisy roots.

APRIL 11

NO ENTRY

APRIL 12

A very rainy day.

APRIL 13

Spent the evening in Ruths room with Mrs Douglas one of the
No 3 sisters whom we knew in Etaples. She told us at length her
experiences since we last saw her at No 1. The first six weeks of
their stay in Lemnos in August 1915 was a nightmare – without
sufficient food unsanitary conditions: & dysentry among their
men & sisters. At first they could not buy food but at last after
much persuasion were able to get each day something from different boats in the harbour. No preparations for their coming
had been made – & the food for their poor patients was awful.
Later however after two sisters & several men had died the food
supply increased. There are sisters not yet recovered from the
effects of the dysentry – in England – in some cases it left a men-
tal condition. No 3 stayed on the island till the last of the evacuation from the Dardenelles, they were then sent to Alexandria for
two months, where at the time things too were very unsettled &
a native rising seemed imminent. When transport became possible they came on here while No 1 Stationary who were with
them were sent to Salonic[k]a.

In the afternoon today in my hours off Miss Brand & I walked
down to see the sick sisters at No 14.

April 14

They are putting up a high wall around our quarters today. Yesterday's mail brought me such a beautiful little Easter message from Granty in the form of a prayer book. Ruth & I had our half days & went to Le Portel on the car. A windy showery day & and we both had headaches. The church the stones for which were carried by the women from the shore below ugly but two or three peasant girls with white caps & black gowns so sweet & fresh: acting as caretakers were most interesting. We walked back to Boulogne by Outreu [Outreau]

A concert by the Lake Hope Party at night.

April 15

Went down town in my hours off with Miss Cooper & bought some more roots for my ward Garden at the market. Also went to see the old Porter of this Jesuit College & got some postcards of the place from him. He is a quaint old figure acting as porter at a boys school on the Rue de Calais – & all his talk is of the wonderful old days when he was Porter at the College & with tears in his eyes he describes the glories of the distroyed monastery.

April 16

This morning a German aeroplane appeared over our camp the guns from the boats in the harbour & the anti air craft guns boomed out immediately & the German flew as fast as possible up towards the sun but dropped a bomb near St Martins Camp which did no damage but fell in a field – The shrapnel from the anti air craft guns fell among our huts. A small bit hit Marie Muir. Ruth & I went out on the ramparts of the old town in our hours off.

April 17

Letters from home & from Granty written April 2nd.

Miss Steele & Miss Lindsay left for Le Treport.

April 18

Miss Corelli & Miss Ledue arrived to stay over with us on their way to a Clearing Station.

A Princess Victoria Concert party in the YMCA tonight.

APRIL 19

A French concert party entertained tonight in the YMCA. Mdle [mademoiselle] Champion & Monsieur Vanderstreeck, the latter of the Opera Comic Paris.

APRIL 20

NO ENTRY

APRIL 21

Good Friday.
I went to part of the three hour service in the town with Miss Bliss

APRIL 22

NO ENTRY

APRIL 23

Easter morning dawned beautiful & fair
I went to the early service in the YMCA hut. In the afternoon as Ruth is still not allowed to go without her dark glasses, She & Stephie & I went down to the Valley together – We took some snaps – then sat in a field & ate biscuits which I brought – then we read the The Brushwood Boy aloud, & finished it as we walked slowly home. In the evening Ruth came in & lay on my bed while I read "the Flellands"

APRIL 24

Ruth taken away to No 14 General infectious section with German measles – Such a tragedy has not yet befallen us.

APRIL 25

In the morning a German aeroplane appeared high up over the camp & circled around over the town. Two bombs were heard & the anti air craft guns & the guns from the boats boomed out many times but did not succeed in hitting the enemy. Nearly noon I was told to go on night duty tonight & as I wanted to give my patients a special treat for tea I went down town immediately after lunch. As I was turning up the lane of Le Petit couchon [Cochon?] I heard the guns again & looked to see an aeroplane circling low near the docks but it soon rose & started sea ward followed by the bursting of shells of many guns all of which failed to do any damage.

This afternoon one of our McGill orderlies lost his eye through the explosion of a soda water bottle on his ward. The sight is completely gone in one eye & the other is badly hurt. Dickie has gone on tonight to special the case.

A beautiful summer day today.

APRIL 26

Last night there was an air raid at Etaples which is now a big base for troops. Several incend[i]ary bombs were dropped near 24 General Hospital & No 1 Can[adian] but fortunately did no harm.

About 9 AM a German aeroplane appeared over Boulogne – the guns immediately fired on it & several times it had a very close call but tacked & turned mounting higher & higher right into the heart of the sun & so got away. Rumour says Boulogne is not using its best guns on these isolated German aeroplanes for by doing so the enemy will discover where they are situated (which is one of the probable reasons for the recent scouting in this line) & so will be able to avoid them.

A summer day today.

APRIL 27

I walked down town this morning with Connie Stuart & P. Babbit. Took my new perscription for spectacles to be filled.

Did not sleep well today.

A very hot day today.

Convoy at 9.30 PM. I only received nine new cases.

Cyril writes on the 21st

"We have just come out of the trenches or perhaps I should say where the trenches used to be, for they are completely smashed to pieces by shells. It has been the worst I have yet seen".

APRIL 28

An uprising in Dublin for which Martial Law has been proclaimed. Sir Rodger [Roger] Casement was captured some days ago. It is announced today that James Connolly the Labour leader is the self styled "Comander in Chief" of the Rebels[15]

Miss Brand & I walked out to the Isolation Hospital at Wimereux this morning & talked to Ruth through her little hut door. She is better & was to get up today. It is very hot & I was very tired when we arrived in camp at noon. Did not sleep this pm.

APRIL 29

Went to bed early today, but could not rest though I stayed in bed all day.

HMS Russell, Capt William Bowden Smith RN flying the flag of Rear Admiral Fremantle struck a mine in the Mediterranean & sank. 124 officers & men missing

APRIL 30

James Connolly died of wounds received during the rising in Dublin.

Other arrests made in Ireland.

Transplanted some of my little plants today.

MAY 1

Could not sleep so got up & went for a walk through the Valley with Miss Cooper. A very large convoy tonight. Into my own ward 18 patients gas poisoning cases were admitted. The Germans with a favourable wind have used this diabolical method again near & about Armentiers [Armentières].

Here in the grounds the Narcissi & Blue bells are lovely now & there are so many of them. The patients pick them and bring them in to the Wards.

MAY 2

Slept well today. All day.

The gas cases of last night tell me that the wind changed suddenly on Sunday & before they could move the gas was upon them. It was sleeping hours & most of the men had to be wakened. Many never waked again.

MAY 3

Went into Boulogne this morning. Got my glasses – Ordered the little "chaplet" for Granty. & then took the car out to Wimereux to see Ruth. She is coming back to us tomorrow but is not looking very well & has neuralagia. I stood at her cabin door &

talked to her for a long time. I was very late getting to bed & did not sleep well. Another air raid on East coast of England last night. No lives lost.

MAY 4

Went downtown this AM with Connie Stuart & Dickie. Got some nice snaps of the Happy Valley taken on Easter Sunday.

MAY 5

Tonight Miss Bagshaw & Winnie Brown who are with the Laval Unit came up to dinner they will stay the night & go on at noon tomorrow to St Cloud [Saint-Cloud] where their hospital is situated – The rest of the MGH [Montreal General Hospital] girls who came over with them are at Shorncliff still but expect to follow to St Cloud soon.

Lecture on the "Campaign in the Dardenelles" by Professor Baillie tonight.

Got up early this afternoon as I could not sleep & took Miss Drake down into Happy Valley. It was her first sight of the Valley & she was delighted. A year ago tonight we said Good Bye to our Montreal friends.

My Need

I & the bird
And the wind together
Sang a supplication
In the Winter Weather.

The bird sang for sunshine
And the trees for Winter fruit
And for love in the springtime
When the thickets shoot.

And I sang for patience
When the tear drops start,
Clean hands & clear eyes
And a faith ful heart.

A.C. Benson.[16]

MAY 6

Went out with Winnie & Miss Bagshaw to Wimereux this morning to see Ruth. Called on our way back at the Louvre to see Blanche Bibby but she was out & as we had to get back to camp for bed we could not wait. The Laval party went on to St Cloud this afternoon

MAY 7

Dug & transplanted some of my flowers in the little beds I have made in front of our hut in the lines.
A rainy day.

MAY 8

A windy rainy day.

MAY 9

Another day of storm wind & rain.
The Convalescent Camp Concert party entertained in the YMCA tonight.

MAY 10

Got up at four o'clock today as it was fine & went down town [with] Miss Cooper. Got a frame for [brother] Robs photograph.

MAY 11

Bycicled out to Wimereux on Connie Stuarts wheel this AM to see Starkey. A lovely morning & a delightful ride down the hills. Returned by Wimille & the Calais Road.
Poor Starkey is in very bad condition. She has had acute rheumatic fever followed by complications. She is such a sweet girl.
Edith Stuart returned from sick leave tonight & a young girl from Montreal Miss Ross also came to take Martha Allen's post in our Mess. Miss Allen is at Shorncliff.

Nurses' quarters, Boulogne. Clare's hut with flower beds.

MAY 12

Got up rather early & went with Stephie down into the lane & gathered pretty red phlox & hawthorn by the side of the brook. A heavy rainstorm came on at 10 PM during which we had a convoy come in.

A party of Red Cross officers & ladies (amateurs all) presented the "Duke of Killicrakie" for our patients tonight. It was very good indeed.

MAY 13

Heavy rain all day: late in the afternoon I put on rain coat hat & rubber boots & went down in the lane to gather hawthorn & the red flowers for the Altar tomorrow. Everything was dripping wet & the hawthorn shook its wetness down all over my face. The brook is almost a torrent today & everything is so fresh & sweet & the birds so happy in spite of the rain.

Later I got such a shock when in the paper of May 10th in the
Casualty List I see Canadian Infantry Regiment – Gass – No: —
— G. (the number is almost like Cyrils – just one figure wrong)
missing – It cannot be our boy!

MAY 14

Went to early service this AM & said a prayer for the poor missing lad whoever he may be. & tonight received a field post card
from Cyril written on the 8th of the month.[17]

MAY 15 – 16

NO ENTRY

MAY 17

Worked in my garden this AM. Slept the rest of the day.

MAY 18

Ruth & I went down town bought one bycicle & ordered a second from the little shop near Trinity Church.

MAY 19

Guns from the direction of the sea heard all night tonight
Connie S & I rode down to Wimereux to see Starky this morning

MAY 20

Bycicled down town with Ruth today & did a few errands.
Among others got flowers for the church tomorrow. In spite of
the heavy gun fire out at sea last night there is no report in the
papers tonight of any sort. It is possible that the guns may have
been bombarding the coast further north.

No 3 Stationary Sisters left for their new abode over the hill.

MAY 21

It is very hot. Did not sleep well today. This morning bycicled
with Connie Stuart, through Rupembert & Wimille to Wimereux
to see Starky.

MAY 22

Went down town & had some alterations made to bycicle. Ruth
had her hair washed

MAY 23

Bycicled with Ruth first to Wimereux to No 14 Stationary with some vases & to Starky with her mail – then on through the sand dunes to Ambletoise [Ambleteuse], then inland through a swampy district & back to the top of the hill above Wimille, down the hill, through the village & back by the Vallé de Denacre. Had coffee & cake at the café before we pushed our bycicles up the lane to camp. Did not sleep well today; though it has been a beautiful sunshiny cool day

MAY 24

Went for breakfast with Ruth to the café in the Valley (omellette, French Rolls, fresh butter, have coffee in one of the little rose arbours in the garden Read The Blue Bird) Came back to camp, went to bed & slept well all day

Red Cross Recreation hut opened today.

MAY 25

Off night duty

Started with Connie Stuart to bycicle to the NS [Nursing Sisters'] Convalescent home at Hardelot, but misconnected in Boulogne & after waiting for her for about an hour, I put my bycicle for keeping in the Red Cross headquarters at the Christol & went out alone in Lady Giffords car. After lunch went to bed. The Villa in which the Sister's Convalescent Home has been arranged is a pretty one in the midst of the woods and belongs to Princess Louise Duchess of Argyle.

MAY 26

Wakened about 6 AM. Read & wrote till breakfast time. Breakfast in bed then went for a walk with an English Q.A. and heard a good deal of their order. Miss Glendenning is here at present – after lunch Miss Glendenning & I & four other sisters walked up to the Condette Church. These roads are like old friends & so beautiful just now. Returned at 6 PM in the car with two English sisters for Wimereux – two Q.A. Civil Reserves.[18]

MAY 27

Ruth brought me my breakfast this AM. Afterwards we went down town together to see the bycicle man on business. Then went back to camp & I washed my hair before dinner. I went to [Ward]N 2 after dinner on duty.

MAY 28

N 2 Ward all day today. Read in my hours off.

MAY 29

Met Ruth in town after five o'clock, & we went to look up the bycicleman —

Had Typhoid inoculation in the evening.

MAY 30

Ruth Dick & Miss Watling went for leave today. It is a lovely day but I am very miserable with my inoculation. Temp 101–102 all afternoon.

MAY 31

Feel better today but not quite myself. Went down town with Stephie in my hours off. Ruth's bycicle not ready.

JUNE 1

Had my half day. Very rather miserable again today so Stephie & I spent the whole afternoon down by the brook with our rugs pillows & books. I slept for quite a long time. A Lecture in the YMCA tonight on "Russia".

Note [?]

JUNE 2

N 2 went into isolation today. A case of measles developed this morning. Rumours today of a frightful battle near Ypres in which our Canadian troops are taking part.[19]

Note from Ruth written night of their arrival in London

JUNE 3

Stephie & I went down town again today to see about Ruth's bycicle. It still is not ready so I cancelled the order hoping she may get one in England. A big convoy of patients from the PPCLI [Princess Patricia's Canadian Light Infantry]'s 4 & 5th CMR [Canadian Mounted Rifle]'s – Also a frightful battle in North Sea reported[20]

JUNE 4

The news of the fighting Thursday, Friday & yesterday is ghastly.
Our troops simply mown down without hope of resistance by
artillery fire. Miss Harrisons brother has come in with a head
wound. Mrs Giffins brother was last seen by one of these men
lying on his face in a trench. Louise McGreer's brother has been
in the thick of it. – & there are thousands of others. It is terrible.
I went down to the Red Cross today with Mrs Giffin in hours off
to see if we could get news of her brother at the Red Cross. We
waited for a long time in the Museum & returned later to the
Cristol but met with no success –
At Sea there has been an enormous battle with terrible loss on
both sides so the papers report
Another convoy came to us last night & another today
We heard from a patient also that Murray Anderson, Ruth['s]
cousin, was reported at one of the Clearing Stations shot
through the lungs.

JUNE 5

Another trip into town with Mrs Giffin to the Red Cross but no
information. She believes her brother is dead.
Louise McGreer had a telegram from the Rev A P McGreer that
her brother is seriously wounded
Heard today from a patient that Lapp is doing most excellent
work in his new post
Note from Ruth tonight written in London

JUNE 6

The tales of the loss of life in the recent fighting around Ypres
increase each day. This is part of a third battle of Ypres. Our
Canadian troops lost their trenches & retook them. It is a ghastly
affair.
I went for a ride around the back roads with Whitney tonight.

JUNE 7

Note from Ruth tonight written in Edinburgh.
Had an operation for tonsils in the ward today so was not off all
day but went for a little ride with Stephie tonight after dinner.

Reported today that Lord Kitchener with his staff is drowned off the coast of Scotland the ship wrecked by a mine or bomb on board or a torpedo during a storm.[21]

Truly Calamity seems to have come upon us. The French people are in despair of this latest mishap.

JUNE 8

Poor Louise heard today that her brother is gone. Poor lad! It is easier to die at present than to live under conditions at the front. His mother of course is the one to whom the suffering comes in this case. The lad's message to his mother was to say to her he had died fighting for his country & to be sure & let the other boys come.

JUNE 9

Mrs Giffin is sure now that her brother is gone too. Cooper moved today.

JUNE 10

Miss Eastwood & I got flowers for the church today. On the whole the War News from our front is better. Our Canadian troops have retaken their trenches, but of course to us this means nowadays the thought of carnage & loss of life. The Russians are doing wonderful work lately.

JUNE 11

Whitsunday. Miss Eastwood & I got up at five & went down town to St John Church for early service. We came back up such a pretty lane to the windmills on our way back to camp.

We have been having convoys continuously all this week.

The Russians have captured thousands of prisoners lately.

JUNE 12

Ruth & Dick & Watling came back tonight. Ruth brought me a dear little Scotch pebble silver trinket box. She is looking much better for her holiday.

I got their room ready for them & then lay down on Ruth's bed & fell asleep. They came at ten & wakened me. Then I got their supper ready.

JUNE 13

Early this morning a patient from the 25th in Ward B (McLeod) sent for me to let me know that Cyril is wounded. The same shell silenced the whole of Cyril's gun crew. This man was able to walk out yesterday afternoon but Cyril had to wait for dark for the stretcher bearers, as he is wounded in the right foot. I've watched every convoy today, but he has not come down.

JUNE 14

Today in my hours off I made enquiries for Cyril at Red Cross Hdqts. without success. A letter from Gerald during the afternoon telling me of his wound. After dinner Ruth & I went from one hospital to another on our bycicles finally when it was nearly dark & we had no success I decided to go to the DDMS [Deputy Director Medical Services] to see what he could do for me. He was very kind & said he would telephone me later. About eleven o'clock the message came Cyril has been admitted to No 8 Stationary Hospital – progress quite satisfactory – a guarded message.
As the clocks have all gone on one hour I could not go down tonight.

JUNE 15

As soon as I had done the absolute necessities on my Ward I went down to No 8 on my bycicle. I could not go sooner as convoy after convoy is arriving & things are frightfully busy in our hospital.
I found Cyril a very very sick boy, with his right foot gone – practically shattered to pieces. they took it off shortly after his arrival yesterday at 4 AM. Miss Griffiths, an English sister I met at Hardelot is looking after him. He is so good & brave but does not know yet his foot is gone. He is too sick to talk very much.
Went down again with Ruth on our bycicles. He is not quite so well tonight. Wrote Mother & Gerald.

JUNE 16

Took my half day & went out to Cyril – Sent cable to Mother. Went with Ruth in the evening again to No 8. Cyril seems a little better. When they told him his foot was off he said Well I suppose I'll have to make the best of it – there's only one thing I dare not do & that's go home to them dead. He is on the list for England.

JUNE 17

Went down to see Cyril for a little while in morning – Saw his dressing –

Gave my isolation patients a party in pm. Went with Ruth again to No 8 in evening. Cyril seems more like his old self tonight.

JUNE 18

Ran down to No 8 in AM just in time to say good bye to Cyril as he was put into the ambulance for England – He was suffering this morning poor lad.

This is first communion Sunday here for the children.

In Evening Ruth & Stephie & I bycicled out to Souverin Moulin [Souverain-Moulin] for dinner. Had Rabbit pie & pancakes. Ward came out of Isolation today.

Daisies, wild roses – honeysuckle – yellow marguarites – corn-flowers & poppies (the latter in smaller quantities than in the sand dune district) in abundance at present. Also the smell of new mown hay is everywhere about the fields

JUNE 19

Spent whole day in doing up my ward again. Everything fresh & clean.

JUNE 20

15 new patients last night – Most of them gas cases from the recent gas attack near Messines & Armentiers. Bycicled out by Bainchin [Baincthun] to Pont de Brique [Pont-de-Briques] after tea

JUNE 21

Weeded my garden tonight after dinner

New orders to evacuate everyone able to travel to England, as a British offensive on this front is expected. A letter from Cyril says he is in the Royal Infirmary Leicester.

On the road to Soverain-Moulin

JUNE 22

NO ENTRY

JUNE 23

Am very very tired these days & go to bed very early after dinner.
No Canadian mail now for over a week.

JUNE 24

Still no Canadian mail

JUNE 25

Corpus Christi Sunday – the streets to the different ou[t]door
shrines are covered with fresh grass & leaves. Ruth & I had last
hours off duty & went for a bycicle ride out the Desvres road
through Mont Lambert [Montlambert] to [blank] where there
were three altars one at the entrance one in the middle & one
on the far side of the village. Here we waited to see the procession which was very picturesque & quaint & might very well have
belonged to the Middle Ages; the girls in their wide dresses
& wreathes of flowers in their hair & the little boys in their sur-
plices singing. Ruth got a picture so after we had our tea in a
field we walked back to camp.

JUNE 26

NO ENTRY

JUNE 27

Cyril's letter seems cheerful & his condition satisfactory.

JUNE 28 – 29

NO ENTRIES

JUNE 30

At last the Canadian Mails have come. I had a lot of letters but all written before the news of Cyril's wound reached home.

JULY 1

A great advance in the Somme district is reported to have started today.[22]

Ruth & I went down to the post office today in our hours off. A little impromptu concert in the Red Cross Hut in honour of Dominion day. I performed, also Williams. Miss Kennedy of the Canteen was the only outsider present. She sang – Capt Piery sang some foolishness.

Miss McMurrich came through today on her way to England for leave. She is with a French Red Cross Hosp. in Belgium near Dunkirk. She will stay overnight with us. Ruth and I took her for a walk down into the Vallée just before dinner.

JULY 2

Ruth & I bycicled in last [h]ours out to Wirwignes to see the little "home made" church which we admired so much last year. We had tea in the Boulogne Woods. Strawberries & bread & butter & were so hungry. Stayed in the church for about half an hour then returned. The road near Wirwignes very very hilly & difficult but from the Woods back to Boulogne a lovely ride.

A report today says that Etaples & Camiers got big convoys last night

We are making preparations for a great rush & all leave has been cancelled.

Amy Baynes came through today on her way to Rouen

JULY 3

We had morning hours so Ruth & I rode down to No 14 to see
Miss Drake who has gone there with a bad throat. We had lunch
in Wimereux & arrived back in camp to find the ambulances
arriving Ruth got a lot of cases. I didn't get any – though my
ward is ready for either surgical or medical work
Glendenning & Fortescue went up to a Clearing hospital tonight

JULY 4

Last night we got 300 cases into our hospital. Many of them very
bad wounds. Most of the minor cases have been admitted to the
CC [Convalescent Camp] so as our wards are still empty Alice
Stewart & I were sent over to the CC to do dressing

JULY 5

Since the first of the month the British have captured Mon-
tauban, Mametz – Fricourt & La Boiselle [La Boisselle] & the
French advance to the r[igh]t of the British has been very extensive – The Italians & Russians are also making great advances.
The great push forward has begun & though the losses are heavy
yet the men are cheerful – but so frightfully weary & so ragged
& dirty – they will go asleep on the benches waiting for their
dressings at the CC. We had 200 cases into the hospital last night
After dinner Ruth & I rode down to see Miss Drake.

JULY 6

Not quite such a big convoy last night – but many cases sent in
from Etaples & must wait here for the boat.

JULY 7

A convoy of six hundred came to us last night & the evacuation
goes on apace.
We are frightfully busy at CC all morning, & then come back
& help out here in PM[23]

JULY 8

We have been highly complemented by the DDMS of the district
as a hospital for the efficient manner in which we have handled
the great number of wounded this week as we have had forty per-
cent more cases in & out than any other hospital in the district.

The War News still continues good

My sweet peas are lovely with fragrant blossoms. We had over 1100 cases in our hospital this morning & are now short about 9 sisters. Still the work is being done well – everyone is proving his or her ablity at present. The patients are for the most part from Albert, Tricourt & La Boiselle.

JULY 9

A busy busy morning at CC. Four of us dressed 200 convoy cases, besides others. After lunch I went to Ward B where Ruth is very busy. 36 patients had just gone to England & their space was to prepare for the next convoy. Then we got teas for the other seventy odd patients after which I went to the Supply room & made dressings for the rest of the afternoon. Ruth is not very well today.

JULY 10

A busy morning again at CC.

We had 78 patients from 11.45 – 12.45 to dress they were straight from the fighting at La Boiselle & so muddy & dirty – some of the wounds were quite bad ones & were marked up for England. A big convoy in our hospital again last night

JULY 11

NO ENTRY

JULY 12

The War News still continues to be good.

JULY 13

The British & French are still advancing slowly in the Somme district & the casualties are coming down steadily to us from this action. Our sisters have started a Canteen for food & hot coffee & cocoa for our men & stretcher bearers who are practically working day & night these days. Ruth & I took it tonight & from 9 PM till 12.30 it was greatly patronized. After that we left the drinks hot on the stove & the sandwiches on the table for them for the rest of the night & we went to bed.

JULY 14

Aleck Trivett admitted to Ward O last night with a bullet in his right upper arm

JULY 15

CC in AM. Red Cross hut all afternoon. Mrs Giffin is having her half day. Went for a little ride up over the hills to the St Omar [Saint-Omer] road with Ruth after dinner till dusk. A little party given tonight for Miss Chisholm. Aleck is going on to England to have his bullet removed as there is no immediate hurry as the wound is clean.

JULY 16

Sal Chisholm is leaving for England today to be married.

JULY 17

After dinner Connie Stuart & I rode down to No 8 to see Miss Griffith but she was out.

JULY 18

Ruths birthday. CC in AM. Pneumonia tent in PM We celebrated in hours off by taking portraits (?) of one another in our rooms. And by a bycicle ride after dinner up over the hill to Rupembert then by new roads straight through to Olington [Olincthun] & [blank] to the Calais Road above Wimille I gave Ruth a little French medal of Jean[ne] D'Arc

JULY 19

NO ENTRY

JULY 20

Went down town in hours off & got my little painting which was framed. Alice Stewart came with me. Letters from home & Granty this evening. War news from Somme district still continues good

JULY 21

All night long terrific & continuous explosions which shook our huts have been going on in the direction of Calais & have lasted with diminishing violence till 10 AM.
Very big convoys of Australians from Armentiers last night also. We admitted 720 patients in our hosp. from 6 PM to 10 AM this

Clare Gass, "portrait" by Ruth Loggie

morning. CC had about 300 cases too. I went to the Red Cross
Hut all afternoon. 46 cases there all bad wounds. These lads had
made an attack in the face of a terrific shell fire. Canteen for our
boys after dinner.

JULY 22

CC in AM

Half day in PM. Alice Stewart & I went for a little bycicle ride
after dinner in direction of Souverin Moulin. Yesterday morning's explosions was from the destruction of the Ammunition
Supply stores just outside Calais in a little village which was practically blown to pieces. Nineteen bodies have been recovered but
there are very many missing

Five aeroplanes appeared over the village about 11 PM &
dropped bombs on the Ammunition sheds. The wires of the
flash lights had been cut by spies & our guns could do nothing
to the German airships which got away leaving the terrific work

Ruth Loggie, "portrait" by Clare Gass

of explosion to go on late into the morning. The loss is about
5 million pounds worth of ammunition besides the village & a
terrible toll of innocent lives.

JULY 23

CC in AM as usual.

Red Cross Hut in PM. It is a busy place.

The Australians are splendid lads. As Capt Evans says "They are
here for the job" After dinner Ruth & I bycicled out to the Souverin Moulin through Rupembert to the St Omer road then
down through the woods by the steep hill to the village & the
Chateau. We had coffee & cake in the tea garden of the café at
the foot of the hill then came back by Wimille & walked through
the Vallée du Denacre back to camp. The Vallée with its summer
coat of thick leafy green is quite a different valley to the early
spring Vallée but just as wonderful.

JULY 24 – 26

NO ENTRIES

JULY 27

Had a half day & went with Ruth, Dickie, Miss Powell & Miss
Bradley for a cab drive through Ambleteuse district to Marquise
& back by Offrethun & Souverin Moulin

Mr. Markham's Concert party in the evening played "Which is
Which"

Today

JULY 28

Cyrils letter of 26th reached me today: he was to have his second
operation yesterday

JULY 29

NO ENTRY

JULY 30

A little note from Cyril says he is allright.

JULY 31 – AUGUST 2

NO ENTRIES

AUGUST 3

Half day & Ruth & I went into town to have our hair washed
& to do a bit of shopping.

AUGUST 4

Such heavy gunfire somewhere to the north last night. No news
of its meaning this morning

AUGUST 5

Ruth & I after dinner rode through the wheat fields & the sunset
to Wierre[-]Effroy, by the Souverin Moulin road. Such lovely
countryside & lovely harvest fields. At Wierre Effroy which is a
pretty village there is a quaint 12th Century Church & a magic
well of St Godeleine to which yearly pilgrimages go. We went
into the church for a little while and it was quite dark before we
got back to camp

AUGUST 6

Took Mrs Giffin for a little bycicle ride this evening down the La
Poterie road.

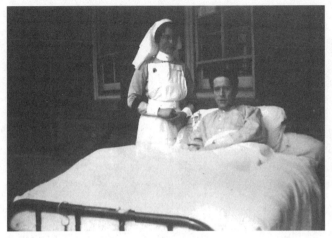

Cyril in hospital, Leicester

AUGUST 7

Tremendous gun fireing somewhere to the north last night. No news of it today

Cyril's last letter tells me he hopes I wont go to England just yet for my leave as he is not yet able to get up.

AUGUST 8

Claire McLeod left us today for England to be married.

The King was in Boulogne today. Some of the sisters & officers saw him. Canon Hanny at CC told us about him. Capt Hodson also told us the story of how he crossed the Channel after his accident last year & how all his attendants were seasick. Capt Evans at CC is asking for special leave today.

Connie Stuart & Kaireen McKay went out on the bycicles tonight.

AUGUST 9

NO ENTRY

AUGUST 10

Some days ago the news that Martha Allen had resigned from the CAMC reached us[24]

AUGUST 11

Half day —
Constance Stuart, Kaireen McKay & I went for a picnic out to
Wierre Effroy on our bycicles. Such a nice afternoon – we rode
through the Souverin Moulin valley then up the hill & had our
tea in the woods back of the village of Wierre; rested for about
an hour there lying on the grass then went round through the
village, stopped for a little while at the church then on to the
Holy Well of St Godeline – where we all drank of the water. Had
Coffee & Pancakes at Café de Souverin Moulin on our way
home. It has been such a nice day.

AUGUST 12

St. Claire's day – Mademoiselle Rose has told us that all girls
have two birthdays in France. One on the real date of their birth
which they call "L'An[n]iversaire" & the other on the day of the
Saint for whom they are named called "La Fête" – so this is "La
Fête" pour moi

AUGUST 13

Last hours today, so Ruth & I & Misses Clark & Gray took our tea
down by the little brook near "the Lane"

AUGUST 14

Walked after dinner with Miss Cooper down to the Cemetary to
find Arthur Pentz's grave, but as it was late we returned without
finding out more than that he was buried there.
Had wonderful baked beans in Miss Clarks room later.

AUGUST 15

The Anniversary of the coming of Notre Dame de Boulogne to
these shores. The grand procession to be held next Sunday.

AUGUST 16

NO ENTRY

AUGUST 17

Stephie & Tate & Miss Brand came off night duty tonight & had
a picnic tea down by the brook, so Ruth & I joined them & we
read Kipling after tea "Below the Milldam" & "They." After dinner we (Ruth & I) went out on our bycicles & explored "Moulin

L'Abbé" [Moulins-l'Abbé] Valley. It is such a peaceful pretty spot

AUGUST 18

NO ENTRY

AUGUST 19

Had my half day & went down town with Ruth. & after dinner went out for a bycicle ride through La Poterie & Wimille & got caught in a storm of rain.

AUGUST 20

Went to Ward W. to open up the new ward there (with Alice Stewart) in part of the old ruin – Such a busy day & some very bad wounds from last nights convoy.

This is the Anniversary Procession Day in Boulogne of the arrival of the Miraculous Statue. I would have liked to have seen the quaint dresses of the Procession but we did not have a minute off duty all day.

AUGUST 21

Very busy all day. No news of my leave though it is now a week since I applied for it

A Navel engagement of which very few details are given is reported tonight in the North Sea. We heard heavy fireing in the direction of the Sea all this morning.[25]

AUGUST 22

Some bad wounds in last night. We have two such nice lads here light duty patients Satinover, an Australian & Cameron a Scottie[26]

AUGUST 23

Heard today that our leave has gone through so expect to go at a moments notice[27]

AUGUST 24

NO ENTRY

AUGUST 25

We left by the 10 o'clock boat, Miss McConnell for Ireland to see her mother who is ill & I for Leicester – Had lunch on the London train. Arrived London 2.30 pm – Went to Matron in Chief's office then back to the Hotel where Mr McConnell had come to meet his sister. Went to see Daddy Long Legs in the evening, walked home from the theatre – such dark dark streets – It seemed almost impossible to find the way at times

AUGUST 26

Left by 9 AM train for Leicester. Arrived midday & after leaving my things at the YWCA went to the hospital to find Cyril in good spirits but very thin indeed & with no appetite or strength, up & about on crutches. Took him into the town for tea & a drive in Abbey Park & stayed with him afterwards till nine o'clock.[28]

AUGUST 27

Sat with Cyril in hospital grounds all morning – in the afternoon took him into town to tea. Met Mr & Mrs Stokes, & stayed with him till dark. – The sister here a Miss Francis has been very kind indeed to Cyril & most courteous to me, She took me over the hospital this afternoon

AUGUST 28

Spent morning in hospital grounds & started with Cyril immediately after lunch for a motor drive into Warwickshire. Such a nice afternoon, first to Coventry, with its quaint old streets & beautifully kept modern town & lovely church spires. The roads around specially beautifully – From Coventry to Leamington & then out to Kenilworth Castle where we left the Motor & explored the old ruin. Cyril doing wonderfully well on his crutches – I took several snaps of the ruin. Back to Leamington & from thence to Warwick – a lovely old town where we had tea after which we went out to see that marvellous place Warwick Castle then along through Shakespeare's country by the quiet Avon passed thatchedroofed cottage[s] & through beautiful country roads & lanes. It was a long ride about 80 miles in all & we arrived in Leicester just as the sun was setting: Cyril was not a bit tired & really had enjoyed the day.

AUGUST 29

Very rainy – I took Cyril up to the Museum in the afternoon & after taking him back to the hospital went into town for my own tea & brought him sandwitches & other dainties for his tea.

AUGUST 30

Sat in Hospital grounds in AM & took Cyril into town for the Moving Pictures & tea – then back to Hospital where I stayed till dark

AUGUST 31

Went to a matinee with Cyril – such a funny play – we laughed heartily at some parts. Tea afterwards & a bit of shopping – we bought a little Queen Elizabeth bell for Mother

SEPTEMBER 1

As it proved rather an uncertain day we went to the pictures again – Cyril likes them – then to tea. He is really looking a bit better & seems to enjoy his meals more than when I first came. In the mornings before it is time to go to the Hospital I usually go for a walk & explore the town. I've found some interesting old churches but for the most part Leicester is a clean well kept modern red brick town.

SEPTEMBER 2

The pictures again this afternoon as Cyril likes them for a change & the weather has not been very certain.

SEPTEMBER 3

A motor drive out into the country by the Stony Gate road, then back to hospital & we talked late into the evening as it was my last day in Leicester[29]

SEPTEMBER 4

Left by morning train for London.
The Kingsley Hotel is full of Canadian nurses recently arrived from Canada. Went out for a long walk in pm & finally ended up in Kensington Gardens for tea. Came back between showers which had suddenly started

SEPTEMBER 5

Loo[k]ed up Muriel, & spent the day with her going in the evening with her & her Aunt to see Chin Chin Chou at his Majesty's a delightful modern version of Ali Baba & the Forty Thieves
Westminster Abbey

Cyril on crutches

SEPTEMBER 6

Left for Folkstone by early train. Went to Queens Hotel & waited there after lunch for B.A. & K.N. – & went with them later to Canterbury where we had a delightful afternoon. The Cathedral is grand.

SEPTEMBER 7

Spent day at Hospital with B.A. & left for France at 7.00 pm. Ruth was down to meet us.

SEPTEMBER 8

Went on duty in Ward W.

Six new Nurses have come during my absence – a Western nurse Miss Jennings is in my room with me; Had supper in Stevies room last night. I went to Ward W. in the old ruin. Very busy there. Found my room beautifully arranged by Miss Ruth Loggie – clean curtains up etc & everything in order.

SEPTEMBER 9

Ruth & I had last hours & went down to old town for tea & shopping for Ruth.

SEPTEMBER 10

A very big convoy last night – mostly Canadians from the Somme. Such bad bad cases. I like Capt Woods' work & he is so kind & good to the men.

Our ward is full & we are sending these patients out quickly which makes for very strenuous work. Miss Jennings & I do all the dressings & some of them are such big ones.

SEPTEMBER 11

Such a busy busy day

SEPTEMBER 12

Orders to evacuate everything possible are in order, & all preparations for a big rush are on.

SEPTEMBER 13

Our Ward is almost empty again so I had my half day & Ruth & I had a lovely long afternoon out in the country on our bycicles out the St Omer Road, through the Boulogne Forest to Le Waast & Colembert where we had tea (most extraordinary tea infusion of tobacco I think). Home by Wierre Effroy & Souverin Moulin – a lovely ride & home in time for dinner

SEPTEMBER 14

Ruth goes on night duty tonight

SEPTEMBER 15

Miss Clark left for Canada today. Her mother is very ill – Three new sisters came today

SEPTEMBER 16

Three big convoys last night. Our ward full again. 110 patients & our own dear Canadian lads – the 2nd Division has lost heavily We have a 21st boy in who came over with us on the boat. Nearly all their officers are gone.

SEPTEMBER 17

We are very very busy, & our patients very sick – terrible wounds & most of them are such bricks.

The weather has become very rainy & miserably cold.

SEPTEMBER 18

NO ENTRY

SEPTEMBER 19

I go on night duty in Ward O & T tonight

SEPTEMBER 20

Have 46 beds in O & 88 in T to look after some medical & some surgical –

SEPTEMBER 21

As usual I cannot sleep in the day

Two convoys tonight

Camiers Aug – Nov 15 –   3,041

Boulogne Feb – July 21 –   14,325

Admitted July 1st to July 21   6,006

    Deaths during July   .42 [30]

SEPTEMBER 22

Went down town this morning with Dick & Ruth – took Ruth's bycicle to get the pedal mended

Guns firing not far south tonight & many search lights & star shells in the sky

SEPTEMBER 23

Heard today that R P Campbell has been killed – this will be a terrible blow to the medical profession in Montreal & the loss to the world of one more good man – a doctor & a gentleman.[31]

SEPTEMBER 24

Last night for a long time the sky in the west was lighted up with fire works. – & the search lights were out in full force. – There was also a great deal of distant gunfireing.

Ruths Australian put in an appearance again last night. He is at the Etaples base.

SEPTEMBER 25

Heard today there was an air raid over south & midlands of England & two Zeps brought down one of which was taken intact & its crew captured.[32]

Rumour says that our friend Lapp has been recommended for

the DCM [Distinguished Conduct Medal].

SEPTEMBER 26

Went down town & had my hair washed this morning.

In my convoy tonight there were a great many Canadian boys.

SEPTEMBER 27

The war news today is very good. Our troops have taken Combles & many prisoners & war material. I hope the casualties are not heavy. The weather lately has been beautiful. Clear September days

SEPTEMBER 28

Went out after breakfast into the dewy fields to pick mushrooms. Ruth & I. Met a little French boy Edward Latteux, such a clever polite child of Modern France. He came with us over the hills in our search. These are his last days of holiday time for on Sunday he goes back to school in Paris. We made an engagement with him to meet him tomorrow morning. We got a nice lot of mushrooms [Marginal notation:] (Me Eduard Latteau College St Charles St Brique Cote du nord Paris)

SEPTEMBER 29

Last night the sky was brilliant at times with the illumination either of gun fire or guide lights. Heavy fireing heard in the distance. In spite of the rain Ruth & I kept our appointment with the French laddie & went for a long tramp in rain coats & rubber boots with him. Brought back a huge basket full & my hat as well. Treated the neighbourhood for supper tonight

As we came in this morning wet & weary, Roy Glennister was singing in our Anti hut. We stayed for half an hour to listen.

I slept very badly today

SEPTEMBER 30

I receive patients in this Ward every night but last night was a specially busy one & as usual I am sleeping very badly

OCTOBER 1

A lovely morning, with heavy dew so Ruth with Alice Stewart & I went for a little ride out the St Omer road then over the hill & down to L'Abbé Moulin, where we took a couple of snaps of the old mill, then went down by the brook among the reeds above the dam & watched the water on the old wheel – then back to our bycicles where we met an old Frenchman in velveteens who spoke very good English & advised us not to leave our bycicles, in full view of passersby, but we told him that all French people were honest & there was no danger. We then pushed up the hill through blackberrie bordered lane to St Lambert [Saint-Lambert] & home by the Desvres road.

OCTOBER 2

On the Somme for these last weeks our troops have been advancing steadily, slowly & surely, but the lists of casualties are large & our hospital has been busy. Also there are a great many sick especially from the Ypres Salient

A rainy day all day today in which everyone slept well.

OCTOBER 3

Went down town this AM with D. R. & W. & while there bought Granty a pretty French dressing gown for Christmas – also some necessities for myself. Another Zepp brought down in England reported today.

OCTOBER 4

Mickys birthday. Went to bed early but did not sleep well. Read nearly all afternoon

OCTOBER 5

Bycicled out to No. 14 Stationary, with Ruth this am to see two Canadian lads that I sent down with [from?] my ward with enteric. They were so glad to see us. – Anderson & King

OCTOBER 6

The weather has been very windy of late, also very showery though on the whole it is better than that of this time last year.

OCTOBER 7

Poor Dicky has heard that he[r] Mother has had a stroke & may linger some time, so has put in her resignation. It will be some time however I am afraid before the War Office will put it through. & the uncertainty of the long waiting is horrible. Miss Mann has just had a similar experience

OCTOBER 8

I got up for service this afternoon at 5.45 PM We had a rather wonderful address from Canon Hanny. Richards took the Service in his own unique style.

OCTOBER 9

Ruth & I went down town this morning & were rather late getting in. Ruth chose paper for her room to cover up the draughty cracks & make it warm for the winter.

OCTOBER 10

Mr. Makeham brought a concert party up for this afternoon & evening. The performance was very good. We went for the first part of it at 5.30 PM.

OCTOBER 11

Got up early this afternoon & went with Stephie & Ruth by car out to 14 Stationary to see our patients there. Took them books & Canadian Papers.

OCTOBER 12 – 13

NO ENTRIES

OCTOBER 14

Ruth & I went down town & had our hair washed this AM. I also got a pair of brass candlesticks (anciens) for Father for Christmas.

OCTOBER 15

NO ENTRY

OCTOBER 16

Princess Victoria Concert Party tonight

OCTOBER 17

NO ENTRY

OCTOBER 18

Following a period of rainy windy weather, it is bitterly cold & clear tonight. Almost like Canadian weather minus the home comforts.

OCTOBER 19

Heard today that Stalky [Pte. Stockwell] Day, who was with us all last year at Camiers (Boysie Wood's friend) who has since taken

his commission & gone up the line, has been so badly wounded,
Compound fracture of upper leg, injury to spine & paralysed – a
dear lad, so full of brigh[t]ness & cheerfulness in spite of everything. If death might only come without all the suffering that
will be his. Boysie came through yesterday on his way I think to
see Day. His brother Chester, is also with him at Rouen.

OCTOBER 20

Am sleeping much better lately. So much so that Ruth & I both
slept in tonight & missed our dinner in consequence. Never wakened till ten minutes to seven.
It is still bitterly cold. We have no stoves in our huts as yet. I
hope they will put them in soon as we are very cold indeed in our
quarters. In the wards we have enjoyed fires for the last two days.

OCTOBER 21

Sunderland the Australian appeared again at Ward S today on
pass from his Etaples base. His advent is interesting to me on
account of Clark's intense dislike of anything Australian. These
patients of Ruth's are very interesting from a physiological point
of view, Sunderland is a big fine looking physical specimen –
with an atmosphere of "winds in the open" about him while
Clark has a narrow clean cut face with regular features & is the
product of one of the great old universities of England. Both
started out equally in Ruth's favour – the former has risen while
the latter's fall is only a matter of moments.

OCTOBER 22

A couple of nights ago with the convoy came a very young New
Zealand lad, a shell shock case – Edney – . His talk in his sleep
was all of "Reg" & "We'll get there yet Reg" the most frequent cry.
Tonight he told me his story – poor laddie – a gentle sweet faced
boy from whom this war has claimed its own.
He & Reg came out from New Zealand a year ago & as Regimental Stretcher bearers have been together ever since – Reg apparently the stronger lad of the two. In the last action while carrying
out a stretcher together Reg was hit & had to give up his place to
another. When Edney returned to his friend after getting his

patient to a safe place Reg was so weak he was unable to walk &
no help was at hand so Edney with all his strength managed to
carry him almost three miles when a great shell burst near him
& when consciousness returned he found Reg still beside him
but the poor lad's head had been severed from his body. Edney
wishing to die also was found by other stretcher bearers & compelled to go to the dressing station & so down to us. He can't
sleep poor laddie & I sat beside him for a long time tonight &
he w[h]ispered the long sad tale to me while the others slept
around us. Then when we had both wept a little over it he
became quiet again & I gave him a sleeping draught & he had a
dreamless sleep till daylight

OCTOBER 23

Off night duty with much relief.
Ruth & I went to Calais by train this morning & had a very nice
afternoon in the old town whose name Mary said was written on
her heart. We went to the Church of Notre Dame an imposing
solid structure of which Peeps into Picardy speaks. Also saw the
house in which Lady Hamilton died & really had a very nice day.

OCTOBER 24

Went to Ward D in the PM. A big surgical ward – with 125 beds –
in the old Assembly hall of the Monastery. Beds on the gallery
stage & main floor. One frightfully sick boy at present – a Canadian laddie, Moore Jackson from Toronto – an English boy
Lusty gave 1/2 pt blood today to try to tide this poor wasted
body over a crisis – I hope it will be of use – Jackson with a red
head lying on the pillow – wasted frame & deeply sunken eyes
two weeks under the awful poison of gas gangreen is fighting for
life – a clever highly strung constitution clinging to life when
another would have secumbed a week ago – one leg is off & the
other is so full of incisions it seems hardly possible he can live.
Such a lovable character – even in his agony he has a wonderful
smile – His poor mother sent him a cake for his birthday today
with a message hoping they would all be together for his birthday in 1917.

October 25

Allen Jackson, such a fine young lad seventeen years old & such a man arrived today – Needless to say he was shocked at his brothers condition. We are all so glad he has come as our boy is much worse. irrational & weaker –

October 26

Our sick Canadian laddie died today.

October 27

Allen Jackson is staying with us till Saturday when his brother is to be buried. Such a brave boy & the only child his mother has left. Please God he may be spared for her. Miss Whitney has been writing Mrs Jackson –

October 28 – 29

NO ENTRIES

October 30

Wrote Ruth invitations in rhyme for her Hallow ee'n party –

October 31

We had such a nice quiet Hallowe'en dinner "en famille" tonight in our mess.

Ruth had a party in her Ward Kitchen for her up patients

November 1

It has rained every day for two weeks with high winds. Our ward is very busy – many bad cases

Have been spending my hours off fixing up my room with Ruth but can't finish up till the men get our stoves in

November 2

The french workmen are putting in tiny coal stoves in our rooms

French lesson with Mickie & Mrs Giffin

November 3

Ruth & I had our half day & in spite of the rain went down town & afterwards went out to Wimereux to see Molly who is in hospital there. She is better & will go on sick leave to England soon.

We had a ride home in a red cross car in the pouring rain.

A large convoy last night.

We got over 50 patients from it.

NOVEMBER 4

A Hallowe'en fancy dress party in the Red Cross Hut tonight. I did
not go but relieved for Francis McKeen who is night nurse in O.
Our room is finished at last & is so nice & cosy
"Romance of the Oxford Colleges" arrived today for Ruth much
to her dismay from Clark

NOVEMBER 5

A frightful storm of wind & rain tonight & all afternoon. Many
small boats wrecked on the coast.

NOVEMBER 6

No mail today – the port closed after yesterday's storm. I have a
very bad headache tonight

NOVEMBER 7

Am still feeling rather miserable so went right to bed when I
came off duty & Ruth brought my dinner down to me. Had several callers tonight Lou Gillis, Naomi Gray & Watling – the latter
going on leave tomorrow
Still no mail.

NOVEMBER 8

Our Ward has been practically emptied in an evacuation to England. so I had the whole day off & slept in this morning as I was
not feeling very energetic. After lunch Ruth & I went to the
cemetary to locate the grave of a patient – after which we went
down town. At Meridews we were waited on by "our friend the
impossible French Youth" in his most patronizing manner. To an
English soldier who came in looking for a book on French gra-
mar, he put on his grandest air & after getting the soldier to
explain several times that he wanted a book from which to study
French, the boy said suddenly "Why didn't you say so at the first"
in his extraordinary manner & disappeared to get it.
Dickie & Mann were to sail on Sat to Canada from Liverpool.

NOVEMBER 9

NO ENTRY

NOVEMBER 10

The Duke of Connaught visited our Ward & the rest of the Hospital today.

NOVEMBER 11

Edney & another New Zealand lad came down from O to see me this morning.

I brought them to speak with our New Zealander Ralph who has just regained his speech. When Ralph came in he was an almost hopeless case but his improvement has been wonderful. Wounded in the head all one side was paralyzed & his speech gone, absolutely two days ago however he began to speak so slowly & badly at first but almost perfectly now. He was pleased to see his fellow country men.

Had two cards from Cyril tonight – one of himself & the other taken with BV [brothers Blanchard Victor] & Athel. The latter he calls "The latest War News" for he has just returned from spending two day[s] in camp with the NS Scottish. Cyril looks well as do also the other boys. Athel is so big & fine & Blanchard as smart a soldier as I have ever seen.

[Later notation:] Ralph died in Eng early in Jan 1917.

NOVEMBER 12

Edney & his friend came in again this morning & after spending nearly an hour with our patient they came to church with Miss Ross & me & our little church parade party – the two Jocks – a Canadian – Albert (who by the way is an RC [Roman Catholic]) & several other Englishmen. Albert has been helping in our kitchen for some time – an Englishman (Yorkshire) a splendid fellow – plain of physique but so gentle & reliable a treasure – He won the DSO [Distinguished Service Order] last year & it was I am sure most thoroughly merited.

NOVEMBER 13

Had half day with Ruth & went out in the car to our old haunts in the Etaples district. Things have changed there in a year. German prisoners camp outside Camiers & they in hundreds & working on a new railroad there. We caught the street car to

Paris Plage – Back to Etaples at 4 PM then walked to No 1 Saw
Dixon, & Miss Young. Of course as usual to spoil our happiness
Ruth developed a headache late in day

NOVEMBER 14 – 16

NO ENTRIES

NOVEMBER 17

Had a real fire in our room tonight. Such a comfort – I got coals
& had it on when Ruth came off

NOVEMBER 18

Ruth & I went down town & did a bit of Christmas shopping on
our hours off. Ruth got a dressing gown, in dark blue material
like Grantys for her mother. Read Dickens with Naomi Gray &
Stephie in the evening

NOVEMBER 19

A rainy day & our roof is leaking badly. Ruth mended it herself
today but not with much effect.

NOVEMBER 20

Heavy rain & roof still leaking. Some very sick patients in our
ward & we are very busy but I love the work with these brave lads

NOVEMBER 21

Ruth & I had our half day. We walked to Souverin Moulin. Had
tea & pan cakes. Went by the Valley & Wimille & back by the
back road – Dark before we reached the Calvary – found two
Australian Soldiers near there lost & directed them.

NOVEMBER 22

Went to Australian Hosp No 2 General with Stephie & Ruth
tonight for dinner enjoyed the visit very much – these are such
frank open hearted women these Australian nurses. We enjoyed
their photograph[s] & tales of their Egyptian experience after
dinner round the fire in Miss Deara's room.
Very busy in our Ward. I am doing all the up patient's dressings
this week on the upper gallery.

NOVEMBER 23 – DECEMBER 15

NO ENTRIES

DECEMBER 16

All week Ruth & I in our spare time, have been getting things together. – for our parcels to the front – & in the evening we have been cracking nuts stuffing dates etc beside our little comfy stove–

DECEMBER 17

NO ENTRY

DECEMBER 18

We sisters have for days now been preparing for Christmas. Now my parcels for the boys at the front are all finished & posted so I can turn my whole attention in my spare time to the preparations in the Ward where I am sister in charge at present. We have been quite busy with a shifting population of wounds of medium severity – a number of those too sick to be moved – & also a number of slight wounds which will stay with us till they are fit for CC or duty again – Among the former are Todd – May – Jock & [blank] who have been with us a long time & among the latter such nice lads who help us greatly in the daily routine – Shafer – Albert – Blanch – Faulkner Cranshaw Price, Osborne – Read – Jock Gray – Parker & four BWI's [British West Indies] or the "Tar Babies" as Whit calls them.

DECEMBER 19

Our convalescent patients have been allowed out to gather holly & greens & the decorating of our ward is proceeding merrily.

DECEMBER 20 – 21

NO ENTRIES

DECEMBER 22

Miss Hoerner & I spent the evening in the Red Cross hut doing up the Christmas Altar in white & gold.

DECEMBER 23

This Eve spent some time in fixing the Church flowers for tomorrow & Christmas.

DECEMBER 24

Everything ready for Christmas day.

At 6 PM as I was crossing the road from our lines being in a hurry to return to the Ward I stumbled & fell in the dark down the flight of steps which lead to the road. For a moment I was stunned by the fall but came quickly to the realization that I was sitting in the mud & a soldier, big & dark against the sky was be[ar]ing down upon me on the left – also that there was an excruciating pain in my rt ankle & that I was weeping. Miss Archibald arriving also at that minute I was helped back up the stairs & on to my bed.

Later having recovered I returned to the Ward where after dinner we sisters trimmed the tree. Went to Midnight service in Red Cross Hut. Such a nice Service. Our little English lad Blanch says the nicest Service he has been to since he was confirmed. We sent forty patients out today & got forty new ones in from the front; Late in our lines stealthy figures might be seen steeling from hut to hut – & the little gifts of one sister to another in transport.

DECEMBER 25

Peace on Earth & the world at war. Yet in spite of this fact we had such a happy, happy day, doing for these lads, our best to make it a Happy Christmas. Blanch promises to write down for me the doings of the day. He, representing the patients made a wonderful little speech after dinner – thanking the sisters.[33] Easton a patient as Santa Claus was a great success. A band from a regiment in town arrived opportunely during dinner & played carols. (I am very uncomfortably lame today but that mattered not at all) & at 6 a[p]m our own convalescent patients sang the carols for the Wards. One of the happiest days I have ever spent. Dinner with our officers in Red Cross Hut in evening

Dec 25th   [1916]

List how they wander the stars among

The first fair notes of the Heavenly Song!

Solemnly sweetly it echoes still –

"Peace upon earth and to men good will."

Tidings of Joy! From all weary hearts

The care that has burdened the night departs.

Tidings of Joy! It is Christmas morn,
And lo, The Light of the World is Born!

DECEMBER 26

Blanch transferred to Annex today & came on Ward as orderly.

DECEMBER 27 – 28

NO ENTRIES

DECEMBER 29

Shafer is to go to the Annex & to Ward A. I had a long talk with the lad today.

December 30

NO ENTRY

DECEMBER 31

Another year ended – a year filled with many sad yet many happy days – In our work in the Hospital we have been happy – the busy days full of interest – so busy that they have flown & the year on looking back has not been a long one in many ways – Yet when one looks at its toll of lives lost then it has been long indeed. Surely this coming year will bring peace to the world.

1917

JANUARY 1 – 11

NO ENTRIES

JANUARY 12

Went to England via Calais & Folkstone on leave. Blanchard met me at Kingsley Hotel London at 6 PM. Dinner at the hotel. Blanchard is such a fine, well groomed manly lad – so big and strong and clever – & so absolutely spick and span –

JANUARY 13

Did a bit of shopping with Blanchard in the morning & to a matinée "London Pride" in which Gerald du Maurier played in pm. Again to see Gladys Cooper in "The Misleading Lady" in the evening.

Between the first performance & dinner time we went down to the little photograph shop on the Strand to get more of the snaps the three boys had taken together. –

JANUARY 14

Went to St Paul's with Blanchard in the morning. Walked back to our hotel by the Law Courts & Chancery Lane.

In the afternoon went for a long walk out to Kensington Gardens & to see Muriel Whalley at Prince's Gate later, Blanchard left 9.30 PM for Witley Camp.

JANUARY 15

Shopped most of day for various necessities & a few luxuries – among the former many cheap books for our patients & among

Lance Corporal Blanchard Gass and Lt Nursing Sister Clare Gass

the latter a few of my favourite authors for myself.

JANUARY 16

Went to Putney to see Muriel in morning; had lunch there & came back to town with her to a matinée in the afternoon, J.M. Barrie's "A Kiss for Cinderella" such a pretty play. Read in my room before a cosy grate fire after dinner.

JANUARY 17

Am still waiting to hear from Athel so put in the time by going to a matinée this afternoon to find on my return (the play was "Romance" in which Doris Keane played) two telegrams one from B.V. saying if I wished to see Athel I must come to Bramshott at once; the other from Beatrice M to say she and Knighty would come to London for tomorrow. They arrived 8 PM.

JANUARY 18

Arose at 5 AM to catch the six o'clock train to Godalming – got a taxi at Godalming & motored 8 miles over good roads & through a beautiful tract of waste lands – hilly & covered with purple broom, through Witley to Bramshott – Found Athel after an hour's search in that enormous camp – saw his Colonel & took him to Liphook the nearest town. Had lunch at the Royal Anchor Hotel & spent the afternoon walking in the pretty lanes there abouts with him. Came back to London about 8 PM – after BA & KN had gone.

JANUARY 19

Met Gertrude Baynes at my hotel at noon. Went with her to the Drury Lane Pantomime after lunch & on our return to the Hotel for tea found Sara McNaughton had arrived from No 3. Sara and I went to see Potash and Pearlmutter in the evening as there was nothing else to do.

JANUARY 20

Gertrude met us at the Hotel at ten & we took Miss McNaughton to the bank & did a bit of shopping with her. Had lunch at the Trocadero & met Muriel & went to see the "Bing Boys" in the afternoon.

Gertrude had tea with us & later Sara & I went out to see "The Private Secretary" together.

Card from Athel tonight tells me he is leaving today from Liverpool for home.[1]

JANUARY 21

I took a morning train to Godalming where Blanchard met me. We had lunch at the King's Arms & then walked four miles to Guil[d]ford where we spent the rest of the afternoon & had tea – Saw Charlie Withrow. & met a friend of Blanchard's – George Lye –. Arrived in London 8 PM.

JANUARY 22

Shopped with Sara most of day & with her went to see Chu Chin Chow at his Majestys in the evening.

JANUARY 23

Left by a 9.45 train for Oxford where we had a lovely day with the Lefroys – Miss Lefroy met us at the station & took us to Trinity & the Divinity Schools & Balliol in the morning. Then we went to Queen's for lunch where the Provost was as charming as ever – After lunch we talked in front of the fire for a while the[n] went to Magdalen – All Souls – Oriel – the Bridge the Botanical gardens & Christ Church Cathedral – then back to Queens to tea & we left to catch the six o'clock train.

JANUARY 24

Went out to see Muriel this morning – then back to do some shopping with Sara in the afternoon

JANUARY 25

Went by 10 am train to Folkestone. Met by BA and Knight – stayed with them at Moore Barracks – talked by the fire in their room in the evening.

BA & Knighty took me out to Canterbury in the afternoon – The Cathedral is marvellously beautiful.

JANUARY 26

Beatrice A & I went into the town in the morning & had our photographs taken.

Left by afternoon boat. A rough crossing. I was very sick.

JANUARY 27

Went on duty at noon. Many of my old friends gone from the Ward.

JANUARY 28 – 31

NO ENTRIES

FEBRUARY 1

With Mrs Giffin Miss Eastwood & Miss Bliss went to tea at Madam Boulier's met Mademoiselle Rose's young brother & enjoyed the visit very much. The old people are delightful. The Grandfather a veteran of 1870.[2]

FEBRUARY 2 – 4

NO ENTRIES

FEBRUARY 5

We have been having wonderful weather (Canadian weather really) clear & cold with bright sunshine & almost half a foot of snow & very very cold – It is almost impossible to keep warm in the huts but Ward D in the old ruin with five stoves is very comfortable

FEBRUARY 6 – 9

NO ENTRIES

FEBRUARY 10

Heard today while on duty that the 85th had arrived in Boulogne. Later a telegram came from Blanchard. Ruth came with me through the snow, first to Anstrove Camp in search of them, then to St Martins where we found them. Saw Blanchard for a few minutes, then had to leave as it was getting dark. Met Major Ralston the Adjutant & Mr Croft.[3]

FEBRUARY 11

Blanchard came to the Ward at 11 am & we went out to lunch together. Miss Stephen came with us. In the afternoon Miss Sedgewick & I went up to the Camp as she wished to see some Musquodoboit lads. I saw Reg Gass – Munroe Lindsay, DeMers, Walter McKenzie.[4]

I went to service in our YMCA later with some of the patients in the Ward then Blanchard came & we went to dinner at the Burgoine.

FEBRUARY 12

I with Stephie went up to the Camp & to the orderly room of the 85th where I met some more of their officers Major Miller, Colonel Finney & one or two others. Blanchard got pass & came out to dinner with us. The English OC of the Camp told me "this is the finest body of men that have been in this camp for many a day." They certainly are a splendid looking regiment. Blanchard spent about a hour with me in my room before going back to camp –

FEBRUARY 13

Heard at noon today that the 85th have left for the front.
Am going on night duty in Ward D tonight.

FEBRUARY 14 – 20

NO ENTRIES

FEBRUARY 21

A shoulder case, Cook, had a haemorrhage today. A very sick boy tonight but such a good patient.

FEBRUARY 22

B.A.M & Knighty & their party from Moore Barracks came through today on their way to Troyes. They came to us for tea, then we walked back to the Louvre with them afterward.
Two amputation cases on the DI list one Paddy – & one very young English boy Holland.5

FEBRUARY 23

Ruth & I went down to the Louvre again this morning but our friends had gone by an early train.
We had breakfast at the Louvre.
Paddy very delirious sang & called out all night. Holland also very very ill.

FEBRUARY 24

Blanchard writes that the 85th are quartered in an old Chateau five miles behind the front line & have been sending working parties up to the trenches. He was out one night when they had two casualties.

FEBRUARY 25 – 26

NO ENTRIES

FEBRUARY 27

A lovely sunshiny morning. Ran down into the Valley before going to bed, Ellen Carpenter & I to see how the spring is progressing. Signs are very few – the trickling of the water down the slopes & the noise of the little brook being the chief signs – spring is later than last year in coming due I suppose to the recent cold weather. Anti-aircraft guns to the north while we were out.

FEBRUARY 28

I have been receiving large convoys of patients every night of late & the Ward has been very heavy & the work difficult. The papers tell us that on a long line of front near Beaupaume [Bapaume] the enemy is retiring.[6]

MARCH 1

A convoy of 55 came into D last night. All Australians from Beaupaume where the Germans are retiring. Such bad bad wounds. My heart aches for these poor lads so far from their home.

Five shot through the chest, one arm blown off. One spine case paralyzed. One fractured pelvis. One pair of trench feet so bad that both feet will have to come off & many other agonizing wounds.

MARCH 2

Day, the Spine & pelvis case in very bad condition.

MARCH 3

Went down the Valley with Ellen Carpenter this morning, crept under the thick hedge & into the old Chateau grounds.

Paddy had a transfusion today.

MARCH 4

Found some snow drops in our little wood this morning.

Paddy greatly improved & has regained his reason

MARCH 5

A letter from BA tonight. They are in Troyes.

A huge convoy today & the ward full of sick patients with very bad wounds

MARCH 6

A frightful wind storm today & very cold.

MARCH 7

A winter's day. Very windy & cold.

MARCH 8 – 10

NO ENTRIES

MARCH 11

A wonderful spring morning. I had the bycicles pumped up by Merrett, our Australian night orderly & Miss Eastwood & I went out for a ride before going to bed, down the Calais road through Wimille to the Wimereux station & back by La Poterie & the monument.

MARCH 12

Orders to clear the hospital in preparation for some special action.

Rumour says Canadian Casualties in the 4th division have been heavy & that a big convoy of Canadians have come to Etaples. We have heard of none in Boulogne.

News today that Baghdad has been taken.[7]

MARCH 13

Off night duty.

Went into town & had a hair wash.

Ruth went on leave to England.

MARCH 14

Went for a little ride with Stephie before going on duty. Rather muddy but otherwise a very nice outing

MARCH 15

Death of Duchess of Connaught in England.

MARCH 16

Rumours today of a revolution in Russia.[8]

MARCH 17

Definite news of a revolution in Russia reached us today. The
people at last are demanding freedom from the many trials
which for years they have borne.

MARCH 18

The Russians have formed a government & peace in St Petersburg is slowly being restored. The blood shed has been compara-
tively small. The Czar has abdigated & his brothers have joined
the people.[9]

MARCH 19

The Czar is a prisoner, as is also his family – the political German spies which infested his court are also in the hands of the
people. The new Government has been recognized by the Allies

MARCH 20 – 21

NO ENTRIES

MARCH 22

The McGill Battery has arrived in Boulogne. They are at St Martins Camp.[10]

MARCH 23

NO ENTRY

MARCH 24

Went to dinner at the Burgoine with Sara McN & Brooke &
Terrance McDermot.

MARCH 25

Arnfield an up patient today developed Spinal Meni[n]gitis
(Acute Cerebro) in our Ward – Such a tragedy a young married
man with two small children. The ward is under orders for disinfection & we are all under observation.

Whit & I rode with Marjorie Ross down to No 14 Stationary hospital to enquire after Arnfield this evening

MARCH 26

Whit & I were unable to accept an invitation to hear the new
orchestra of CC patients at No 7 CC C this afternoon but the
Matron and Mrs Hutchison went & took our apologies to our
patients who were anxious for us to go.

Foxy Reid our new MO in a hut in which we are isolated at present during the cleaning of D.

MARCH 27

Ruth came back today I went down with W[h]itney to meet her but we missed the boat so she came up to the hospital before us. Miss McMurrich and her friend Miss Warner also came to us tonight on their way through for leave.

MARCH 28

Miss Whitney went today for five days leave to see her uncle who is ill in England.

MARCH 29

NO ENTRY

MARCH 30

Arnfield is no better our orderly went down to enquire today

MARCH 31 – APRIL 1

NO ENTRIES

APRIL 2

Moved back to ward D now thoroughly cleaned: & ready to receive a convoy. A windy cold winter's day with snow & rain

APRIL 3

NO ENTRY

APRIL 4

A large convoy of wounded to D.

APRIL 5

NO ENTRY

APRIL 6

Rumours of a great attack at Vimy Ridge near Arras[11]

APRIL 7

NO ENTRY

APRIL 8

Early service .. 6.30.

APRIL 9

Late this pm the news came, that Vimy Ridge has been taken by the Canadians
Miss McN & I are alone on the ward

APRIL 10

This morning hundreds of Canadian wounded admitted, so
tired, but the majority with only slighter wounds –
In D – we received over one hundred & fifty & had stretchers &
mattresses on the floor for the lighter cases.

APRIL 11

We received the stretcher cases from Vimy this morning – many
sick men – ....
Over 100 of yesterdays walkers went to Eng[land] – Munroe
Lindsay admitted to Ward W & Ralph Proctor of the 85th to L.
The 85th on the 9th at 6 PM went over in support to attack
strong positions not captured in the first advance.

APRIL 12

We are still very busy & the wounded are being admitted to
Ward D daily – Many 85th men but most of them of D
Co[mpany]. I can get no news of Blanchard though C & D Co
both went over without a barrage on the evening of the 9th.
Munroe said he last saw Blanchard on the eve of the 9th as they
were filing down the tunnel

APRIL 13

I went this evening to write some letters for Ralph Proctor who is
shot through the chest & spine & is in serious condition. He also
asked me to send a cable to his father –

APRIL 14

NO ENTRY

APRIL 15 AND APRIL 16

The casualties though reported as small from last week's action
have simply filled all the hospitals hereabouts to over flowing.
Robert O'Callahan who is at an English hospital in Wimereux
says he never saw worse wounds than those they have & some of
ours are heart breaking – Gas gangrene is very prevalent & we
have lost several cases. We have had no hours off for a week &
have been on duty late at night & are beginning to feel the
effects of the extra work.

APRIL 17

Ralph Proctor is no better & is going to have an operation for an empyema tomorrow

APRIL 18

Laurie !

APRIL 19

NO ENTRY

APRIL 20

A letter from Gerald this morning in which he says "Blanchard is gone, he was killed on the 9th I think" I cannot believe it.

APRIL 21

NO ENTRY

APRIL 22

The Colonel received a telegram for me from headquarters. It reads "L/Cpl B.V. Gass killed in action April 9th"
I also heard today that Laurie died of wounds in a field ambulance hospital. I thought that Laurie at least with his big guns was safe – but no one is safe these days – none of our boys[12]

APRIL 23

Boysie Woods brought me word that a Lt McCrae of the 4th Amm[unition] Park had gone to see Laurie before he died – I am glad for his poor Mother's sake.
No further news of Blanchard – Saw a boy from the 85th in the Ward yesterday & he knew B.V. & knew also he was reported killed but no more –
(Two months to practice that in which with a years and a half's training he had become proficient !)

APRIL 24

Nancy Morewood has developed Diphtheria & gone to No 14 Stationary hospital.

APRIL 25

Had a half day off duty & for the first part went to see Proctor & write some letters for him.
Later dug in my garden for a while then went for a walk to L'Abbé Moulin with Ruth & Miss Eastwood & Miss Bliss

APRIL 26 – MAY 3

NO ENTRIES

MAY 4

Had letters today from Maj[or] Ralston telling me of the last day of B.V. our Happy Warrior & from Lieut. McRae telling me of Laurie's last day on earth.

MAY 5 – 23

NO ENTRIES[13]

MAY 24

Bycicled with Helen Matthew & Ruth out to Wierre Effroy & the Holy Well. Had a picnic tea at the Souverin Moulin on the way back

MAY 25 – 27

NO ENTRIES

MAY 28

A letter from Cyril today says "It is heart breaking to see Mother & Father broken down but time is a great healer & nothing can stop its progress" The remark is so typical of old "wise head."

MAY 29 – 30

NO ENTRIES

MAY 31

A letter today from Mrs Proctor says that Ralph's brother Athol has been killed Father's letter too tells me of Ralph Read's death. He was a lieut in the 85th.

JUNE 1

NO ENTRY

JUNE 2

Took our tea & [Private John] Valentine down into the fields back of No 7 CC this afternoon Miss Whitney Miss McNaughton & I.

JUNE 3

NO ENTRY

JUNE 4

Took our tea out to L'Abbé Moulin. Madam boiled water & gave us the milk. Had our tea table down by the old moss covered mill wheel.

JUNE 5

Night duty tonight in Ward D.

JUNE 6

NO ENTRY

JUNE 7

Tonight's report says Messines has been taken

JUNE 8

Messines – Wytschaete & Oostaverne in the hands of the British. A great victory. The wounded from these places have been coming in all day The Messines Ridge is in British Hands after many vain attempts in the past on our part to get it The Germans have lost it now, let us hope forever. By this victory part of the Salient of Ypres is considerably straightened NZ, Irish & English took part in the attack[14]

JUNE 9 – 13

NO ENTRIES

JUNE 14

Tonight with his full kit on his back, leaving his stripes on our desk Valentine left us for the 42 Batt. A good boy he has done good work for us – but has been dissatisfied with the injustice shown to him by those in authority We are all very very sorry to see him go.[15]

JUNE 15

Tonight we heard that the recent Zeppelin raid which distroyed a business street in Folkstone had also killed three hundred Canadian Soldiers in that district.

JUNE 16

Some Canadian soldiers were killed in the Folkestone raid but not 300 as reported.

JUNE 17 – 18

NO ENTRIES

JUNE 19

Ward D has been very heavy so far this month. Such sick sick men & many of them. A large percentage are Australians & New Zealanders –

JUNE 20

NO ENTRY

JUNE 21

Written in a sister's autograph album & original.
Oh sister in those radiant
wards, where God
Your recompense will give,
May I not miss
That faithful fellowship as when
I trod
A bruised and battered casualty
in this !

JUNE 22

The King of Greece has abdicated in favour of his second son
Alexander.

JUNE 23

The Ward has grown light at last. I have very few patients but do
not sleep well – all day long I dream – frightful dreams, in most
of which Blanchard comes in difficulty & danger –

JUNE 24

Tonight Blanch came in to say Good Bye. He expects to leave
the Base tomorrow on his way to his Regt. He is such a fine lad –
back to danger and perhaps death – with all his possibilities he
may go into the far country to meet there the thosands of other
young lads – with equal promise – who have gone before him –

JUNE 25

Capt Hepburn came in tonight & talked at length of his life in
the trenches.

Cpl Fry on his kit leave also came – He is to be a lieutenant in
the 42nd –

We are not busy.

JUNE 26 – JULY 2

NO ENTRIES

JULY 3

Queen Mary visited the hospital today
A severe haemorrhage in the Ward tonight.
Russians have had a great victory after months of inaction –
Many prisoners taken.

JULY 4 – 11

NO ENTRIES

JULY 12

Gerald came today Such a great pleasure In afternoon We went down to the Wimereau shore & sat by the sea on a hill side to talk Tea in Wimereau[16]

JULY 13

Bycicled with Gerald and Stevie out to Souverin Moulin Sat down by the brook all afternoon & had dinner at the Souverein M. Estaminet A lovely day[17]

JULY 14

Picnic with Sara & Miss Burt & Gerald down in the field. We all enjoyed it very much –

JULY 15

Took Gerald out for a change to La Portel. Sat on the beach & watched the people all afternoon. I went in bathing.

JULY 16

NO ENTRY

JULY 17

Went out to La Portal for a bath & with Marjorie & Gerald in the afternoon & took tea & had it on the beach afterwards.

JULY 18

Sara & Fitzie & I were Gerald's guests for dinner at his billets tonight. Played bridge afterwards

JULY 19

Had a picnic in the fields this afternoon with Ruth & Stevie & Cooper & Gerald.

JULY 20

Gerald & I had dinner tonight with Marjorie & Sara at the Bourgoine. Played Bridge afterwards.

Clare and Gerald Gass, July 1917

JULY 21

Gerald left tonight for his train which goes out at 4 am. I think he has enjoyed his holiday & I have certainly enjoyed having him here.

JULY 22 – AUGUST 21

NO ENTRIES

AUGUST 22

Left Boulogne 8 PM. Reached London 11 pm

AUGUST 23

Out shopping in Am in the now familiar London streets. Went to see General Post at the Hay Market theatre in the evening Saw Beverane twice once in the Bank & once in the street

AUGUST 24

Shopped in AM. Lunch at Lullus on Regent St
Madam Toussaud's in the afternoon.

"The Maid of the Mountains" in the evening at Daly's. Saw Molly unexpectedly in the street – She is on her way to a Convalescent home. Also saw Jessie Sedgewick on her way home to Canada

AUGUST 25

Left 9.30 Euston Station for Scotland, came through Rugby to Manchester to Lancaster & Carlisle:– through Gretna Green Goat Bridge Stirling Bridge of Allen [Allan], Auchterarder (of Cameron fame) to Perth. Spent night at Perth

AUGUST 26

Left P[erth]. 9.45 for Inverness The country so beautiful through Dunkeld Pitlochry & Blair Atholl – mountains thickly wooded with a shallow rushing river over a rocky bed at their foot & in amongst the trees pretty house with gardens in full bloom

After Blair Atholl the hills become barren: & covered with the lovely purple heather without a tree – sheep dotted – lonely shepherds huts

Inverness stayed Station Hotel 2.45 PM

AUGUST 27

Saw the town & outskirts & bought one or two souvenirs in the shops of the Capital of the Highlands. Left by boat 3.30 for Fort Agustus [Augustus]. through the locks first then on into Loch Ness a beautiful lake. Castle Urquhart at its more beautiful part – Gaelic shepherds with their dogs on the boat – Rainy after leaving Inv & rained at intervals all afternoon Sun came out as we entered Fort Agustus – bay. Fort A in a sheltered valley surrounded by mountains very lovely. A Benedictine monastery occupies sight of old fort.

AUGUST 28

Train to Fort William – passed Aberchalder & Loch Oich to Invergarry & the old castle ruin then Loch Lochy & the mountains grow higher & more stern as we go on. so barren, so vivid with their covering of purple – & the purple mists around their peaks – Then the river Spean & Lochy to Fort William – Walked into Glen Nevis & viewed that stern old giant – but did not have time to climb it. Lunch at Highland. then left by Spean Bridge & Tulloch for Loch Lomond. At Tulloch the rushing highland rivers are the most beautiful I have seen. To our right near Rannock [Rannoch] the mountains of Glencoe can be seen. Passed Moor of Rannock of Kidnapped after which though the mountains are still high they loose something of their sternness. Till happier Tarbet comes in view.[18]

AUGUST 29

Bonnie Bank of Loch Lomond
In the morning went for a long walk through pretty lanes by Lake side. 1.30 PM took boat to Inversnaid a lovely spot. there from 2 – 5.15 walked out to Rob Roy's cave. Such a rocky wooded shore here rises from the lake. Several overhanging rocks form caves in the district. Saw two nice Canadian boys from 5th Div[ision] on leave – also seeing Rob Roy's country. Met two Canadian officers later in pm who were also at the cave.[19]
The journey down Loch Lomond was lovely. Reach Balloch at sunset.

AUGUST 30

Left Balloch 8.40 for Sterling [Stirling]. Took taxi to castle. Castle very interesting & beautiful. On to Callander later (10.42 am). Arrived 11.20 & took coach immediately for Trossac[h]s. A beautiful day, passed Loch Vennachar [Venachar] – Achray & Brig of Turk & on to Loch Katrine around which the country is very very lovely. "Where twines the path in shadow hue, round many a rocky piramid." Lunch at Trossach Hotel. Back to Callander in pm. Train to Edinburg[h] in evening.
The Highland cattle in Trossach very nice looking.

AUGUST 31

Royal British Hotel
Edinburgh
Lovely airy open city filled with history & interest. Mary Stuart the most picturesque figure of all. We went up to Calton Hill in am. where a funny old guide told us many things about the city. By train to Melrose in the afternoon Taxi to Melrose Abbey –

Abbotsford Dryburg[h] Abbey. Went through Edinburgh castle
also in am also saw St Giles Cathedral and onsite shops

SEPTEMBER 1

Started early for High St Cannon Gate & Holyrood. The Cannon
gate is the most fascinating old street I have ever been in. The
sight seeing of this morning is a long ago wish realized – Marys
rooms – the old chapel ruin – the street & grounds so often travelled by the Stuart Queen, John Knox's house etc. Went to Forth
Bridge in pm by motor bus. British Men of War everywhere – the
place thronged with sailor boys.

SEPTEMBER 2

Took bus to Roslin [Rosslyn] Castle went to morning service in
the loveliest chapel I have seen. Afterwards explored the ruin of
the old feudal castle – parts of which are intact. Lunch at Roslin.
Went for car ride in pm in Edinburgh & a walk. Left 10 pm for
London. Miserable night in train without a sleeper

SEPTEMBER 3

Slept for short time in am. Met Molly. Saw the Matron. I went
shopping & to tea with R.O. Molly & Sara & I went to see "Inside
the lines" at the Adelphi theatre in pm –

SEPTEMBER 4

Went to Bank in Am & shopping afterwards. To see "The Invisible Foe" at the Savoy in pm HB Irving & Fay Compton a thoroughly enjoyable play – though of a serious character. Fay Compton is very beautiful –

SEPTEMBER 5

An air raid in our immediate district last night. Bourne &
Holling[s]worth [Department Store], the Charing Cross Hospital
& parts of Thames embankment bombed. & considerable damage done – Our Hotel was all awake & downstairs & out side. – I
slept through most of it as I was tired. Back to France in PM.

SEPTEMBER 6

Arrived Boulogne 6 pm
They had a bad air raid here tuesday night also Several houses
on the Rue de Calais smashed to pieces – & all the upper part of

the Rue de la Paix is in ruins – As it was so near the Hospital the shrapnel came down like hail on the roofs of the huts but no one was hurt here – Several of the towns people were killed & many injured.

SEPTEMBER 7 – 27

NO ENTRIES

SEPTEMBER 28 AND SEPTEMBER 29

We have had many air raids this month. Two new anti air craft guns have been placed in the field to the left of Naps. monument & these with the help of the old ones have driven the enemy away. We had however two casualties from St Martins Camp both privates one killed & one badly injured during one raid & have also had several slight wounds from stray shrapnel most of these in No 7 CC.

SEPTEMBER 30 – OCTOBER 14

NO ENTRIES

OCTOBER 15

Our dear boy's birthday [brother Blanchard]
He would have been nineteen today.

OCTOBER 16 – 26

NO ENTRIES

OCTOBER 27

Fathers letter tonight tells of a very serious operation for Cyril. from what I can understand it is appendicitis with perforation & peritonitus Poor laddie – surely he has suffered enough. Went with Ruth to hear the orchestra at the Central YMCA tonight

OCTOBER 28

Valentine is here today. He had with [him] several others of his platoon been specially recommended given a stripe & ten days leave.[20]
He is a good boy & was very glad to see Ward D again.

OCTOBER 29

The news that Italy has lost thousands of men & hundreds of guns to the Austrians is very startling. I cannot see when or where the awful war is going to end.[21]

One of the essential qualities of a nurse is to be always pleasant.
To show one is in a scot is to have a depressing effect on the patients
To have a pleasant expression has the opposite effect.

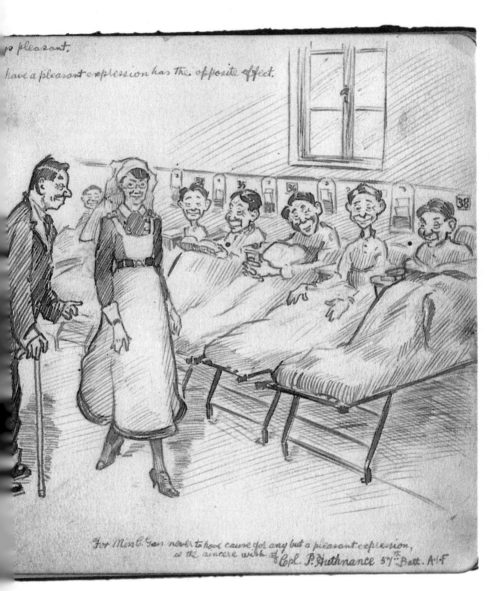

For Miss Gass never to have cause for any but a pleasant expression, is the sincere wish of Cpl. P. Huthnance 57th Batt. A.I.F

For Miss C. Gass never to have cause for any but a pleasant expression, is the
sincere wish of Cpl. P. Huthnance 54th Batt. A.I.F.

OCTOBER 30

NO ENTRY

OCTOBER 31

News came this am that I am to leave together with Mrs Giffin
for No 2 Canadian CCS [Casualty Clearing Station] early tomorrow morning.

Went up to St Martins Camp for our gas masks with Miss Hoerner in the afternoon. Ruth had half day & helped me to pack.

Went over to Red Cross Hut for an hour this evening to see the
fancy dresses

NOVEMBER 1

Left No 3 at 8.30 am, Ruth came to station to see us off. Arrived
at Calais at 11 am but had to wait there as our luggage had not
come. Left 6.45 with luggage for Hazebrooke [Hazebrouck]
arrived 11.30 pm. RTO [Railway Transport Officer] asked us to
wait in his office where he made tea for us & we had supper
from Miss Ross' box of sandwitches & cake

Ambulances arrived 2.30 am on to the frontier through a driving rain. Arrived No 2 at 3.30 am.[22]

NOVEMBER 2

Went on duty at noon. We are living in a marquee from which
Whit[ney] & G. De Cou are leaving for England. Whit looks
wretchedly!

This country is flat & uninteresting at first sight – but the traffic
of troops is tremendous.

NOVEMBER 3

Am to go on night duty tonight as a Supply.

NOVEMBER 4

Had quite a busy night in the "gas" tents most of time. Such sick
sick men from the recent gas attacks

The Canadians have recently come up to Ypres from Lens so I
hope to see Gerald

NOVEMBER 5

This has been a dreadful time at Pas[sc]hendael[e] & our Can.
boys have done wonderful feats of endurance & fighting against

No. 2 Canadian Casualty Clearing Station

almost impossible odds.[23]

NOVEMBER 6 AND NOVEMBER 7

Spent the morning with Drake – a lovely morning – "lorry hopping" – through Monts des Cats [Mont-des-Cats], Westoulte &
Locre to Kemmel – At Kemmel which is a picturesque village in
ruins we saw the grass grow in trenches of last spring's activities
still intact but overgrown with the summer's greenness. Went
into the shattered Church in the village, then on up the hill to
the observatory – on Kemmel Hill – Here we found two NZ sisters who shared their breakfast of sandwitches & their field glasses with us. Through the glasses the Messines Ridge & the

Wytschaete Ridge the scenes of the early summer's fierce fighting can be seen & on the left Dickiebush [Dickebusch] Lake & beyond that Ypres The day was clear and sunshiny & I enjoyed the outing. Kemmel Hill is one network of old trenches & dug outs still used for observation purposes.

NOVEMBER 8

I hear Miss Hoerner arrived at No 3 today.

NOVEMBER 9

NO ENTRY

NOVEMBER 10

"Hun" planes came over tonight & dropped bombs but I have not yet heard of damage done.

Col McLean the OC of No 1 CCS was killed several days ago near Dunkirk by a bomb. There were other casualties there as well.

NOVEMBER 11

Walked in to Pop[eringhe] this morning before I went to bed – this town has been badly shelled at times & many of the houses though occupied again have the marks upon them Little restoration has been made. Rode home in a lorry

NOVEMBER 12

Miss Hoerner came over to tea this pm. I escorted her part of the way back.

At 6 pm went to a concert by "the Maple Leaf party" It belongs to the 4th Div (Canadians) & is such a clever performance. Such good voices.

NOVEMBER 13

Our bombardment today & last night has been tremendous; It shakes our huts & is continuous. Col Davis leaves this hospital today. Col Brown is the new O.C. I go to the Officers Ward tonight. Miss Holland comes off.

NOVEMBER 14

Walked to Boeschepe this morning with one of the English sisters attached here before we went to bed. The morning was lovely for this time of year & though the mud was thick I enjoyed the

Maple Leaf concert party

walk very much. We came back on a lorry.

NOVEMBER 15

Went to Bailleul this morning with Miss Drake & Miss Regan
Walked part of the way & rode on lorries the rest Went into the
old church there & into a few shops. The town was heavily
shelled last week. Some casualties but not much destruction of
property. The church & old belfry tower are intact
Miss Woods Capt McKim & Capt Yates came up tonight to take
the place of Capt Dixon, Miss Davies and their team.

NOVEMBER 16

Such a heavy bombardment from our guns this morning which
probably means our men will attack again. Rumour says we have
cut off 4 divisions of Germans by our heavy shell fire the last few
days. Fire directed behind the enemy lines to cut off their
retreat.

NOVEMBER 17

Terance MacDermot & his friend Clark came down yesterday to see me. Brooke could not come.

NOVEMBER 18

The guns along the front are quiet once more. That awful continuous thunder has ceased for the time being. An occasional explosing where some ammunition dump has been bombed is all that disturbs the quiet & in the night the continuous flares along the horizon the only sign of warfare.

NOVEMBER 19 – 22

NO ENTRIES

NOVEMBER 23

Terrance MacDermot came again today. Alone this time. I took him over to No 3 to tea, where I think he quite enjoyed the afternoon. Miss Hoerner asked him to play which he did. He plays wonderfully well.

NOVEMBER 24

Valentine came tonight "a bruised and battered casualty" with a piece of shrapnel in his face & his face very much swollen. He was on his way from an English CCS back to his regiment.

NOVEMBER 25

NO ENTRY

NOVEMBER 26

The Wards have been very quiet of late with little doing on this front though persistant rumours of the Germans massing for an attack are rife

NOVEMBER 27

News of a wonderful British Victory near Cambrai. thousands of prisoners including 182 officers & many guns. Tanks & cavalry went over without a barrage in a surprise attack.

News from Italy still none too good. Still the Italian line is beginning to be strengthened.[24]

In Palestine the British troops are three miles from Jerusalem.

NOVEMBER 28

The Tsar's second daughter Tatiana has escaped from Russia via Japan & is on her way to USA.

NOVEMBER 29

Mrs G[iffin] went in to Pop this morning while I went with Drake & the Padre to Hazebrooke & Aire in the ambulance for the Laundry & other errands for the Mess. Aire is a quaint little town with its Canal & Red & barges & other boats. The church is very fine. Hazebrooke is quite a little town. The Padre stooped at Marie Salad's & a grocers there.

About 30 Km to Aire.

NOVEMBER 30

The Germans have been shelling Poperinghe heavily since noon yesterday. Also the whole road from Ypres to Pop. making it impossible to get troops in or out. There are also shells being dropped this side of Pop near the Cross Roads beyond No 3 CCS. where the railway runs. Many Casualties were brought in from Vlamerbughe in the afternoon & last night. The men say there have been direct hits on the Pop station.

DECEMBER 1

NO ENTRY

DECEMBER 2

A Report today of a German counter attack at Cambrai successful with great losses on our side 1000 men & 2 Batteries so the papers say.

Our poor lads !

DECEMBER 3

"Fritz" has been overhead all night tonight. There is bright moonlight & wind blown clouds which hide the planes from our anti air craft guns About 10 bombs have been in the direction of the Air dromes near Proven.

Later –

I have got several cases in from the bombs which were dropped. They fell in a camp near Pop. where the Midland Regt are billetted

DECEMBER 4

Air ships have been over all night tonight probably observing for more shelling.

DECEMBER 5

Today about noon the Germans began to shell the Cross roads again one shell smashed the Estaminet at the corner into bits & several Belgians & soldiers were impaled there. Another shell burst just outside No 3's Mess Hut. But fortunately no one was hurt. The sisters were all at lunch. Hallie Carman just coming up to lunch was very near & throw her out on the ground. She is unhurt.

I was asleep when the shelling began but the whir of the first shell overhead awakened me. The explosions shook the ground. I voted for the Union Government in Canada – this am.[25]

DECEMBER 6

A heavy bombardment from our guns began about 2 am this morning – Enemy planes have been over head all night. I though[t] I saw one brought down in the distance but am not sure. Three 12" shells whistled over the hospital about 6 am: one went directly over Ward H. where Mrs G is night nurse – broke the telephone wires at the tracks & exploded in the field beyond – about 100 yds away. No damage done but a great shell hole in the field

DECEMBER 7

Fathers letter tonight brings the sad news that [cousin] Lou Miller who has been missing since May has been located in an Insane Hosp from Shell Shock.

DECEMBER 8

NO ENTRY

DECEMBER 9

The ruling party at the moment in Russia have brought about an armistice to consider peace with Germany, which from all appearances will come to nothing.

The military Faction under Kaledin & Korniloff are rebelling & have already interfering with the carriage of the wheat crop from Siberia[26]

Today the news of the most colossal disaster of the war reach[ed] us. Halifax is destroyed from the explosion of an ammunition ship in the harbour[27]

DECEMBER 10

German planes have been over head all day with our planes engaged in battle & bombs were dropped in the distance

In the evening we had warning for "gas" attack preparations but nothing came of it.

The casualties in H[alifax] are estimated at 2000 dead & 8000 injured

DECEMBER 11

A heavy bombardment from our guns is in progress tonight

———

Thousands (Twenty) people in Halifax are destitute & the loss of Property estimated at £4,000,000

As usual the USA is ready immediately with offers of help & trains of nurses doctors & supplies, trained engineers & other workmen are already in Halifax & at work. Besides our own local workers who are already there.

DECEMBER 12

Giffin & I went "Lorry Hopping" this am and finally arrived at St Omer [Saint–Omer] at 12.30 Wandered around the town till 3 pm. then went to the traffic sentry to get a Lorrie back finally got an Ambulance to Cassel & from there a lorrie belonging to Signals to Boeschepe & home. We were very cold tired & sleepy but got back in time for dinner.

DECEMBER 13

Hazebrooke has been heavily shelled both yesterday & today about one hundred shells each day – the town is badly destroyed & there are many casualties.

On duty in Ward D today.

DECEMBER 14

Officers Ward in PM.

DECEMBER 15

Officers Ward all day.

DECEMBER 16

Had a day off duty & stayed in bed all day.

It is bitterly cold

Had such a nice bunch of Canadian letters in the evening – also
one from Gerald & a snap taken in Paris. He had his leave in
Paris & Lyon – & enjoyed it very much.

DECEMBER 17

On duty in the Officers Ward.

DECEMBER 18 – 23

NO ENTRIES

DECEMBER 24

A wonderful hoarfrost over trees & earth this morning. The
Country is like Fairy land.

A little concert given by the men of the Unit in the evening after
which the Christmas stocking[s] were given out to them & to the
light duty patients after which we distributed the stockings to the
different wards

DECEMBER 25

Early service at 6.30 am.

DECEMBER 26 – 31

NO ENTRIES

1918

JANUARY

The Cup of War
Are ye able to drink of the cup that I shall drink of ?
And they say unto him: We are able.[1]

JANUARY 1

The Huns watched the old year out with a little air raid here
The anti air craft were very active for about an hour 11.30 PM to
1.30. A quiet day in the Ward today
Went to No 3 to dinner

JANUARY 2

We are very busy with the staff lacking three sisters & no hope of
their being replaced till there is some readjustment at headquarters of Nursing Affairs in France. There are only twelve of us
here & the hospital is full all the time.

JANUARY 3

It is bitterly cold with about 2″ of snow on the ground except on
the roads where the lorries and ambulances have long since
worked the two ingredients – snow & mud into a smooth paste –

JANUARY 4 – 8

NO ENTRIES

Staff, No. 2 Canadian Casualty Clearing Station

JANUARY 9

Night duty in the Officer's Ward.

JANUARY 10 – 30

NO ENTRIES

JANUARY 31

Off night duty Went with the Ambulance to Dunkirk. The road after Berque [Berques] is reached is beautiful – running as it does along the bank of the Canal which is at present used a great deal for hospital Barges. Berque itself is the quaintest little town I have seen in France – a walled town with its Canal running through & its moates intact.

FEBRUARY 1

Went in the Ambulance to Boulogne today with Mrs G & Miss J Johnson – the latter going on leave.

FEBRUARY 2 – 3

NO ENTRIES

FEBRUARY 4

Ward D this morning

FEBRUARY 5 – MARCH 8

NO ENTRIES

MARCH 9

On night duty in Ward D. Howel & Barker – night orderlies.

MARCH 10 – 14

NO ENTRIES

MARCH 15

There has been shelling in the neighbourhood for the last week past nothing coming in near at hand but quite distinctly heard & felt.

MARCH 16

Rumour says messages have been dropped from Hun planes warning civilians to leave Poperhinge as it will be heavily shelled also the districts surrounding

MARCH 17

Shells dropped on the Pop – Abe[e]le road tonight & several in the field behind No 3 & 17's Sister quarters – some of my patients were very nervous & frightened.

MARCH 18

Kemmel Hill in the Ambulance this morning for a birthday outing but the district was being shelled so we did not stay long on the top of the Hill The destroyed village is full of Australians. Shells are still coming into the field behind 3 & 17 – but I slept well today in spite of the noise being tired.[2]

MARCH 19

Last night continuous shelling of our camp began about 9 pm. Some fell in the field as before & others in 17 & 10's lines near the brook the soft mud saving casualties. The sisters spent the

189

night in our Mess which is across the back road. All patients
evacuated this morning & we were called at noon & bundled off
to St Omer in a hurry.

MARCH 20

St Omer – In the empty wing of the old Convent used by the Sisters of No 10 Station[ary] as Nurses Home. It is very cold &
damp in our wing but otherwise we are alright although we have
only the bare necessities of clothing with us.

There was an air raid here tonight.

MARCH 21

The great German offensive begins

News today says the Germans have broken through at Bullicourt
[Bullecourt] & surgical teams are being sent out. Miss Johnson
of our party & Ellen Carpenter from 3 went off in the night.
Capt Beggs & Aikenhead from 2 Maj Scrimger & Capt Lisle from
3. The Germans have also attacked Dunkirk from the sea & air –
without success.[3]

MARCH 22

Hazebrooke is being heavily shelled. Our lines at Remy are still
getting shells & the Pop road is badly destroyed. The Colonel
brought news & letters today. Other hospitals in the neighbourhood are over crowded & our men have gone to them. Miss
Magnus went off on a team tonight to the Bullicourt district.
Another air raid here – a small boy badly wounded. One sister
killed by shell at 58 CCS & several wounded

MARCH 23

Hazebrooke has been heavily shelled again & is now practically
deserted. Pop & Abeele are also suffering Miss Boultbee went
back to No 2 today to see about getting our luggage but
although they brought the equipment for some of the Sisters the
Col did not send either Mrs G's or mine thinking he will be able
to open up in the near future.

MARCH 24

The war news today is very discouraging. Peronne & St Quintan
[Saint-Quentin] have been captured by the Germans & 25000

prisoners & 400 guns have been taken The Germans seem to be making a desperate effort all along the line Long distance shelling of towns that have escaped for months has begun in every sector.

MARCH 25

The Sisters from two more English CCS's shelled out are arriving here today & two [CCSs] on the Peronne front have been captured with all their personelle so rumour says.[4]

MARCH 26 – 27

NO ENTRIES

MARCH 28

Returned to No 2 Can CCS today.

The Wards have all been cleaned & the walls stained & they look awfully well. I return to Ward D in the afternoon where five very sick patients await me. Barrie has been with them during our absence

MARCH 29

Abeele as we passed through yesterday is absolutely deserted. All civilians are gone & there are no signs of military activity

MARCH 30

NO ENTRY

MARCH 31 [Easter Sunday]

Went for a walk by the brook today & picked such pretty yellow blossoms – cowslips daisies & anemones

APRIL 1

NO ENTRY

APRIL 2

Our Ward is Comfortably busy. Barrie & Millard[?] are there.

APRIL 3 AND APRIL 4 AND APRIL 5

The [German] advance on the Somme is to us who know nothing of the inner plans – an appalling disaster. Albert has fallen & the Huns are threatening Arras – Capt Beggs & Miss Johnson, Capt McKendrick & Miss Magnus & their teams have gone back with the retreat.

It is said that half of all our rolling stock has been captured. Miss

Clare Gass, spring 1918

Johnson specially & Ellen Carpenter who went on a team from
No 3 CCS have had thrilling experiences. Capt Aikenhead &
Capt Beggs after carrying stretchers for hours evacuating the
patients, marched 30 Km camping on the roadsides for sleep
with the retreat. finally setting up a dressing station somewhere
with Miss J's help in a henhouse

APRIL 6
(This tale we learned later)
It is said that their orderly Ray – went about among those dying
patients they were obliged to leave behind & gave each in turn
1/2 gr Morphia at the risk of being himself being left behind
& taken prisoner

APRIL 7
NO ENTRY

APRIL 8

Our Miss Young came today to No 2 CCS.

APRIL 9

Miss Young came to ward D.

Rumours of great activity at Armentiers & Messines

APRIL 10

Armentiers has fallen & the Germans marching on to Bailleul -
Estaires & Merville are taken Also Ploegsteert – The rush of
Ambulances here is tremendous –

We are very busy.

APRIL 11

The news is very discouraging – our men seem to have no support from the guns around Bailleul. The Huns are advancing
rapidly

APRIL 12

Our Ward is still very busy & the OR is working night & day.

Some shelling in the neighbourhood tonight

APRIL 13

NO ENTRY

APRIL 14

We were sent away at a half hours notice & arrived at No 13 CCS
at Arneke [Arnèke] on duty in pm. Giffin & I doing dressings
for the walking wounded[5]

APRIL 15

I have a little infection of my right thumb They are not busy
here at present

Walked into the village with Miss Young & Louise McLeod this
pm. No news – no papers

APRIL 16

The British Matron &[in] Chief & Miss Ridley came today

Went for a long country walk in pm.

The paper says Bailleul is in flames –

Rumour says we have retaken some of our lost points –

APRIL 17

Conflicting rumours about the battle on this front The French seem to be taking over this part of the line. A french RTO came to Arneke today We are to join No 2 tomorrow

APRIL 18

We came by Ambulance to Esquelbecq this AM Our hospital tents are nearly all in place Some of our Sisters are quartered in billets in the village

Eight of us are to go into a very dirty school room in the school house

APRIL 19

After cleaning two schoolrooms today & making them habitable we are told tonight we must move in the AM as French GHQ are coming here & must have these rooms There seems to be no place for us in town as the French are crowding in.

APRIL 20

Moved this morning into different billets in the Village. Miss Young & Giffin & I are in a house together –

APRIL 21

The news is not at all reassuring. Rumour tonight says Kemmel Hill has been taken by the Huns. Went to church in the evening with Miss Young

APRIL 22

Kemmel Hill has been taken also the villages of Locre & La Clyte by the Huns.

APRIL 23

I am working each day at the equipping of the new line of tents which will correspond to the Post Operative Ward of our old hospital Ward D Line 5

APRIL 24

The traffic through the village of Esquelbecq is tremendous – both French & English – guns ASC [Army Service Corps], & troops. At night we cannot sleep for the shaking of the windows & the noise on the street

April 25

Miss Young & Miss Boultbee & Miss Hegan left today to sail for Canada where they expect to be Matrons.

April 26

We received heavily today both French & English patients. So many many hundred. Miss Gee & I are alone on the Ward. We are very short of Sisters. Those who have gone have not yet been replaced.

April 27 – May 3

NO ENTRIES

May 4

Our billets are not altogether satisfactory. Madam does not want us there & makes no scruples about saying so.

The other houses are not so bad but they are filled with French officers –

May 5

Our old hospital site at Remy is knocked to pieces. Ward H. the mens dining room & the kitchens are no more. The Medical stores are smashed as is also the Estaminet at the Corner.

May 6

I am very tired. Breakfast 7.30 & dinner at 8.30 at night with not a spare moment in between except the hurried lunch at noon & we have taken in steadily & very heavy cases this past week

May 7

Fortunately the war news is better. The British line now seems to be holding firmly with its allies the French. Kemmel Hill is no man's land being so heavily shelled by both sides that no human being can exist there

May 8 – 9

NO ENTRIES

May 10

We have been very very busy for the last two weeks. Today how-ever things are lighter.

MAY 11 – 19

NO ENTRIES

MAY 20

Went with Louise McLeod who is leaving the unit Giffin, Peggy Rose & Capt Streight to Boulogne today had a wonderful day & came back through most beautiful country in the moonlight. Had dinner with Capt Streight in town

MAY 21

A dreadful air raid at Etaples Sunday night 1000 casualties rumoured 4 of whom are sisters.[6]

MAY 22

NO ENTRY

MAY 23

The Canadian Railway Troops are having a sports day tomorrow Barrie is preparing to enter the races

MAY 24

A steady rain all day The sports were not held.
I go on night duty in Line 5 Ward D tonight

MAY 25

A heavy bombardment all along this front tonight

MAY 26 – JUNE 6

NO ENTRIES

JUNE 7

Came off night duty We moved in the morning from our billets in the village to a fine big room in the farmhouse near the hospital. Stayed up for a concert in the afternoon & went to bed early.

JUNE 8

Went to Berges this pm.

JUNE 9

Went to Recussitation Ward this morning.

JUNE 10 – 11

NO ENTRIES

JUNE 12

Barries birthday today

JUNE 13 – 20
NO ENTRIES

JUNE 21
Back to Line 5.

JUNE 22 – JUNE 28
NO ENTRIES

JUNE 29
Left No 2 CCS for Boulogne & McGill

JUNE 30
NO ENTRY

JULY 1 AND JULY 2
Pneumonia Hut for me
An air raid of a severe nature last night. 8 bombs fell very near the hospital & 7 CC but no one was hurt only cows & horses in the field were killed. In Outreau a french gun & its crew were exterminated & about 40 casualties came in from the Henriville Camp

JULY 3 – 4
NO ENTRIES

JULY 5
Etaples & Paris Plage today with Sara Mrs Giffin & Sally Watters Met Reg Gass also late in afternoon He has just returned from England where he has taken out his commission.[7]

JULY 6
News of the sinking of our Canadian Hosp Ship Lan–dovery Castle reached us today
All the Sister[s] are lost[8]

JULY 7
NO ENTRY

JULY 8
Ruth returned from leave today.

JULY 9
Miss Pearl Fraser, Miss Fortescue & Gladys Sare were all on board the Hospital Ship Llandovery Castle

JULY 10

Col Elder left today to be consultant in the Rouen Area. With his leaving the McGill Unit is practically dissolved. The Vision Book & the gift cigarette box have been sent home. The McGill has come out of brackets 9

JULY 11 – 14

NO ENTRIES

JULY 15

A great German offensive in the South – successful – district near Soissons & Chateau Thierry [Château-Thierry]

JULY 16 – 17

NO ENTRIES

JULY 18

The tide seems to have turned & successes to the Allies are reported in different parts of the line

JULY 19 – 24

NO ENTRIES

JULY 25

The War news from the south is good. The French Americans & English are closing in on the Salient & the Germans have been obliged to retreat. In the North Meteron [Méteren]retaken by our troops[10]

JULY 26

Typhoid Inoculation today.

JULY 27 – 28

NO ENTRIES

JULY 29

The 3rd Div (Canadians) Concert Party gave us a performance in the Red Cross Hut tonight. Such an enjoyable evening. One of their girls is specially clever & they have some fine voices.

JULY 30

The 1st CanR Troop [Canadian Railway Troop] have started a bomb proof tunnel in our lines

JULY 31

Col Drum the new OC came today.

Mr Kingman of the General Hospital & Sir Wm Peterson are also here[11]

AUGUST 1

A Hun plane over in AM.

There was a very bad air raid 11.30 pm until 1 next morning
Much loose shrapnel fell around our quarters & many patients came in from the town & the stretcher bearers camp down the road

One bomb fell in our field by the Hindoo cemetary

AUGUST 2 AND AUGUST 3

The Hotel Derveux British headquarters is no more the result of an Incendiary Bomb the fire is still raging. St John's Church & the Palais de Justice fared only slightly better. With much injury to houses round about & many people killed. The Wards here are caring for many severe cases – soldiers only – some have died.

A bomb also fell on the street just by the "Port des dunes".

St Martins houses are badly shattered by a bomb & an aerial torpedo, but the casualties there are slight. No 2 Stationary at Outreau was shaken badly

AUGUST 4

Miss S P Johnston came from 2 CCS today. She is attached here.

AUGUST 5 – 6

NO ENTRIES

AUGUST 7

Effie Boulster & Miss MacFarlane went on leave today

AUGUST 8

NO ENTRY

AUGUST 9

The French & Canadians have made a wonderful advance on the Somme.[12]

We are all so proud of our Canadian Soldiers

AUGUST 10

The Canadian 4 divisions were moved in absolute secrecy down to the Somme under a pretence movement to the North.[13]

AUGUST 11

NO ENTRY

AUGUST 12

Stevie has gone to No 4 CCS.

AUGUST 13 AND AUGUST 14

A very bad air raid here last night. Many people killed over near the Wind Mill Camp, one poor lad from No 1 CC out without leave had his head blown off on the 1 CC road. A french officer was also killed there. Two of our Tunnelers were wounded by shrapnel from the bomb which fell by 1 CC's canteen. We were all in the new tunnels in spite of the gas & mud & water there[14]

AUGUST 15

An air raid warning tonight. Heavy fireing in the direction of Calais by [but] the raiders did not reach Boulogne.

AUGUST 16

A cloudy night No raid
Sara went to No 1 CCS today

AUGUST 17

A rainy night
The paper says there is heavy enemy fireing in the Mt Rouge [Le Rouge-mont]

AUGUST 18

Restless rumours of all sorts afloat today.
3 Stationary going to Russia
all three year War Nurses to be returned to Canada
Sealed orders for several sisters etc etc.
The Canadians & French are nearing Roye.

AUGUST 19 – 21

NO ENTRIES

AUGUST 22

The tunnel in our lines is finished today. The sisters gave the men of the Co a supper party in the Red + hut. The 4th Div

Concert Party (Maple Leaves) entertained them afterwards.
Jess Sedgewick & Pidgeon down from 2 CCS for the day with
Forbes & Holland who are going to the Forrestry Corps hospital

AUGUST 23

1st performance of the 4th Div Concert party for the unit

AUGUST 24

A letter from Walter Blanch's sister today saying their boy has
been missing since March 22nd
Ruth goes to 3 CCS tomorrow. Also Marjorie Ross.

AUGUST 25

Ruth left this AM.
A very bad air raid in Boulogne & vacinity last night. A big fire
from an incendiary bomb some where in the town lit up the
whole sky with a different light to the bright moonlight
We went to our tunnel for the first time.

AUGUST 26 – 30

NO ENTRIES

AUGUST 31

Late tonight my orders for England arrived.

SEPTEMBER 1

NO ENTRY

SEPTEMBER 2

Had a wonderful dinner at the corner Estaminet as Mrs Giffin's
guest – John who returned to France today was there & Miss
Hoerner & Hallie Mrs Austin Sallie Watters & Louise McGreer

SEPTEMBER 3

Left Boulogne for London to report to the Matron in chief to
await transport duty. A beautiful calm crossing & a comfortable
journey in the train to London. Went to 66 Ennismore Gardens
for the night[15]

SEPTEMBER 4

Met Molly at the Bank at 10.30 after having visited the Matron
in Chiefs offices at 10 AM. Miss Cains told me to report again on
Saturday. Molly & I went to Edith Leslie's wedding at 11 & the
reception at 66 Ennismore Gardens after – Shopped in PM &

Farewell to Boulogne

went to "The Title" at the Royalty in the PM.
Mrs J B Gass' 40th anniversary [Laurie's mother]
Saw Louise McLeod at the wedding

SEPTEMBER 5

Came to Browne Hotel last night
Went to the Bank early & shopping with Molly after. Tea at No 1
Hyde Park with Whit & Fitzie.
Ellen Carpenter married today
Say[w] Gertrude Elliot in "Eyes of Youth" at St James' Theatre
tonight with Molly.

SEPTEMBER 6

Molly left this AM for Hastings to see Brooke I went out to see
The Purple Mask at the Lyric with Miss Galbraith tonight. Had
tea with Whit at RumpleMayer's on St James' St this afternoon
& walked out to the Park with her afterwards.

SEPTEMBER 7

My letters contrary to instructions were sent on to Ennismore
Gardens so I declined leave this morning before I got my invitation.
Transferred to 66 Ennismore Gardens Lodge. Went to M[atron]
in Chiefs office this morning. Have been posted to Can Special
Red Cross Hospital – Buxton – on Tuesday. Saw Capt McCusker
at 133. He is a patient at Matlock Baths. Went with Nancy Morewood to see Nurse Benson at night (Marie Lohr)

SEPTEMBER 8

Met Helen Cassels at Hyde Park St Pauls in AM with Nancy &
Jackie. – tea at No 1 Hyde Park Place where Bobbie Morewood
met us (Bobbie has a very badly injured rt eye)
Dinner with them at the "Rende[z]vous" with them & a concert
for troops at the Palace theatre afterwards (Beatrice Lillie).

SEPTEMBER 9

Shopping all morning. Met Nancy & Bobbie at the Rendevous
for lunch & went with them to the matinée "Going Up." Tea at
RumplMayer's Stayed in & rested in the evening

SEPTEMBER 10

Nancy came to train with us. Left for Buxton 12.15 – arrived
4.50 pm.

SEPTEMBER 11

This is a light duty hospital: all convalescent patients. Went on
duty at noon.
Very high
Pretty country & Buxton situated on the hillside & in the valley.
It seems to rain continuously with high winds.

SEPTEMBER 12

Met Col Burnett & his officers at the tea hour.
Yesterday letters from Father & Elsie[16]
Tea today at Northwood Home for Sick Sisters. Saw Miss Carr

SEPTEMBER 13

Letters from Giffin, John & Howell today

SEPTEMBER 14 – 15

NO ENTRIES

SEPTEMBER 16

Walked up to Solomans temple & through wood in PM Went to dinner with Wishie (Mrs McLean) & enjoyed the evening. She was alone.

SEPTEMBER 17

Saw Valentine on street tonight. Photographs taken today
Miss Blott A/[ssistant] Matron went to London today & I have been left in charge.
A meeting in the room at which I was present to discuss a Dance to be given by the different units here. Saw Miss [Vivian] Tremain[e] for the first time
Went to the movie met Maj Robson[17]

SEPTEMBER 18

NS Wishart went to Liverpool this AM for Hosp Ship duty with leave to Canada

SEPTEMBER 19

Saw John Valentine today
He is on his way back to Canada to finish his Medical Course.

SEPTEMBER 20

NO ENTRY

SEPTEMBER 21

On the street behind the hospital here there is a little old fashioned shop with Miss Pilkington Fancy Repository above the door.

SEPTEMBER 22

Went a lovely walk to a waterfall & chasm called "Lovers Leap" – late this afternoon. It is so pretty thereabouts & the actual ravine very sinister & grand. The story connected with the name is of Cromwells days

SEPTEMBER 23

NO ENTRY

SEPTEMBER 24

Went by train to Rowsley & from there by taxi to Chatsworth

"I have been left in charge"

House & Hadden Hall. Enjoyed the sight seeing very much
indeed especially the paintings & tapestries at Chatsworth & the
romantic historical atmosphere of both gardens & house at Hadden Hall

The country is really very beautiful.

A letter tonight from J S says that 2 CCS has moved back to
Remy

SEPTEMBER 25 – 26

NO ENTRIES

SEPTEMBER 27

Flora Robsons for tea

Went with Miss McGrath to Pools Cavern – a huge cave through
which the river Wye runs. It will hold thousands of people & was
in early days used by Poole a robber who was brought to justice
afterward. The formation of the rocks through the dripping of
the water is most interesting

Mary of Scotts while in captivity in Buxton visited this cave

Remains of Roman occupation have been found in abundance
here

SEPTEMBER 28

NO ENTRY

SEPTEMBER 29

Walked with Miss McGrath 6 1/2 miles to the Bull & Thorn Inn
on the London Road. Had tea & then returned to B[uxton] by
the same route It rained all the way coming home

SEPTEMBER 30

War News from all fronts is good. We are advancing everywhere.
In Belgium the line of ridges from Passchendael[e] to Wychette
[Wytschaete] have been retaken.[18]

Bulgaria surrendered to the Allies reported Damascus has fallen

OCTOBER 1 – 2

NO ENTRIES

OCTOBER 3

Bulgaria terms for peace are severe if they are accepted

OCTOBER 4 – 7
NO ENTRIES

OCTOBER 8
Bulgaria has surrendered unconditionally to the Allies

OCTOBER 9 – 11
NO ENTRIES

OCTOBER 12
The incurable treachery of the Hun is again at work to try to get peace or an armistice to enable them to recuperate. Now that our armies are victorious everywhere, they put forth their cries for Peace.

OCTOBER 13
NO ENTRY

OCTOBER 14
The name Capt A.G.C. McDermot is in the Casualty list (killed) today
To have lived through four years of this darkness & to die just as the dawn seems to be near. His poor mother!

OCTOBER 15
Had BV lived he would have been 20 yers old today.
A wonderful 8 miles walk this afternoon by the river path to Miller's Dale. Never have I seen more gorgeous autumn colouring. The walk was a wet one but so lovely. We came back by train
The Matron in Chief came to dinner

OCTOBER 16
Five of our Sisters at Bishopsdale were told this morning they were to go to the Segragation Camp in North Wales to help with this awful plague of Spanish Influenza which has broken out there. I offered my services in place of another who does not wish to go[19]

OCTOBER 17
Kinmel Park Military Hosp. We arrived 10 pm last night in Rhyl. Met by Can headquarters car & went to bed in a ward hut.
A very busy day today Miss Beard & I on a 30 bed ward. Such sick sick men. Many of them will die.

OCTOBER 18 – 21
NO ENTRIES

OCTOBER 22

A letter today from [brother] Reg. dated Sep 30 saying Father has broken his arm.

OCTOBER 23 – 29
NO ENTRIES

OCTOBER 30

Turkey surrenders to Allies

OCTOBER 31 – NOVEMBER 2
NO ENTRIES

NOVEMBER 3

Austria surrenders to Allies

NOVEMBER 4 – 9
NO ENTRIES

NOVEMBER 10

Abdication & flight of the Kaiser to Holland.[20]

NOVEMBER 11

Capture of Mons by the Canadians.

Germany surrenders to Armistice terms

NOVEMBER 12 – NOVEMBER 16
NO ENTRIES

NOVEMBER 17

Went to Miss Jones' for tea with Miss Reid. Met a New Zealand & a South African Cadet there. Nice lads who liked the jolly tea table conversation.

NOVEMBER 18 – 26
NO ENTRIES

NOVEMBER 27

Miss Pemberton & Miss MacDonald also John saw me off in the taxi.

Left Rhyl for Buxton a very tiresome journey. Miss Melburn came to Rhyl. Changed at Manchester & again at Stockport. Mrs Growshaw had a nice supper tray ready for me when I arrived at Bishopsdale at 9 PM.

NOVEMBER 28

Left 7.30 AM for London Little Whitney & Kathleen Knight came down to train to see me off. Reported at office of DGMS [director general medical services] & Matron in Chief at 2 pm. Afterwards went out to 66 Ennismore Gardens

NOVEMBER 29

Went to bank & did some shopping in AM. London is wonderful as ever but I have such a stupid companion this trip
Went with Miss Upton to see 'the Boy' in the evening at the Adelphi

NOVEMBER 30

Reported at Transportation Office 2 pm.
We are to go to Southampton for the Olympic on Monday. Went with Miss Upton to see The Luck of the Navy at the Queens theatre.
Telegram from Rhyl saying Gerald was in London & is going north to see me.

DECEMBER 1

Stayed in all day & rested for the morrow as it is raining & I am not feeling too well

DECEMBER 2

Left London 11.30 – Waterloo Station. Miss Hargraves introduced a Mr Charteris who was very kind on the journey down. Arrived Southampton 3.30. Cannot go on board till tomorrow staying at the South Western Hotel. Miss Benjaman [Benjamin] has lost her bag: 2nd offence since we left Rhyl.

DECEMBER 3

On board Olympic after lunch. After settling down I went out with Miss B to send a telegram to her people. She is the most helpless individual I have yet seen. Wrote a couple of letters after dinner

DECEMBER 4 – 13

NO ENTRIES

DECEMBER 14
Arrived Halifax Harbour 8 AM
DECEMBER 15 – 31
NO ENTRIES

[Inside back cover, 1918; undated:]
People have been a long time learning that thoughts are things
to heal, upbuild, strengthen or to wound, impair or blight.
After all we can't do much for many people, no matter how hard
we try but we can contribute to their usefulness & happiness by
holding for them a kind thought if we will.[21]

Appendices

CLARE GASS CHRONOLOGY

1887	18 March, born at Shubenacadie, Hants County, Nova Scotia, Canada. Baptised Lelia Clare Gass.
1901–05	Secondary education at the Church School for Girls, Edgehill, Windsor, Nova Scotia
1909–12	Nursing training at the Montreal General Hospital, School of Nursing, Montreal, Canada. Graduate no. 384.
1912–15	Private duty nursing in Montreal
1915–19	Lieutenant nursing sister, Canadian Army Medical Corps, No. 3 Canadian General Hospital (McGill)

1915 May–July: Etaples, France temporarily with No. 1 Canadian General Hospital

1915 July–December: Camiers, France

1915–16 December–March: Cliveden, England, temporarily with Duchess of Connaught Canadian Red Cross Hospital, Taplow

1916–17 March–November: Boulogne, France

1917–18 November–June: No. 2 Canadian Casualty Clearing Station, Remy Siding, on the Belgian border

1918 July–September: Boulogne, France

1918 September–October: Canadian Red Cross Special Hospital, Buxton, England

1918 October–November Segregation Hospital, Kinmel Park, Rhyl, Wales

1918 December: Transport Duty, England–Halifax

1919 January–November: Ste-Anne-de-Bellevue Military Hospital and train transport duty across Canada

1919 November: Demobilization

1920–21 District visitor, Family Welfare Association, Montreal

1921–24 Secretary, Family Welfare Association, Montreal

1924–52 Director, Social Service Department, Montreal General Hospital, Western Division

1952 Retirement; volunteer acting director, Social Service Department, Canadian National Institute for the Blind, Montreal

1953 Return to Shubenacadie; volunteer work in the community

1968 5 August, death from cancer at Camp Hill Veterans' Hospital, Halifax, Nova Scotia; burial at Shubenacadie

INSTRUCTIONS

FOR

MEMBERS OF CANADIAN ARMY MEDICAL CORPS NURSING SERVICE

(WHEN MOBILIZED) [1]

DISCIPLINE AND DUTIES

1 As regards medical and sanitary matters and work in connection with the sick, the matrons and sisters are to be regarded as having authority in and about Military Hospitals next after the officers of the C.A.M. Corps and are at all times to be obeyed accordingly, and to receive the respect due to their position.

MATRON-IN-CHIEF

2 The Matron-in-Chief will be required to be thoroughly acquainted with the organization, mobilization and administration of the entire Nursing Service and will exercise supervision thereof. She will keep the records and confidential reports of the matrons and sisters. She will perform such other duties as from time to time will be determined by the D.G.M.S., and will be a member of the Advisory Board for Standing Orders. She will submit to the D.G.M.S.. recommendations for the appointment, promotions, distribution, and resignations of members of the C.A.M.C. Nursing Service and will take action in connection with such measures as are approved.

3 She will, under the direction of the D.G.M.S., perform such duties as may be allotted to her, including general supervision, and she will by frequent inspections keep herself acquainted with the administration of the Nursing Service in the various Military Hospitals.

4 She will be responsible for maintaining a sufficient staff to carry out, in the event of emergencies, all nursing arrangements.

5 She will receive the applications of all ladies desiring to join the C.A.M.C. Nursing Service, and will obtain the necessary references as to suitability of candidates.

MATRON

6 The matron will be responsible for the general nursing arrangements of the hospital, for the due performance of their duties by the sisters and nurses, and for the maintenance of good conduct, efficiency and discipline amongst all members of the nursing establishment, as well as for the cleanliness and good order of the wards under their charge. She will not be responsible for nursing in wards which are set apart by the administrator of the hospital for cases which he may consider unsuitable for female nursing.

7 She will be responsible for the supervision of the sisters' quarters and its domestic economy the equipment, housekeeping, and upkeep of the Home; care and management of the nursing and domestic establishment; the official method of dealing with the establishment when sick; arrangement of their respective duties and times off; the regulations with regard to pay, warrants, travelling and other claims, arrival and departure reports.

8 She will be responsible for demanding from the quartermaster a sufficient supply and for the good condition and cleanliness of the bedding and linen in the nurses quarters and the wards under her nursing charge.

9 She will take over from the quartermaster or steward the equipment shown on the ward inventories in wards nursed by her sisters, and will be responsible for the same to the quartermaster.

10 She will take over from the quartermaster the regulated quantity of bedding for each ward nursed by her staff and will keep a bedding book (A.B.. 54), in which all bedding drawn from or returned to the store will be accounted for. All transactions must be entered and signed in this book as they occur, and she will be responsible for the balance of bedding shown therein.

11 She will frequently inspect the equipment and bedding to ascertain whether any damage has been done thereto, and will check them with the inventories periodically.

12 She will see that all orders and instructions of the medical officers treating the cases are duly carried out by the sisters.

13 In all instances of difficulty she will apply to the officer in charge, who will render her every assistance in the performance of her responsible duties.

14 When she is informed of any neglect of duty or impropriety of conduct, whether on the part of sisters, N.C.O.'s, men, patients, or visitors, she will at once report it to the O.C.

15 She will fix the hours of duty, meals, and recreation for sisters and nurses, subject to instructions from the matron-in-chief, in such a manner as will comply with standing orders.

16 She will see that proper medical and nursing attendance is provided without delay for sick members of the nursing establishment.

17 She will keep the books and accounts connected with the nursing establishment; and a monthly record of the messing will be kept together with a statement of the cost, vouched by bills of expenditure; the special allowances drawn by the nursing establishment under the Regulations being entered in liquidation thereof. The register is intended as a permanent record, and will be vouched by the signature of the matron, and inspected periodically by the matron-in-chief.

18 Should the period of mobilization be prolonged, she will make arrangements for the annual leave of sisters, reporting thereon through the O.C. to the matron-in-chief.

19 She will forward a confidential report upon all sisters serving under her. These reports, covering nursing and administrative capability, tact, zeal, judgment, personal conduct and general fitness, will be forwarded through the O.C. to the office of the Surgeon-General: they will be made when a sister is transferred from one hospital to another (except for temporary duty) on the termination of her services, or annually if the period of mobilization be prolonged.

20 She will at the end of each month forward to the matron-in-chief the sick report of members of her nursing staff.

SISTERS

21 Every sister in a Canadian military hospital will be under the immediate supervision of the matron, and directly responsible to her in all matters relating to conduct and discipline. She will receive and carry out such orders and instructions relative to the treatment of the sick as she may receive from the officer in charge of her wards, whom she will accompany in his visits. She will be responsible for the nursing of the patients in her wards, and for the cleanliness, ventilation, lighting, warming, as well as good order of her wards and annexes.

22 Before going off duty each sister is required to put in writing in the night memorandum-book any notes on special cases, or other important matters which may be necessary for the guidance of the night nurses and orderlies, or which it may be desirable to bring to the notice of the night-sister. The night-sister will see that these instructions are carefully carried out, and will record the hours of her visit to each ward, noting in the night memorandum-book any information she may wish to bring to notice.

23 Sisters will be detailed in rotation for duty as night-sister for a period of not less than one month, as the matron may decide. A night-sister will report herself to the matron to receive instructions; she will visit the wards frequently through the night, and, on coming off duty, she will report to the matron on the condition of the patients.

24 A sister must comply with the instructions of the matron and officers. She must daily report to the matron as to the condition of her wards, or of the various departments of which she is in charge. She must be careful to mention any irregularities which may have occurred, or other matters to which attention should be directed.

25 Any neglect of duty or impropriety of conduct, whether on the part of N.C.Os., orderlies, patients, or visitors, will be reported by her to the matron. In cases of emergency she will apply for the assistance of the officer or N.C.O. on duty.

26 When in doubt or difficulty in any matter she will at once inform the matron, who will, if necessary, bring it to the notice of O. C., or, in his absence, to the officer on duty.

27 A sister is not, at any time, to go to wards in which she is not working, except on special business; she is not to remain in her own wards, or visit in any other wards, when off duty.

28 A sister may not allow nurses or orderlies to visit in her wards, except on business, or by special leave of the matron.

29 She is to adhere punctually to her time-tables, and to be most particular in returning to her wards at the exact time specified.

30 The sister is personally responsible for the correct measurement of all drugs employed for hypodermic injections, sleeping-draughts, and strong poisons.

31 She will ensure that all poisons and external applications are kept in

their appointed place, and that the special poison-cupboard is kept carefully locked, and the key removed.

32 She will keep the keys of such store-closets and lock-up places in the wards as may be required for the carrying out of these duties.

33 The sister must give the matron the earliest possible information of any serious cases of operations connected with her wards, or of any other matters of importance affecting the welfare of the patients under her care.

34 If a sister deems a special nurse or orderly necessary, she must immediately report the fact to the matron. At night the night-sister will act for the matron, mentioning full particulars in the report.

35 She will take over from the matron the regulated quantity of bedding for her wards, and the equipment shown on the ward inventories and will be responsible for the same to the matron.

36 A sister must take care that there is no waste of provisions, coals, gas, water, or other articles. She must exercise the strictest economy compatible with the adequate supply of the patient's needs, in the use of mackintosh, bandages, tow, lint, cotton-wool, and all surgical dressings.

37 A sister is responsible for the linen allotted to her ward, and for its good condition.

38 In cases of fresh admissions into her ward she will ascertain when the patients last had food and see that they are not kept waiting for suitable nourishment.

39 She will cause to be drawn from the steward the personal equipment required for each patient on admission, and will be responsible that it is returned into store on the patient's discharge or death. A list of these articles is given in Standing Orders for C.A.M.C.

40 When a patient is able, she will obtain his signature on the counterfoil on A.B. 42, as an acknowledgment of having received these articles, but when he is so ill as to be unable to look after his equipment, she will cause the ward-orderly to endorse the book.

41 When a patient is too ill to look after his regimental clothing, the sister will cause the articles to be handed into the pack-store with the clothing, and will countersign the cheque from A.B. 182.

42 When any case of illness or accident is brought to hospital, or in the event of any accident, emergent illness, or attempted suicide, resulting

in personal injury, occurring in the hospital, she will cause a medical officer to be at once informed, and, pending this arrival, will take such steps within the limits of her training as may appear to her to be necessary to meet the requirements of the case.

43 She will be responsible that patients who have been allowed up throughout the day are in bed by 8 p.m. in winter and 9 p.m. in summer.

44 She will see that the discharged men leave her wards in sufficient time to be present at their parade.

45 She will visit her wards at meal times and see that the diets are properly distributed and served and that the patients conduct themselves in an orderly manner. She will communicate any irregularity to the officer on duty.

46 The sister will daily receive from the steward the wines, spirits, or malt liquor ordered for the patients in her wards, and be responsible for their correct distribution, in accordance with the orders of the officers.

47 When the daily diets and extras have been entered on the diet-sheets by the officer, she will complete and sign the Diet and Extra Sheet Summary (A.F. F734). She will then check and countersign these forms and transmit them to the steward. Prescriptions and requisitions for Drugs must reach the Dispensary not later than 11 a.m.

48 She will immediately report to the quartermaster all damage or deficiencies, as well as breakages of crockery or table glass, or any damage to library books.

49 She will submit all applications from patients for writing materials, tobacco, etc., to the officer in charge of the ward for approval, and will arrange for such indents and for letters to be sent to the officer in charge of the hospital for disposal.

50 She will be careful that money, articles of food and drink, books, tracts, pictures or articles of equipment are not introduced into the wards without the previous sanction of the administrator.

51 Sisters and orderlies should unite in showing special sympathy and kindness to the friends of those patients who are on the "dangerous list."

52 Sisters are earnestly requested to interest themselves in the home circumstances of men being invalided as permanently unfit, and make such representations as may be necessary to the matron.

53 She will be most careful in noting the religion of patients under her charge, and in the event of serious illness, she will see that the Chaplain of patient's denomination is duly notified.

54 When a death takes place the sister in charge of the ward will see that the body is reverently prepared for the mortuary, and will then inform the senior N.C.O., who will proceed in accordance with Standing Orders, C.A.M.C.

55 A sister is not permitted to accept presents of any kind from any patient, or friend of any patient, whether during his illness or after his death, recovery, or departure.

56 She will, by every means in her power, afford the orderlies ample opportunity for learning their duties, and endeavour to awaken their interest in all that pertains to nursing. As far as the exigencies of active service permit, she will endeavour to impart to her orderlies a knowledge of the following subjects:

    (I)   Personal cleanliness,

    (II)   Cleaning of ward, dusting, sweeping, cleaning, baths, tins, brasses, taps, etc., mackintoshes.

    (III)   Cleaning and disinfection of all utensils, beds, and lockers.

    (IV)   Bedmaking-draw-sheets, changing of sheets for helpless patients.

    (V)   The correct reading of measure glasses and other measures used; with constant practice to see that the quantities indicated are really known.

    (VI)   The accurate use of the clinical thermometer; the pulse and respiration; registering the same on charts.

    (VII)   Names of instruments in constant use in the wards, and how to use them (syringes, enema apparatus, etc.)

    (VIII)   The padding of splints of all kinds; making of different bandages; abdominal, many-tailed, etc.

    (IX)   The application of every sort of bandage.

57 The sister is held responsible for reporting to the matron if any of the nurses serving under her are not well, and if they appear to need medical or surgical attention.

58 Uniform is to be worn on all occasions, both indoors and out of doors,

except when on leave out of garrison, or by special permission of the matron. Jewellery is not worn with uniform.

59 Sisters are not to visit each other after 10.30 p.m. but must retire to their rooms by that hour, unless special permission for late leave be obtained. Their bedrooms are to be neat and orderly and all lights are to be extinguished therein by 11 p.m., unless special permission be given.

60 A sister is not to absent herself from meals without permission. Except at the recognized "off duty" times she will not absent herself from the hospital or quarters without permission.

61 She will be careful to exercise due courtesy and dignity in all her relations with officers, N.C.Os., men and patients.

62 She will bear in mind that unquestioning obedience and loyalty to her superior officers are an obligation.

APPENDIX A

PATTERNS AND MATERIALS OF UNIFORMS.

Uniforms will be purchased by the members themselves, an allowance for this purpose being granted. The establishments selected to supply it will be intimated to them, and all details furnished on application to the matron-in-chief.

The following instructions are published for guidance in connection with the purchase and provision of uniform:

Full Dress: Should not be worn whilst actually engaged in
                  ward duties; otherwise interchangeable with
                  working dress.

Navy bue cloth, scarlet collar and cuffs, with
                  white piping.

C.A.M.C. buttons and belt clasp.

Two stars on each shoulder.

Shoes and Stockings Black.

Working Dress: Permissible at all times, summer and winter.
                  Linen, mid-blue, washable.
                  Buttons: Gilt C.A.M.C.

Rank Badges: Two stars.

Belt: Tan coloured leather with C.A.M.C. clasp.

Collars: Eton. Cuffs: Bishop pattern.

Aprons: White.

Caps: Muslin (one yard square).

Shoes or Boots and Stockings: Tan coloured.

Great Coat: Navy blue cloth.

Raincoat waterproof: Navy blue.

Cape: Navy blue cloth, lined with crimson.

Hats, winter wear: Navy blue felt with C.A.M.C. badge.

Hat, summer wear: Panama, Navy band with C.A.M.C. badge.

Helmets may be worn when serving in hot climates.

For State ceremonies and entertainments matrons are responsible that uniformity of dress is maintained.

Mufti: (a) For golfing, riding, tennis and other games.

(b) When on leave, outside Garrison areas.

(c) The wearing of mufti in France is not permissible at any time.

APPENDIX B

Articles of Field Equipment with which Members of
the Nursing Service will provide themselves
when ordered on Active Service.

1   Steamer Trunk, not to exceed 36 x 24 x 12 inches, with name and service painted plainly.

1   Sweater, mid-blue.

1   Waterproof Apron.

APPENDIX TWO

CAMP KIT

The Kit will consist of the following in addition to three general service blankets, to be obtained free under regimental arrangements from barrack stores:

1 Telescopic Cot Bedstead.

Dunnage bag with name and service plainly painted on.

BAGGAGE OF OFFICERS AND NURSES PROCEEDING OVERSEAS
VIA FOLKESTONE AND BOULOGNE

1. In view of the confusion which at present exists when Officers and Nurses claim their baggage on arrival at Boulogne, it has been decided that each piece of baggage shall be conspicuously addressed with the rank, name and unit of the Officer or Nurse owning the baggage. All such baggage will be taken in charge by the Railway Company, and arrangements made with the Embarkation Staff at Boulogne for its delivery in proper order to the owners.
2. The Railway Company will not take charge of any baggage which does not comply with the above instructions.
3. These instructions will take effect from the 25-6-17, from which date the registration of the baggage of Officers and Nurses travelling by the above route will cease.
4. The attention of all Officers and Nurses should be called to these instructions, which should periodically be republished in Command, etc., Orders.

(Auth. G.O.C. R.O. 1717 d 15-6-17)

APPENDIX THREE

CLARE GASS'S OVERSEAS CORRESPONDENCE

20 May 1915 [postcard to her father: the sea front, Boulogne-sur-Mer]

We are still here but expect to move on to our work tomorrow. Miss Lindsay, one of our number was out yesterday & says we are going to be very comfortable in tents & huts & that the situation is beautiful. I am starting a long letter telling you of my doings but am too unsettled just now to finish it

21 May 1915 [postcard to her father of Porte des Dames, Boulogne]

...When I get time to think out my wording carefully I will write you all my news but at present feel too unsettled to write very carefully.

[May–June 1915] [postcard to her mother of L'Ancienne Eglise Notre-Dame, Etaples]

Give her [Bell] the coat or anyone the things you like. By the time I get back they will all be old fashioned. Keep the old green suit. It is alright for certain things.

24 July [1915] [postcard to brother Blanchard of a statue at Paris Plage]

[congratulations re school examinations] I hope you will work well next year as well for though you are big & strong you are really too young to enlist & you are serving your king & country far better just now, by studying & preparing for the future. As I have seen more of the troops from the front I have realized how foolish it is to come over here till you are twenty at least & you are only sixteen yet so don't tease Mother any longer to enlist for you will really prove a braver boy if you stay at home with her & work at school.

28 August [1915] [extract of letter to her mother]

I am still on night duty & am writing at my desk. I expect to come off a

week from tonight – I love the work as our convoys of patients always
come in at nights but I hate the days trying to sleep & not succeeding.

[three names of locations censored]

...Mother don't allow Blanchard to enlist. he is far too young; he is not
seventeen yet. His duty to his country at present is to play the man at
home & stick to his lessons to fit himself for his service later. – when it
comes to a time of a dearth of men in Canada – then will be time enough
for old men & lads to enlist. The British War Office in its far seeing wis-
dom in this very matter has ordered all Fifth Year Medical Students back
to their universities to finish their year knowing that their help will be
needed later on. In the early part of this war too many young lads in their
enthusiasm enlisted under false pretences of being eighteen – but until it
is an absolute necessity – which it is not at present – I think it is very
wrong – Until the government requires sixteen & seventeen year old boys
to enlist – it is wrong for them to go surely? There is no doubt about the
final outcome of this war, but we still have to think of the future of the
nation & these young boys ought to be preparing to take the places of the
men who have given their lives for the cause & whose places will have to
be filled when the war is over.

...

I have been so hard on my boots since I came to France! – being able to
wear one pair nearly a year as a rule I have worn two pairs completely out
since April & was on my last pair when I got Granty to send me another
pair from Gales just like the others I got there. Beatrice is going back to
Montreal in October. I am glad as Granty is very dull without us all.

...

It is going to be frightfully cold here in the winter. Already here in the
nights I am wearing all the clothes I possess including a sweater & am con-
templating very soon sending to Granty to purchase flannels for me, luxuries which as you know I do not usually indulge in.

...

I will never forget these wonderful moonlight nights lately. I often stand at
the door when I am not busy & the sight of this great sea of tents in every
direction is a wonderful one.

24 October [1915]   [extract of letter to her mother]

...one parcel contains only a Paris doll for [cousin] Marion

···

the rest of the packet I would like you to keep closed till Christmas day – I have been collecting these little things all summer at different times – since the weather has settled down to rain & wind we will be confined more or less to camp

···

I don't mind the cold but it is almost impossible to keep things from getting wet in these tents in rainy weather. Tonight it is pouring & bitterly cold with a north wind. I am in bed Granty sent me nice warm underwear – thick gloves – bed socks & warm stockings from Montreal & I got an eiderdown quilt from England so I am pretty comfortable but the winter here both in the trenches and out is going to be miserable. If only this dreadful war could end speedily.

···

I owe about a million letters at this moment & it is generally too cold to sit in this tent & write – the only warm place is – bed.

7 July [1916]   [letter to her brother Cyril, enclosing one
                      from their father to Clare, 21 June 1916]
This note from Father has just come so I am sending it on to you. We come honestly by what pluck we have don't we? Isn't he a brick?
No let up in the work just yet. If the early days of June were bad from the Ypres district these early days of July have been worse from another district & of course the war news continues to be good.
You see my cable reached home just in good time for a Montreal letter which came tonight tells me you were reported in the Montreal papers of the 23rd as wounded; those papers would not reach Father till the 25th & very shortly after that my letter would come to them. So it all worked out well. I hope your leg is getting on well. I am so pleased to hear it has cleared up so quickly. We are very fortunate dear lad! I haven't heard from Gerald yet this week but trust he is all right as there does not seem to be much doing just now at his part of the line. I've been intending to go down to No 8 to see Miss Griffiths but have been really too busy lately. Wasn't it lucky that my ward was in isolation while you were here.

[enclosed letter to Clare from her father, 21 June 1916]
Your "Marconi" "saying Cyril wounded in hospital here, progress
satisfactory Don't worry Am writing particulars" just to hand.
I gather from this that the wound is a serious one, but not dangerous and
that he is in your hospital for all of which I am very thankful.
I know you will keep me well advised as to his welfare and let him lack
nothing.
Mother and Reg send their love to him and best wishes for his recovery.
Let me know at once how he goes along and I will try for a furlough home
for him when he is fit. That is if he wants it – He has done his share like a
man and I am proud of him – He needn't worry if he is disabled. With his
head and mine we can pull through.
I am sending a "Chronicle" that will cheer him up as I think my boys are
as gritty as I.
Tell him for me not to worry to let me know what he wants and he will get
it or the hair will fly somewhere.

22 July [1916]   [postcard to her brother Cyril]
We are still busy as ever. ... I wish these Shubenacadie boys would let me
know if they come to Boulogne wounded. There are so many things I could
do for them. ... We are getting Australians in here by the hundreds these
latter days. they have been getting just what our C[anadian] troops got in
the early part of June. Let me know what day you are going to have your
operation & write as soon as you feel able after it is over & find out if you
will stay in this hospital till you get your new foot or if you will go to a CC
[Convalescent Camp] in England or wait to get your foot at home.

[July 1916]   [postcard to her mother of a painting by
                     Francis Tattegrain, "Marie la Boulonnaise"]
...Am also trying to write a little article for the Edgehill magazine but am
not really in the mood nor have I proper time these days. I usually write at
night in bed & get so sleepy over it that it really isn't worth much

26 August [1916]   [postcard to her father of Ruins of Leicester
                          Abbey]
Found Cyril looking fairly well & up & about on crutches. We went for a

long drive this afternoon & had tea together in town

19 September [1916]   [postcard to her mother of Canterbury
                        Cathedral]
I have been very busy since I came back from England. Our own Canadian
boys just now some of them with heart-breaking wounds – I go on night
duty tonight so want to get this card off before I lie down for a afternoon's
rest.

                              ...

I've had beautiful pansies this summer & have gathered a few seeds which
I'm enclosing – my other flowers were lovely but not exceptional but these
pansies were wonderful & I'd like to see if you can get some plants like
them

31 January 1917   [postcard to brother Cyril of a scene from
                    Lady Godiva]
[glad he's home; Athel will soon be there] I had a very rough crossing
back to France & was very sick. We are very busy just now but feel the better for my holiday

2 September [1917]   [postcard to her father of Edinburgh Castle]
I have loved Edinburgh ... we leave for London tonight. France on Tuesday. I hope before another leave is due this horrible war will be over

[September 1918]   [postcard to her father of Buxton from
                     the Slopes]
This is a light duty hospital. Very little to do & what there is very uninteresting. The Matron is going to London tomorrow for the week & I am to
be left in charge. And as all my war nursing so far has been actually with
the sick & wounded & I know nothing about official lists & reports – I am
not looking forward to the week especially as I hardly know this hospital
routine yet or my way about.

25 September [1918]   [postcard to her mother of Peck Hydro
                        Buxton Canadian Hospital]
Absolutely no news. Think I am probably established here for six months

or a year before I will hear anything more of transport duty. We sent a lot of patients home from here this week.

[October 1918]   [postcards # 2 and 3 to her [mother?] of St
                        George Village near Abergele, Wales]
...seven wards for the sick Canadians

...

While this influenza is prevalent there will be no chance of my coming home as England is very short of nurses at present.

...

We are busy now so it doesn't matter but it would be a very dull place if the hospital were slack. The Mess too is a tragedy We are not getting nearly enough to eat & there is no place to buy. However I am well, so have much to be thankful for

14 January [1919]   [postcard to her mother of Windsor Castle
                         but mailed in Canada]
The ADMS won't let me go home. Says he may place me in 24 hrs. Probably at St Anne de Bellevue. Will write as soon as I hear. Will need my thick uniform which is in the empty front room

"TO THE MEN OF THE CAMC"[1]

At this time, when our boys are returning with honour to their homes, there are many among them in the Medical Corps of whose actual work at the front, little is known by the civilian population of our land. The following verses written in 1917 at a Canadian Casualty Clearing Hospital give a glimpse at least of the nobility & faithfulness of the soldiers in this branch of the service.

We sing of a band of workers whose praise is seldom heard
On whom no decorations or honours are conferred,
No battle rush inspires them, no lust to win & slay;
These are the quiet fighters we are honouring today!
The struggle always with them is to leave & join the throng
Of soldiers in the trenches where 'tis said mens' gifts belong
Yet they have never failed us & of their best they give
That maimed & battered comrades may retain the strength to live

Some of them come from our prairie with its wealth of golden grain
Where daily toil has prepared the soil for sunshine & sweet rain
And now their mighty endeavours are not for the wealth of the farm,
But to see that comfort is given to a fractured leg or arm.
How have they learn[ed] the secret, they who have tilled with the plough?
Secrets supposedly womens' in days that are past until now?
Into each heart Christ's sorrow – sorrow for war's despair –
Has planted a seed of his gentleness & He will harvest it there.

Some were our city school boys with all their love of Romance
Ready & eager to join in the battle in far off France
These were the flower of our country – so straight of life & limb
Energy, loyalty, & keenness, with uniforms wonderfully trim:
And they have been posted to duty, here in our hospital ward
With none of the exultation & glamour of musket & sword

And here in their disappointment in the midst of the agonies real
They give of the strength of their young arms & their purity of ideal.

Some are our men of business dealers are these in gold
Financiers wise & crafty where things are bought & sold
These were the steel of our nation & have given up all for the Cause
Money & homes & children – to carry out Honour's laws.
And these are working at bedsides, untireing through the long day
Awaiting the call to the front line which will bring them into the fray
Calculating minutely that which is needed here
And helping with firmness of courage our boys to meet death without fear.

Some come from the silent Northlands, warriors tried are they
Men who could match their prowess with Prussian guards today,
Men, whom the trail has cultured, men whom the silences taught
Lessons of skill & endurance with sterness & labour wrought:
And here in the day of battle & far removed from the strife
They arrange the hospital tables to prepare for the surgeon's knife.
Or with willing & quiet footsteps at the sound of the faintest moan
They bring a drink to a bedside & gentlest sympathy's shown

So have they given their service in ways that were not their choice
So have they shown us their manhood nor given their grievances voice
Some have been killed at their duty when the bombs rained death from the
sky
Some have contracted diseases & were not afraid to die
And some go on in the workings though the days & the years are long
And are still the truly gentle & are still the truly strong.
These are a band of heroes! God guard them still we pray
These are the quiet fighters we are honouring today!

LIST OF THE MEMBERS OF THE ORIGINAL UNIT,
NO. 3 CANADIAN GENERAL HOSPITAL (MCGILL)[1]

COMMANDING OFFICER
Colonel Herbert Stanley Birkett
SECOND IN COMMAND
Lieut.-Col. Henry Brydges Yates
OFFICER IN CHARGE OF SURGERY
Lieut.-Col. John Munro Elder
OFFICER IN CHARGE OF MEDICINE
Lieut.-Col. John McCrae
(Appointed from the 1st Brigade, Canadian Field Artillery)
OFFICER ATTACHED
Lieut.-Col. J.G. Adami
Major John Lancelot Todd

SENIOR OFFICERS
Major Edward William Archibald
Major Walter Henry Hill
Major Allan Campbell Howard
Major John Campbell Meakins

OFFICERS
Burgess, Capt. Henry Clifton
Browne, Capt. John George
Dixon, Capt. Howard Chancellor
Ewing, Capt. William Theodore
Francis, Capt. William Willoughby
Henderson, Capt. Arthur Theodore
Hingston, Capt. Donald Alexander
Howell, Capt. William Boyman
Hutchinson, Capt. John William
Law, Hon. Capt. David (Q.Master)
Little, Capt. Herbert Melville

Macdonald, Capt. Ronald St John
MacMillan, Capt. John
Malone, Capt. Reginald H.
McKim, Capt. Lawrie Hamilton
Pirie, Capt. Alexander Howard
Reford, Capt. Lewis L.
Rhea, Capt. Lawrence Joseph
Robertson, Capt. Russell Butler
Russell, Capt. Colin K.
Stevenson, Hon. Capt. George Henry (Dental Officer)
Thornton, Hon. Capt. Lawrence H. (Dental Officer)
Tidmarsh, Capt. Frank Wendell
Turner, Capt. William George
Wickham, Capt. John Cuthbert
Wilkins, Capt. Walter Ashby
Osler, Hon. Lieut. Edward Revere

MATRON
Matron Katherine Osborne MacLatchy

NURSING SISTERS

Archibald, N/S Cora Peters	RVH	1909
Armitage, N/S Beatrice Louise	MGH	1913
Austin, N/S Mrs Maud Emilie	RVH	1912
Babbit, N/S E. Pearl	MGH	1913
Bliss, N/S Mary	RVH	1911
Bradley, N/S Eva	RVH	1910
Brand, N/S Louise J.	RVH	1909
Carman, N/S Harriet E.	MGH	1910
Carpenter, N/S Ellen E.	RVH	1914
Chisholm, N/S Sara	RVH	1914
Clark, N/S Muriel Maud B.	MGH	1908
Cooper, N/S Alice Mary	MGH	1912
Cotton, N/S Dorothy McL. P.	RVH	1910
Davies, N/S Isabel	MGH	1908
De Cou, N/S F.I. Gertrude	MGH	1913

Dickie, N/S Elizabeth Lillian	MGH	1910
Drake, N/S Harriet T.	RVH	1907
Duncan, N/S Jennette F.	MGH	1904
Eastwood, N/S Victoria	RVH	1909
Engelke, N/S Mary Evelyn	MGH	1912
Enright, N/S Nellie J.	RVH	1909
Fitzgibbon, N/S Olive	RVH	1913
Forgey, N/S Bertha	RVH	1909
Fortescue, N/S Margaret Jane	MGH	1906
Gass, N/S Clare	MGH	1912
Giffin, N/S Mrs Edna Jane	MGH	1913
Gillis, N/S Louella Louise	MGH	1909
Glendenning, N/S Jane	RVH	1914
Gourlay, N/S Roberta	MGH	1914
Graham, N/S Ruby Rutherford	RVH	1913
Gray, N/S Lilly Naomi	MGH	1913
Handcock, N/S Eleanor	MGH	1913
Harrison, N/S Constance W.	RVH	1910
Hoerner, N/S Sophia Mary	MGH	1898
Jack, N/S Charlotte Christina	RVH	1914
Lindsay, N/S Mabel	RVH	1898
Leslie, N/S Edith	RVH	1912
Loggie, N/S Ruth	MGH	1910
MacDermot, N/S Mary Langdon	MGH	1911
Macdonald, N/S H. Hilda	RVH	1915
MacIntosh, N/S Margaret I.	RVH	1902
MacKay, N/S Kaireen	RVH	1914
MacKeen, N/S Frances	RVH	1913
MacLeod, N/S Claire S.	RVH	1913
MacLeod, Katherine A.	MGH	1914
Macnaughton, N/S Charlotte Louise	MGH	1904
Mann, N/S Jane Elora	MGH	1914
McConnell, N/S Rachel	MGH	1914
McDiarmid, N/S. Anne B.	RVH	1908
McGreer, N/S Louise	MGH	1912
McLeod, N/S Louise Frances	MGH	1908

Morewood, N/S Anne Saumarez	MGH	1914
Muir, N/S Mary Middleton	MGH	1913
Park, N/S Margaret F. S.	RVH	1914
Pidgeon, N/S Lilian	RVH	1913
Robertson, N/S Seaborn	RVH	1914
Rodd, N/S Janet M.	RVH	1913
Ross, N/S Julia Marjorie	MGH	1914
Sampson, N/S Violet Eleanor	MGH	1907
Sedgewick, N/S Jessie M.	RVH	1914
Sewell, N/S Hope	RVH	1914
Stark, N/S Anne	RVH	1914
Steele, N/S Mary F.	RVH	1902
Stevens, N/S Louise Myrtle	MGH	1914
Stewart, N/S Alice Mary	RVH	1913
Stuart, N/S Constance Mary	MGH	1912
Tate, N/S Annette M.	MGH	1914
Watling, N/S Christina Mary	MGH	1909
Watters, N/S Everetta	MGH	1910
Whitney, N/S Eveline Mary	MGH	1913
Woods, N/S Margaret J.	RVH	1914
Wright, N/S Maude	RVH	1912

OTHER RANKS

Abell, Pte. Murray Clement
Adams, Pte. George Frederick
Apps, Pte. Carl O.
Archibald, Pte. William Charles
Baby, Pte. George Raymond
Bache, Pte. Joseph Henry
Bale, Pte. Thomas William
Bankier, Pte. John Patrick
Barnes, Sergt. Ernest
Bausch, Pte. Charles Joseph
Baxendale, Pte. Albert
Belanger, Pte. Philippe Bernard

Bell, Pte. E.H.
Benger, Pte. Manfred
Beveridge, Pte. William Wentworth
Bieler, Pte. Jean Henry
Billington, Pte. Horace Winsland
Bisset, Pte. George William
Bissett, Sergt. James
Blunden, Pte. Denis Alfred
Bolland, Pte. William
Bowie, Pte. Gordon Harper
Brand, Pte. Maxwell Stanley
Brooks, Pte. Charles L.
Budd, Pte. Henry William J.
Chapple, Pte. Hugh
Chisholm, Pte Alexander Neil
Christie, Sergt. David Semple
Christy, Pte. Arthur
Church, Pte. Cyril Klock
Clarke, Pte. George Ernest
Collingwood, Pte. Gordon Francis
Craigie, Pte. Charles
Craik, Pte. Oliver Stanley
Crediford, Pte. Harry Thomas
Crichton, Pte. James
Culyer, Pte. Bertram William
Currie, Sergt. George Selkirk
Davidson, Pte. Walter M.
Day, Pte. Chester Sessions
Day, Pte. Henry Stockwell
Demuth, Sergt. Otto
Dodge, Pte. William
Drummond, Lance-Corpl. Alfred J.
Duley, Pte. Walter Albert
Eaton, Pte. Harry Edward
Eberts, Sergt. Harold F. H.
Egan, Corpl. Hugh Arthur

Elder, Pte. Herbert Munro
Elsmore, Pte. Hugh Cochrane
Evans, Pte. Harry Ilsley
Farlinger, Pte. Anderson C.
Farquhar, Pte. John Alexander
Fauvel, S/Sergt. Bertram Auguste
Felix, Pte. Gordon Adolphe
Fitzgerald, Pte. William Victor
Fraser, Pte. John Weldon
Freeman, Corpl. Frederick William
Fry, Pte. Henry Stevenson
Gall, Pte. George Lockhart
Gallagher, Pte. Cedric Aubrey W.
Gardner, Pte. Alexander John
Gareau, Pte. Urban J.
Gibson, Corpl. Lawrence
Gibson, Pte. Percy Leopold
Giroux, Pte. Joseph
Guiou, Pte. Norman Miles
Hadley, S/Sergt. William George
Hale, Pte. Richard G.
Halley, Pte. John Lockyer
Hartwell, Pte. Arthur
Hefferman, Sergt. John Maurice
Henry, Pte. Charles Blanchard
Hermon, Pte. George Ernest
Hersey, Pte. Eric Mason
Hobart, Pte. George Maxwell
Holman, Pte. John
Hopkins, Pte. Robert Charles
Hume, Pte. George Edward
Humphreys, Pte. William James
Hunter, Pte. William Andrew
Hutchison, Pte. Keith Ogilvie
Jenks, Pte. Archie Nathaniel
Johnson, Lance-Corpl. John

Johnston, Pte. Hugh Alston
Kean, Sergt. Cecil Darling
Keeping, Pte. Benjamin Charles
Kelly, Pte. Frederick Joseph
Kendall, Pte. Carson J.
Kennedy, Pte. Archibald Philip
Kennedy, S/Sergt. George Lionel D.
Kinsman, Pte. Reginald Price
Lalonde, Pte. Lionel
Laing, Sergt. George Frederick
Lapp, Pte. Victor R.
Laurin, Pte. Earl M.
Learmonth, Corpl. James
Learoyd, Pte. Douglas R.
Le Bel, Pte. Moise William
Leeson, Pte. Lavell Hall
Lefebvre, Pte. John Gordon
Lennox, Corpl. Norman
Lockhart, Pte. James R.
Logan, Pte. Herbert Lemuel
Lowry, Pte. Wilbur Clouston
Lyons, Pte. George Albert
Macaskill, Pte. John
Macdonald, Pte. Douglas Ogilvie
MacDonald, William Alexander
Mack, Pte. Harold James
MacKechnie, Pte. Richard Edey
Macnaughton, Pte. Benjamin F.
Macguire, Pte. Ernest Warren
Malcolm, Pte. Charles Gordon
Manning, Pte. Clinton Edgar
Marshall, Sergt.-Major Albert F.
Marshall, Pte. William David
Martin, Pte. Leslie John
Martin, Pte. Max
Matthews, Corpl. Frederick

Mathewson, Pte. Cornelius Kelly
McCleery, W.O. Edward Jenner
McCormick, Pte. Robert Roy
McCusker, Pte. Emmet Andrew
McDonald, Pte. Hugh Reid
McKenzie, Sergt. William
Michell, Pte. Robert Lee
Miller, Pte. Fred Gus
Mitchell, Pte. Horner Dean
Mitchell, Pte. William Hector D.
Montgomery, Pte. Lorne Cuthbert
Mungall, Corpl. William Silvester
Neilson, Pte. Henry Kenneth
Nolan, Pte. Joseph
Offord, Pte. Robert James
Ord, Pte. William Erling
Owers, Pte. William Heath
Paine, Pte. Henry George C.
Palmer, Pte. John Hammond
Parmalee, Pte. Arthur Granville
Parsons, Pte. Walter Stanley
Payne, Corpl. Thomas Albert
Pedley, Pte. Frank Gordon
Peterson, Pte. Clyde Forington
Phillips, Corpl. Archie Lovell
Poirier, Pte. Henry
Price, Pte. Reginald Francis
Ramsay, Pte. Irving Daniel
Rankin, Pte. Archibald James
Redman, Pte. Rupert Cheesman
Reid, Pte. Loudon Corsan
Richards, Pte. Archie Loveluck
Rigg, Pte. Charles Henry
Riley, Pte. Richard
Robertson, Pte. John
Roman, Pte. Charles Lightfoot

Rose, Pte. William Harold
Rose, Pte. Walter James
Rosenthal, Pte. Solomon
Ross, Pte. Alexander G.
Ross, Pte. Dudley E.
Scriver, Pte. Walter de M.
Sharp, Pte. Albert Davies
Simkins, Pte. Henry Charles J.
Simms, Pte. Hans
Skinner, Pte. Bernard Woodworth
Slack, Corpl. Harry
Smeall, Pte. James Edward
Smith, Pte. Frederick Samuel
Smith, Pte. Herbert Henry
Smith, Pte. James Henry
Smith, Pte. Lee
Smith, Pte. Stanley Rowan
Spiller, Pte. Albert John
Spohn, Pte. Henry Gordon
Stewart, Pte. Charles C.
Stewart, Pte. James Reid
St George, Corpl. Stewart F.
Stockless, Pte. Willis George
Suter, Sergt. Albert Ernest
Templeman, Pte. William
Tennant, Pte. Percy S.
Terry, Corpl. Gilbert Shire
Thomson, Pte. Roswell
Tinling, Corpl. Charles Burnaby
Toovey, Pte. Kennedy Hamilton
Trefry, Pte. Harold Scott
Valentine, Pte. John Baptist
Vaughan, Pte. Arthur Cecil
Walcott, Pte. Francis Sharpe
Walsh, Pte. Cecil Owen
Warner, Pte. James Harrison

Warner, Sergt. Joshua William
Wert, Pte. Harold Clifford
White, S/Sergt. Frederick
White, Sergt. Harold
White, Pte. William Horace
Wienke, Pte. Charles
Wilkes, Sergt. Alfred Burton
Wilkinson, Pte. William Henry
Williamson, Pte. Harold Freeman
Williamson, Pte. Norman Trenholme
Wilson, Sergt. Robert D.
Woods, Pte. Charles Halkett C.
Wright, Pte. Henry Stanley
Yates, Pte. Christopher Montague

MATRON MacLATCHY'S RECOLLECTIONS

No.3 Canadian General Hospital. Sailed from Montreal
on the Metagama, May 6th, 1915.
The personnel consisted of 35 officers, 73 nursing
sisters, 130 rank and file

By Matron K. O. MacLatchy

Our send-off from Montreal was most enthusiastic and took away a little of the sadness of farewell. The second day out the news of the loss of the Lusitania by enemy submarines caused us to think seriously about "the demons down under the sea." The voyage was fairly smooth and quite enjoyable. Several cases of illness broke out and several emergency operations were performed. Sisters were detailed for duty and the patients well cared for. When we reached the danger zone, we were again reminded of the dangers that lurked unseen. Bands ceased playing, no lights were allowed on deck, port holes were closed and heavily curtained, and there was a general air of suppression. All arrangements for action were made should the boat be torpedoed. The last night at sea all retired partly dressed and with our life belts beside us and waited for what might happen. However, a peaceful and radiant dawn came at length and the sight of the green hills not far away caused us to thank God and take courage.

We arrived at Devonport about 4 a.m., May 15th, disembarked at 1 p.m. and entrained for London. The railway journey through the most beautiful part of England, including Devon (glorious Devon) was thoroughly enjoyed, and the panorama of the smiling landscape with the meadows and gardens in their riot of colour, thatched cottages, ivy-mantled towers and castles, beautiful trees, rivers and hedges, crowded out the unpleasant memories of the old ocean's grey and melancholy waste.

The Sister[s] and I were met by the Matron-in-Chief, Overseas Canadian Nursing Service, and we were conveyed in charabancs to hotels to await orders. Orders were received on the 18th for 56 sisters to proceed to France. 15 were detailed for duty with the Canadian Red Cross Hospital,

Taplow. I remained in England until June 13th, and on that date proceeded to No. 2 Canadian General Hospital, Le Treport, France, to await orders to rejoin No. 3 Canadian General Hospital. My orders came July 17th to rejoin hospital at Dannes, Camiers. The sisters were recalled, and in a few days we were together again and the work of making a hospital was begun. The weather was ideal and our tents were pitched in a pleasant valley, at the foot of high hills upon which the grain fields, with pop[p]ies and cornflowers intermingled, flourished and the ever varying shadows passed. From the summit of these hills the view was delightful; the peaceful village, the long stretch of sand dunes, the plaza, the restless ocean. After our little grey homes, i.e. bell tents, were made habitable, the work of equipping the hospital wards was begun. Sisters were detailed to each line of tents and the sisters in charge drew the linen and equipment, and the wards were soon ready for reception of the sick and wounded. The sisters and orderlies converted empty Red Cross boxes into linen cupboards, medicine closets, bread boxes and what not. Each bed was equipped with hospital kit, towels, wash cloths and soap, and a Red Cross bag containing useful articles was hung from the head of the bed. Our first convoy arrived August 8th – 36 cases. The excitement was intense, and we felt that we had begun the great work for which we had left our homes and country. During our stay at Camiers we received 3000 sick and wounded, the busiest time being the Battle of Loos.

About the 1st of October the bad weather began – fog, rain, gales and penetratng cold. The tents leaked and mud was terrible. The entry in my diary for October 25th was: "Very windy, with driving rain. Pools of water all over the camp. Nearly blew out of bed last night. Hospital tents all leaking, several condemned. Sisters mess tent almost up in the air. Outlook not cheerful."

November 7th, we received orders to close up, and the patients were evacuated to England. Some of the tents had blown down and the mud was almost impassable. The closing up and turning in of equipment occupied some time. The unit was again broken up and the sisters detailed for duty in England and France. Wooden huts had been commenced for sisters' quarters and were ready for occupation December 8th, and we left our little bell tents without regret. During these months of rain and mud the health of the sisters was excellent, their cheerfulness under such dampening circumstances was wonderful, and they showed early in the game the stuff they were made of. The only heating apparatus each had was a small blue flame oil stove, and that winter of 1915–16 was cold and blustery.

January 3rd, we again rejoined our unit in Boulogne. The site of our hospital was the grounds of an old Jesuit College, previously the site of the Indian Meerut Hospital. The sisters were recalled and again began the preparations for the sick and wounded. This time, the accommodation was in galvanized iron, wooded and asbestos huts, tents, and part of the old college, which provided room for 2000. The outlook was dreary enough when we took over, but some alterations and a great deal of soap and water finally made the place habitable, and on February 14th we received the first convoy in Boulogne. Small convoys each night during the winter and spring months kept us comfortably busy. With the spring and summer the aspect of the hospital grounds changed. The beautiful trees, with ivy-mantled trunks, the spring flowers which carpeted the grove, the stone covered with ivy, made the hospital a thing of beauty to the men who, a few hours before, were in the filth of the trenches. On the 24th May, the Red Cross recreation hut for convalescent patients, "erected, equipped and maintained" by the Canadian Red Cross, was formally opened, the Princess Victoria concert party giving an excellent concert. This hut had facilities for reading, writing, two billiard tables, gramaphone and piano. It was beautifully situated in the grove in the hospital grounds, and from its wide verandah the view was delightful. The convalescent patients enjoyed the hours spent in this hut and the many concerts by the concert parties from England and army divisions.

July 3rd, 1916, brought a change in the quietness of the hospital. The battle of the Somme had begun, 8374 patients being admitted during the month. July 10th, 836 were admitted and 420 evacuated. Large convoys daily in August. The battle of Vimy Ridge also brought many casualties. April 18th, 1917, over 200[0] were in hospital, and large convoys were received daily durng the month. These figures will show the work there was to do during the many large battles.

The following figures may be interesting: Number of patients admitted to hospital, 1915, 3,039 (August to November); 1916, 35,640 (January to December); 1917, 48,465 (January to December); 1918, 42,191 (January to December); 1919, 4,233 (January to March); detained for the night, 9,684. Total, 143,252. Total number operations performed, 11,395. Number returned prisoners of war (Nov., 1918), 1,533.

The personnel was increased after the first year, the number of nursing sisters allowed for a 2000-bed hospital being 112. The number actually on duty varied with sickness or leave, and when the great battles were raging, several would be sent to reinforce the nursing staff of the Casualty Clearing Stations near the firing line, returning when their services were not required.

The cheerfulness of the patients was remarkable, which helped those who were attending them to carry on and endure the sights and suffering caused by enemy guns. A large wound would be called "a scratch," and the usual remarks were, "Have I a blighty?" "It's good to 'get between sheets'"; "Give me a fag"; etc. During the battle of Vimy Ridge we received many Canadians, and they were one and all jubilant over their wonderful achievement. It was a great privilege to get our own soldiers, but the Imperial, Australian, New Zealand and South Africans were all alike, brave and uncomplaining, and all felt it an honour to minister to them.

During 1918 the visits of the Hun by aeroplane were very frequent. My diary records about 40. The anti-aircraft guns, with deafening boom, kept him at a distance, but did not prevent him from dropping bombs dangerously near our hospital, and often casualties from the raids were brought into our hospital. During these visits all were supposed to "take cover," as the shrapnel and unexploded bombs were dangerous. Several times "duds" fell in our grounds, and, on one occasion, part of the shell casing crashed through the roof of the ablution hut and buried itself in the concrete floor. During an air raid in March, 1918 a bomb was dropped in our hospital grounds, tearing an immense hole. Windows were broken in the hospital huts and in the sisters' quarters; there were no casualties, as the trees and stone wall afforded protection to the huts. In August, 1918, bomb-proof dugouts in the sisters' quarters were completed. These were excavated through rock and clay, and three entrances were protected by sand bags. Forty steps connected these entrances with the chamber, which accommodated about 200. Sisters off duty were supposed to remain in the dugouts until the "all clear" was sounded.

The work of the Red Cross cannot be too highly praised. Its help to the hospital was incalculable. There was no need it could not supply, and the feeling that we had only to ask to receive was cheering in these days when our hospital was full of the recently wounded. The Matron had charge of the

Red Cross supplies and was responsible to the officer commanding the hospital. Indents as required were forwarded to the Canadian Red Cross stores at Boulogne, and the cases received were placed in the Red Cross stores on our own grounds. Indents were submitted to the Matron daily by the sister in charge of each ward, who distributed the articles received when needed.

Among the thousand and one useful articles were socks, pyjamas, sweaters, pneumonia jackets, dressing gowns, utensil bags, bandages, dressings, etc., etc., etc., and, of course, the most appreciated by the patient were the cigarettes, chocolates and gum. A "fag," when a large and painful wound was being dressed seemed to help him keep his nerve.

The cases of apples, oranges, jam preserves, canned peaches, jellies, etc., deserve honourable mention. Each apple was wrapped with tissue paper and packed with greatest care, so that they arrived in perfect condition, and the jams, jellies and preserves showed the same loving care. I am sure the women who prepared these delicacies felt that possibly a husband, son, brother or sweetheart might receive a portion of his favorite preserves. The devotion of our noble women at home will never be forgotten, and each one deserves the "Well done, good and faithful servant."

Just a word about the nursing sisters with whom I had the honour and pleasure of being connected. About 400 had duty for long or short periods with No. 3 Canadian General Hospital. The sisters' one thought when on duty was the comfort of their patients, and many francs of their own money were spent for delicacies for the seriously ill and treats for the convalescents. These attentions helped them to forget for the moment their horrible experiences. There were many inconveniences to put up with, and often the hours were long and work heavy. Night duty on active service, which came about every three months, was most difficult and nerve racking, especially during the long, dark, stormy night. The convoys of sick and wounded usually arrived during the night, also the evacuation to England took place. During the long battles the night nurses often had 100 or more heavy surgical cases under their care and these had to be watched vigilantly for haemorrhage and gangrene. Often these duties were performed with the enemy plane overhead, amid the deafening noise of our own anti-aircraft guns. The only light allowed was a shaded lantern until the "all clear" was sounded. The courage of the sisters on these occasions was remarkable and won the admiration and respect of the patients. In the Great War the nurse was truly "a ministering angel", an inestimable source of comfort to the "broken soldier" in his hours of suffering, "even unto death." Our days over there were not all work and no play. Durng the quiet times the sisters had extra time off and availed themselves of the opportunity of visiting the neighbouring towns and lovely valleys near the hospital. They also derived a great deal of pleasure from the tennis court and the occasional dances in the Red Cross recreation hut. Our own officers and many from the line who were at Rest Camp attended, and all were better for these diversions. And there was the two weeks' leave about once a year to England, Scotland, Ireland, and later to Paris and the south of France, which refreshed and invigorated. The health of the sisters was excellent, considering the strain and the periods of pneumonia and influenza epidemics when the wards were full of infection. We left two of our sisters sleeping in the land of poppies. One of our original staff is "asleep in the deep" with those brave souls who stepped into immortality when the Llandovery Castle was torpedoed. The ineffable sadness of the haunting notes of the "Last Post" at the graves of our well beloved will never be forgotten, and in these days of "Peace on earth" our thoughts are often of those who

"Short days ago, lived, felt dawn,
"Saw sunsets glow, loved and were loved."

NURSING SISTER MABEL CLINT'S RECOLLECTIONS[1]

1918. BOULOGNE AND AIR RAIDS

After this interlude, it was with personal joy, and the envy of many that two of us received orders on April 12th., our application for service in France being approved. It was an emergency call for nurses, as the consequences of the break in the line, the terrific carnage of the close fighting, the confusion of the retreat, and the congestion of hospitals in all areas, needed relief after weeks of overwork and menace. I think we reached London on a freight train, for I remember we were in a little compartment with two benches at the rear of trucks, and saw no conductor, and rattled and jolted, and stopped frequently till 4 a.m., when we ran into the Midland station. The hotel, depleted of its staff, had only one sleepy old man behind the desk, but we literally fell into bed, and knew nothing more till a jangle of church bells at 11 roused us. We needed several articles of equipment, and it was Sunday. A telephone call to the shop where our uniforms were made elicited the fact that two cleaners were there, and would let us in if we knew where to find what we wanted. We selected them in the dim, sheeted showrooms, and I verily believe could have loaded a lorry with goods and driven off. Were we not Sisters, and Canadians? Our name stood high in England since Ypres. With that baffling English trust in honesty, we were allowed to depart without payment, one of the men offering to parcel our merchandise, and come back at 5 P.M. to hand it out, and receive our cheques. And there he was to the minute.

How happy we were to see once more after a long absence the silhouette of Boulogne Cathedral, the gray walls of the massive citadel, the irregular pile of hotels, and steep, roofed houses along the quays, the masts of the fishing boats, the curving break-water and the light house.

No. 3 Canadian General Hospital was formed originally of some of the most distinguished surgeons and physicians of Montreal and McGill University, the first such unit to be enrolled in the Empire. The nurses came chiefly from the two largest hospitals there, the Montreal General and Royal Victoria. And the first summer medical students had volunteered as orderlies and dressers. It was therefore a more homogeneous Unit than others that had preceded it. No. 1 General or Base Hospital at Etaples, and No. 2 General at Le Tréport had been carrying on a steady service since the spring of 1915, and these Base Hospitals got all the worst cases in the area behind a particular sector. Organized for "the duration", they had not the constant uncertainty, movement and evacuation of patients in the Stationarys, (a quaint misnomer) but after a severe engagement their work was extremely heavy; operating day and night, and after care of wounded tested all resources, for which of course they were more fully equipped. They expanded to 2000 beds on occasion. Some men could not be moved for months. Throughout the four years the Canadian Medical Profession was proud to hear general praise of the lay-out, ward arrangements, surgical and nursing skill given to all Casualties in these two representative Units, and patients were united in grateful acknowledgment to doctors, nurses, and orderlies.

"McGill" had been established for some time at the summit of that two mile long hill, which had seen so many thousand British troops march up it to the tune of "Tipperary", since August 8th. 1914, till want of breath silenced them. The site of the huts was amidst trees, and included the semi-ruins of a Jesuit College, which was utilized as operating theatre, etc., with a post-operative ward adjoining. Capacity was 2400, M.Os. 28, staff 300, and the Sisters numbered about 110. Since the enemy advance of March, they had been working at high pressure, and as the Germans retook ground that had been British since 1914, even Boulogne became fairly near the front, and emergency dominated all actions.

At various times for services at the Clearing Stations, Canadian Medical Officers had been gazetted awards of the V.C. [Victoria Cross] and M.C. [Military Cross], and more such recognitions of valour and duty were won in 1918. To these weeks also belongs the story of the heroic conduct of Sisters who remained to the last minute in these Clearing stations, and as they fell back, continued to assist the surgeons in tents set up by the wayside, doing what they could for the wounded, till ordered to Boulogne, unable to risk capture by an enemy who did not respect the Red Cross. Those men who had a chance for life went down in the trains, and ambulances (many driven by women) which came up to the firing line, but many had to be carried out on stretchers, and left on the grass to die, for neither time nor conditions allowed evacuation of all. I wish these ex-sisters would combine their experiences in a brochure for record in the Canadian Nurses' Association.

It is a thrilling chapter in the history of the C.A.M.C., which should be set down before all is obliterated. Some of these Sisters were attached to what had become known as Surgical Teams, which did good work over a wide area. They were composed of Surgeon, Sister, Anaesthetist (often a Sister) a non-commissioned officer and an orderly, and were sent as a mobile unit to whatever points their services were most required, remaining a certain number of weeks before relieved. They had to have a practical "gas-mask course" before they left.

Close to No. 3 rose the tall Colonne de la Grande Armée, looking out to the Channel, where below Napoleon had assembled his regiments for one of those carefully planned invasions of England which never materialized. However there was the Column, in memory of the intention, and all around it for miles British camps, hospitals, cemeteries, marching men, guns and stores, on such a scale as even Napoleon never dreamed of .... "the nation of shopkeepers" come to the aid of his erstwhile subjects, and for their own existence, to bar the way against an equally boundless ambition, and more ruthless foe. Lower again, on the beach at Ambleteuse, Caesar's Cavalry are said to have embarked for England. He had more luck, but got such a fierce reception that it was ninety years before Romans again invaded the White Island.

Up to the month of July the situation was so complicated and obscure on the new trench alignments that the hospital was turned into a huge Clearing Station in itself. As many as 670 were once admitted in 24 hours, fed, put to bed, dressed, operated on if necessary, and 469 sent across the Channel the same night. We had constantly to be ready for rush orders, but there were also periods when the expected did not happen, and we were idle. There always remained several wards where the fractures unable to be moved were concentrated and where all the appliances and treatments evolved by war surgery were in use. One hut which required good nursing care was that set apart for chest cases, mortality among such being high. Mustard gas too provided us with a large number of suffering men, few of whom probably were curable. Later too the Influenza epidemic almost filled every hut with medical cases, and the daily work became more like that of a civilian city hospital, with the greater proportion of the patients in bed for days. Infected wounds and gas gangrene were the most serious and difficult cases to treat for months in 1918, amputations being more numerous than at any other period, and tetanus prevalent. Surgical and nursing skill were united in effort to save life and limb amid the appalling wastage of war.

On May 19th.-20th. occurred the shocking affair at Etaples twenty miles away, the deliberate bombing by a score of enemy planes of English and Canadian Hospitals, full of helpless patients, supposed to be protected by the Red Cross. There were 171 casualties, 56 fatal, many from machine gun bullets, and among them seven Canadian sisters, of whom four died. As one London paper put it: "This is one of the most diabolical crimes that Germany has committed. Let us hear no more of German Airmen's 'chivalry.'" These incidents do not properly come within the scope of these pages, as I was not present, but I cannot refrain from mentioning them. One who was there said of the Sisters: "I was proud of them." There was no panic. Those not on duty lay under beds to avoid breaking glass. Amid darkness, explosions, noise, and bursts of flame, no one made any outcry, and the Matron and five Sisters received the soldiers' decoration, the military medal, for bravery in action. One Sister went out to get morphia for a companion bleeding to death, and others rendered first aid, literally under fire. "I thought the girls were splendid", wrote an eye-witness: "Sister W . . . . dying out on the hillside, and knowing it, yet begging them not to bring stretcher bearers into that inferno, when it could not save her. All of them saying, just as the men do, 'Don't bother with me; I'll be all right. You people will be exhausted'. All the blackened faces."

The Canadian Hospitals involved were Nos. 1 and 7 General, and 7 and 9 Stationary. Attacked again later, the destruction was so great that Etaples was evacuated within two weeks. Lives of several Sisters were saved by one, perhaps the heroine of the night, who went back over and over again, and insisted on getting her comrades out of a hut which had taken fire unknown to them. A long procession wound through the great Etaples military cemetery two days later, (12,500 graves there) and there the names of the victims may be read among the stones bearing the Maple Leaf. We heard the bombardment distinctly, and the Hun planes had passed over us, but had no missiles left on their return. About a month after this outrage we heard with horror and incredulity of the sinking of the Llandovery Castle hospital ship, fortunately without patients, and the drowning of fourteen Canadian Sisters and others in an open boat. Ten New Zealand Sisters had previously met a similar fate in the Marquette. The number of Imperial nurses drowned must have exceeded this total, and many were torpedoed and rescued.

Boulogne was bombed almost nightly that summer, chiefly to destroy the morale of the population, as well as deal a blow at the British line of communications. It was pitiful to see the French, young and old, wending their way at nightfall to the galleries opened under the broad walls of the fortifications. Some died there, some were born, and at 5 a.m. back they tramped again to daily work, worn, sleepless, but resigned as ever to passive resistance. On June 30th water and electricity were cut off for some hours by bombing damage to the main conduits, and the enemy airmen circled so low at times that it seemed they proposed to land in the grounds. Shrapnel fell like rain, and five terrific explosions smashed glass far and near. On this occasion discussion arose as to how best to show up hospital areas at night, and orders were posted to lay out a large pebbled or white-washed square on the ground, with the Red Cross in the centre. Many argued however that this merely supplied an easy target for the enemy airmen, and the latter speakers from evidence accumulated were apt to be right.

To us also it was a nerve-racking time, as we were disturbed once and twice nightly if the weather was clear, and about five nights a week. Usually about 11 P.M. a maroon would sound the alarm, "Huns over lines." The second signal informed us the enemy airmen were at Calais, and the third that they were in our own area. All lights were immediately extinguished, and an eerie silence awaited the first crash. It was not so much the noise as the concussion on the ground that was most terrifying, and speculation never could be sure of the direction, and who or what had been hit. Breaking of glass, shrapnel from French anti-aircraft posts, sharp machine guns in action, and "Lizzie" close at hand increased the din. From a German prisoners' camp nearby came cries of terror, and demands to be released from the attentions of their own craft!

I seem to recollect that when a number of us foregathered in the dark in some central hut on these occasions, and Sisters off duty were *doubling up* beneath beds in twos and threes, that the site I selected was quite popular. For never being able to fit *under* an army cot, I had to remain on top of one, and there was quite a competition for the extra protection of the lower storey! ...

One particular night, August 14th., it was estimated 80 bombs fell on the town and vicinity, in an attack which lasted one and a half hours, over an area of perhaps three by one and a half miles, such a raid as even London had not experienced. Several hospitals were hit that night, and nurses and patients killed at Wimereux, a St. Johns' Ambulance party, just back from unloading a Red Cross Train, were wiped out, an ammunition plant was struck, a railway dump and British Officers' Headquarters practically destroyed, the docks hit, and the Casino hospital set on fire. Several other fires also started, which with star-shells, flares and search-light beams, the continuous barrage, and the chatter of the 'Archies', made it appear that all Boulogne was doomed. Forty were killed, and stretcher bearers worked amid the burning ruins, collecting the casualties with death overhead. Among those who had stationed themselves with their own cars in various quarters of the town to convey wounded to hospital in these raids, were a number of English women, whose courage and prompt aid saved many a life, and won the admiration of the inhabitants. We ourselves were fortunate, No. 3 getting only a 'dud' shell, and another which burst in the sunken road between the hospital and the Sisters' Quarters. There was a dug-out of sandbags in the corner of our ground then, but two of us preferred, if we were about to die of Hun frightfulness, not to be smothered, and sitting at the door of our hut, had a good view of the weird scene. The red glare of fires, bursts of firing from the defence positions, the shaking of the ground under us, shrapnel pattering on our roof … a nose-cap whacked on to our doorstep … made an appalling ensemble. To walk down the Grande Rue next day, with its gaping hotel rooms, its blockage of bricks and stone, the great holes in the fields, ruins of walls and gardens, yawning windows, would have resembled nothing but an earthquake, had we not become familiar from photos with such scenes of devastation.

Sir Robert Borden came over just then, and ordered timbered dug-outs to be prepared for sisters off duty, as it was at last realized that the Germans would observe no rules of war whatever. There was some suggestion that sisters should be withdrawn from night duty but as it met with strenuous opposition it was never put into effect. The tunnel, built by Canadian Railway troops, and finished by German prisoners, was 22 feet underground, with 10 feet of earth above. Two entrances, screened by sandbags, provided escape if necessary. It was a cold and clammy shelter to slide into from a warm bed. It was "an Order" that everyone must repair to this retreat at the second maroon. One night when I had warned a new arrival from Canada, who was all excitement, and inclined to think air-raids were great fun, that she must not linger, she still stood at the entrance, bound to see the first attack anyway. A bomb crashed, and she came hurtling down the slippery mud steps, on top of me, stuttering: "Was ... that ... a b ... b... bomb?", while the whole place quivered, and stones clattered outside. Sundry small articles were scattered about our floors when we came up, and the next field had a hole in it the size of a cottage. We had to be always on the alert at 11 p.m., and more often than not the Alarm sounded. A scramble for boots, a grasp at a kimona and military coat, and we joined the parade of the tired, angry company of pigtails and pyjamas. Scarcely had the "All clear" been sounded by a bugler on the walls of the town, and we were lying dressed and muddy on our beds, (for we knew 'Fritz' would be still about) than the Alarm would ring out again, and the performance be repeated. Often a third time the "Alert" roused us, and perhaps it was 3 a.m. before we got to sleep, to rise again at 6, and go about our duties. It was extremely fatiguing, but did not succeed in breaking our spirit. Sisters from the Clearing Stations, spending a night on the way to leave, declared ours appeared to be the real front, as far as air attacks went. We could always tell the difference between an enemy machine, which had a wicked throb, and our own, which droned or hummed.

Everyone preferred to be on duty during air-raids. There were things to do, even in the dark. We carried morphine, hypodermic and tourniquets in our apron pockets. The worst cases were visited, and rounds made to see that no light was visible. I saw a speck at the end of a ward one night, while the enemy was above us, and on remonstrating, an apologetic voice of a lad of 18, replied: "Sorry, Sister, never thought. It was something to bite on." To those who lay helpless in splints, it was a greater ordeal than fighting, waiting for the next 'hate' to mangle already crushed frames. On the whole, however the soldiers slept through raids, and my waking those who had beds up in a great attic under some skylights, where they might lose their eyesight, was not really popular. No air fighters could be spared from the front at that time for defence of back areas. At the end of August we were able to remark that we hadn't had a raid for a week, and the enemy become too occupied then with the great offensive of the Allies to spend the nights annoying us. They had failed in their objective, paralyzing Boulogne harbour, and shaking the fortitude of the Boulognais. But two more of our nurses had been murdered in the meantime in another dastardly attack on British hospitals there. At Doullens in No. 3 Canadian Stationary a night operation was in progress, and as the German aircraft flew back and forth overhead, they finally with machine guns killed patient, surgeons, sisters and attendants. No. 7 and 9 Stationaries were practically wrecked, and personnel had to be withdrawn.

On Sunday June 30th., both men and nurses proceeded to various cemeteries to decorate Canadian graves for Dominion Day. The first British cemetery which we had visited at the top of the hill in Boulogne in November, 1914, was now closed, and in beautiful order, but alas! the immense increase in the green mounds, the long straight rows of trenches, the little crosses arm to arm, the names of thousands added, since, during the far-flung course of duty, we had last stood there. A short united service was held, and the Last Post sounded.

One of the most fantastic sights of the whole war happened each evening at Boulogne. A row of fat, 'sausage' balloons would rise irregularly to the east of the town, wavering and inflating themselves in an awkward, sluggish fashion, like great, brown pigs. They carried an invisible wire net, and were for the purpose of entangling enemy aircraft, like chains in the Straits of Dover for 'U' boats. Opinion was divided as to their utility. They may have stopped a few planes, but others got through or above them. The Silver King and Silver Queen, British Observation Balloons, floated gracefully above the Channel most days, and it was a great relief to see each morning a group of our planes soaring over camp towards the lines. The first year of lack of guns, ammunition, *and an army*, were a terrible strain even to the non-Combatants. Only – as we counted each 'bus,' we felt it told its tale of the previous day's losses. Our clever Canadian Concert party the "Dumbells" had been giving entertainments in the reserve lines for a long time, and our patients enjoyed a visit from them, and "shows" nightly in the Y.M.C.A. Hut. The "Maple Leaves" also entertained us later.

The hospital huts of No. 3 were on the whole more commodious than others in which I had served, central aisle was wider, and at one end a small office was provided, and a compartment for preparation of diets, from which also meals were handed out after being received from the main cook-house; washing of dishes was done in the wards. A patient was selected in each hut and given a week or so longer of convalescence before being marked for "Con. Camp." Among these, as a rule, easily the best were the "Jocks." These Scottish boys seemed to have been home-trained to be useful, enterprising and faithful in little jobs. I don't know what we should

256

have done without them. One kept my "primus stove" going for two weeks. I think he got out of bed at midnight to take a look at it, and had a pride in helping to 'run' the ward. Canadian Sisters always had a great deal more physical work to do in the wards than the English Nurses, as their trained orderlies accomplished a large amount of routine care of the patients in the latter hospitals. One of the 'Jocks' could not sleep one night after admission, though hot drinks, etc. had been given him. Replying to the nurse's enquiry as to what was the matter about 3 a.m., he said: "I'm quite O.K., Sister. It must be the bed. I haven't been in one for seventeen months." I admit this was the one and only occasion when I heard of "rest in bed" keeping a soldier awake! German prisoners were employed in outside duties in various camps, being marched over from their barbed wire enclosures daily. Our patients used to throw out cigarettes to them, and they were chiefly at this time young men who had been school-boys before 1914, stolid, expressionless, and dull. Though these youths had no personal share in preparation for hostilities during previous years, they had all formed part of the compulsory school navy league bands, and had been educated in every possible manner to glorify the fleet of the Vaterland, and contribute their pfennigs to its increase for the purpose, as they were told, of rending from England, that arch enemy, the command of the sea. It was therefore not to be wondered at that they were all ready and looking forward to "The Day".

We had too in 1918 some American patients from Calais who had met with accidents or were ill. I was surprised to find that among them was a considerable percentage of illiterate young men. Most of the Americans who had fought with the Canadian contingents I think elected to remain with them after the entry of their own country into the war. Personally I believe Canada had a great deal to do with U.S.A. final participation, through interest and admiration for the achievements of this Dominion, publicly and privately expressed. It was only in 1919 that we learned for the first time 'WHO HAD WON THE WAR'!

"McGill" also was the hospital to which the Portuguese sick were sent, and they averaged about 600 listed during most of 1918, over 5000 in all receiving medical attention.

A few statistics of a General Hospital in war may prove informative for comparison.

From Aug. 7th. 1915 to April 1919.

Total cases admitted:	143,762
Wounded:	52,389
Sick:	81,689
Died:	986
Operations:	11,395
Admissions wounded one night,	490
Passed through, busiest month	46,000
Operated on one month,	2,300

A reminder of Lemnos came on Oct. 31st. when a brief despatch announced that General Townshend had signed an Armistice with Turkey in Mudros Bay, some little consolation for the ills endured there. Other Armistice rumours reached us with regard to the western front, but were scarcely heeded, for "They say" had long lost authority. Also the victorious advance of the last three months, in which Canadians took a glorious part, must, we thought, be continued into Berlin.

Notes

NOTES TO INTRODUCTION

1 Nicholson, *Canada's Nursing Sisters*, 96, 98; National Archives of Canada (NA), MG 30, E45, Margaret Clotilde Macdonald Papers, "History of Nursing Services," Ch. 6; "Correspondence," Macdonald to W.R. Landon, 12 May 1922; Gunn, "The Services of Canadian Nurses and Voluntary Aids During the War," 1975. Census of Canada 1921: 5,476 nurses in 1911 and 21,162 in 1921. The total death number for CAMC nurses is 46; 39 is the overseas number. Nursing numbers vary by source and location, from 2,000 to 3,000. Those giving the higher number usually include about 500 nurses serving with the military in Canada and another 400–500 serving overseas with nursing organizations other than the CAMC.

2 Information on the Gass family background comes from conversations with nieces, nephew, and a cousin in Nova Scotia in the spring of 1999: Elizabeth Anderson, Geraldine Brenton, Trudy Henderson, Roslyn MacPhee, John Gass, and Marion Walsh, as well as from telephone conversations and correspondence with nieces Catherine Germa and Mary Brown in Ontario in the autumn and winter of 1999–2000. A chronological outline of Clare Gass' life, pieced together from the research for this book, is included as Appendix 1. For mobility of Nova Scotian women, see Brookes, "The Provincials by Albert J. Kennedy," 94 and Beattie, *Obligation and Opportunity*.

3 Edgehill *Calendar*, 1903–4, 1904–5. According to the handwritten Edgehill ledgers for 1902 and 1903, Robert Gass Esq. of Shubenacadie was

paying $75 a term for his daughter's board and tuition and a varying amount, usually approaching $25 a term, for extras. The major extra expense was "pianoforte" at $12 a term. Annual school expenses therefore would be $300. Family recollection has it that the Gass daughter was the only child in the family to receive this kind of schooling.

4 Clare Gass belonged to the "second generation" of nurses trained in Canada. See McPherson, *Bedside Manners* 19, 30, 39.

5 McGill University Archives (MUA), RG 96 MGH School of Nursing, Container 424, File 685 "Probationers." She was one of thirty-three probationers allowed to continue their training that year from an initial group of fifty-three chosen from close to six hundred applicants. MUA, *Annual Report of the Montreal General Hospital* 1909, 81.

6 MUA, RG 96, MGH School of Nursing, Admission Registers, Container 417, File 611 Register of Student Agreements.

7 Ibid., Container 416, File 608, Register of Nurses and Probationers Employment; Container 427 File 688 Nurses' Register and, the same volume reversed, Register of Nurses' Work, 1909–12.

8 Ibid., Container 429 has a sample of student record cards from 1911, although Gass's file was not among them. A printed assessment form was available, with the personal information severed by the University Archivist.

9 Nicholson, *Canada's Nursing Sisters*, 45.

10 Ibid., 46–7

11 Morton, *When Your Number's Up*, 183.

12 Canadian Nurses Association Archives (CNA), Nursing Sisters Association of Canada Papers (CNATN), Secretary [Jean Gunn] to R.L. Borden, 21 December 1914; H.M. Jacques to Jean Gunn, 15 January 1915.

13 MacDermot, *History of the School of Nursing*, 59. The formal *Instructions for Members of Canadian Army Medical Corps Nursing Service* is included as Appendix 2.

14 Fetherstonhaugh, *McGill*, 42–9. A list of the original members of the unit is included as Appendix 5. In addition to the General and Stationary Hospitals, Canada had six Forestry Corps Hospitals, four Casualty Clearing Stations, and one Field Ambulance; Morton and Granatstein, *Marching to Armageddon*, 278.

15 G. Allard was the first to draw the connection between nursing training

and military life ("Les infirmières militaires," 68–81).

16 J.Cameron-Smith, " The Preparation of Nurses for Military Work," 556.

17 NA, Macdonald Papers, "Pay for Nursing Sisters," NA, Canadian Expeditionary Force, RG 150, Acc 1992–3/166, Box 3436–16, Clare Gass personnel file, pay sheets. The extra allowances amounted to $18.60 a month while a nurse was "in the field" (duty in France) and $30 a month for the costs of the nurses' "mess," their eating and social centre. Clare's pay sheets show her earning between $108 and $111.60 per month, of which she assigned $50 a month to a bank in Montreal. Travel allowance usually meant vouchers for first-class train travel, although the latter was not always available.

18 Gass Diary, 2 March 1916.

19 The McGill University Library and the Canadian War Museum both have collections of war posters. Desmond Morton has gathered a number of slide reproductions of posters and photographs which he kindly allowed me to view. A good sampling of British posters is found in Haste, *Keep the Home Fires Burning*. Feminist historians have begun to untangle the gendered nature of war propaganda along the lines I suggest here. Two of the best examples are Susan Kingsley Kent, *Making Peace* and Nicoletta Gullace, "Sexual Violence and Family Honor."

20 The Canadian military nurses' uniform is described in detail in the first appendix of the nursing *Instructions*, see Appendix 2. For an analysis of early nurses' uniforms in Germany, see Poplin, "Nursing Uniforms." The reaction of Londoners to the Canadians' uniform appears in Bruce, *Humour in Tragedy*, 3, and Clint, *Our Bit*, 21. One Canadian nurse found the uniform very unappealing and praised Matron-in-chief Margaret Macdonald for allowing the nurses, once they arrived in London, to shorten the garments and refashion the hats, Wilkinson, "Four Score Years and Ten," 16. Another Canadian, serving with the Americans, had quite the opposite reaction, although she was describing the working as opposed to the dress uniform: "Their [the Canadians] uniforms are very pretty, bright blue with brass buttons and they wear veils like the V.A.D.s [Voluntary Aid Detachments]. We'd all love to wear them too if we could"; Bongard, *Nobody Ever Wins a War*, 31 (entry for 12 February 1918). At least two of Clare Gass' nieces recall being confirmed with one of their aunt's nursing veils as head cover.

The nurses were, of course, not the only ones to refer to the soldiers as "lads" and "boys." Male officers did so too, the nomenclature accentuating the lower rank of the common soldier. In a military hospital system that placed middle-class, mostly single women in charge of soldiers' bodies, that lower rank needed to be accentuated.

21 McGill University, Osler Library of the History of Medicine, Edward Archibald Fonds, Dr E. Archibald to his wife, 21 August 1915.

22 NA, Macdonald Papers, "History of Nursing Services," Ch. 4, "Appendix to Headquarters Canadians Routine Order No. 2330 of 28 August 1917. Fetherstonhaugh, *No. 3*, 163.

23 Fetherstonhaugh, *No. 3*, 155, 194; *McGill Daily*, 21 December, 1916; Fetherstonhaugh, *No. 3*, 149.

24 The forbidding of dancing for British nurses appears in Haldane, *The British Nurse*, 221; Osler Library, Archibald Fonds, E.A. Archibald to his wife, 1 July 1916; NA, Macdonald Papers, "History of Nursing Services," Ch. 6, "Report on Work in France," 10.

25 The research interest appears in Dr Archibald's letters to his wife, as well as in NA, RG 9, III D-3 vol. 5035 (also MCF T10925 and T10926), War Diary of No. 3 Canadian General Hospital (McGill). The meeting of the Medical Society (20 September 1917) is also recorded in Fetherstonhaugh, *No. 3*, 128.

26 Desmond Morton traces part of this path in *When Your Number's Up*, 186.

27 The War Diary for No. 3 CGH records its nursing numbers, 30 June 1918. One of the drowned nursing sisters has received biographical notice: Rena Maude McLean in *Dictionary of Canadian Biography* 14 (1911–20): 723. One of them is also depicted in more universally recognizable attire (which she would not have been wearing) on the war poster illustrated at page xxiii.

28 The cleansing solution was a variant of sodium hypochlorite, the traditional one being Dakin's, with two new ones, Eusol and hypertonic salt solution, added during the war. Fetherstonhaugh, *No. 3*, 60. For a graphic description of wound cleansing and treatment, see "Memorandum on the Carrel-Dakin Treatment of Wounds," *The Canadian Nurse* 15, 11 (November 1919): 2107–11.

29 The use of women as anæsthetists was so successful that British hospitals sent their nurses to be trained by the Canadians; Fetherstonhaugh, *No. 3*,

154. Women doctors who were anaesthetists saw action in France with the Scottish Women's Hospitals; Crofton, *The Women of Royaumont*, 255.

30 The "small attentions" is a Gass phrase from her diary, 18 August 1915.

31 The numbers of patients at No. 3 CGH (McGill) from 7 August 1915 to 12 May 1919 were as follows: 81,689 sick, 52,389 wounded, and 9,684 admitted from detained hospital ships, for a total of 143,762. In that total were 11,395 operations, 409 deaths from illness, and 577 deaths from wounds; Fetherstonhaugh, *No.3*, 249. See Appendices 6 and 7 where Matron MacLatchy and Nursing Sister Mabel Clint quote similar numbers.

The battles whose names came to resonate across the twentieth century are Ypres, Festubert, and Loos in 1915 (the first two before the opening of No. 3 CGH); St Eloi, Mount Sorrel, Sanctuary Wood and the Somme in 1916; Vimy, Ypres, Messines, Hill 70, and Passchendaele in 1917; and Moreuil Wood, Amiens, Canal du Nord, and the Canadian advance to Mons in 1918.

The comparison of Canadian nursing work with that of English sisters is from Clint, *Our Bit*, 118. Two Canadian nurses who served temporarily with a British hospital in 1915 commented unfavorably on the English nurses. "The nursing is punk, in fact is not nursing at all," wrote Ruby Peterkin to her sister, 20 June 1915 (NA, MG 30, E160, Irene Peterkin Papers). And Laura Gamble confided to her diary that although the [English] sisters were kind, "to our way of thinking not what we would call good nurses" (NA, MG 30, E510, Laura Gamble Papers [10–11]).

Fetherstonhaugh, *McGill*, 50, quotes the student who cleaned wounded soldiers.

32 One of the oldest gendered divisions of labour is man as combatant and woman as non-combatant. Nursing sister Sophie Hoerner refers to three officers – one the chaplain – being left to guard the few remaining nurses at Camiers early in January 1916; (NA, MG 30, E290, Sophie Hoerner Papers, Hoerner to Mollie, 8 January [1916].

Colonel Birkett's concern about the effect of billeting is in NA, Department of Militia and Defence, RG 9, III C-10, vol. 4571, file 1, folder 3: H.S. Birkett to Matron Macdonald, 4 December 1915. Later in the war, Birkett also objected to the proposal that women take on clerking tasks at his hospital in order to release the men for active duty. He thought the hours and the late nights required of the clerks were too much of a physical strain for women, "apart altogether from the cardinal consideration of morals and discipline." Ibid., folder 5: Birkett to A.A.G. Canadian Section. GHQ, 20 June 1917.

33 Desmond Morton mentions the soldiers breaking ranks in *When Your Number's Up*, 187. Lapp's letter to Gass, dated 4 October 1916, is in the possession of Elizabeth Anderson, formerly of Porter's Lake, now of Windsor, Nova Scotia. The poem, handwritten and tucked loose into the diary, was "written in 1917 at a Canadian Casualty Clearing Hospital" (preface to the poem); I have deduced that the author is Clare Gass. The poem is reproduced as Appendix 4; the original is in the possession of Elizabeth Anderson. Praise for the nurses comes from NA, War Diary, No. 3 CGH, 18 January 1917, and Macdonald Papers, "History of Nursing Services," Ch 5: "The Canadian Casualty Clearing Stations Nos 2 & 3" by Matron Cameron-Smith, 5.

34 Personal and career information from Clare Gass military personnel record at the National Archives, from conversations with the family members named in note 2 and with family friend Coreen Flemming of Toronto, all of whom had specific memories of the summers, and from Clare Gass's own handwritten "School and Work Record" in the possession of Trudy Henderson of Halifax. See Appendix 1 for a chronological ordering of Clare Gass's life. Re post-war jobs for nurses, see CNA, Nursing Sisters' Association of Canada Papers, CNATN President J. Gunn to Sir James Lougheed, Minister, Department of Soldiers Civil Re-establishment, 27 March 1919.

35 The American Association of Medical Social Workers granted emeritus membership to Clare Gass in 1955 (letter from President Pauline Ryman to Clare Gass, 28 June 1955, in the possession of Trudy Henderson of Halifax).

36 NA, Macdonald Papers, "Correspondence," A.F. Duguid to Mrs Alex McMurtry [Isabella Strathy] 25 August 1923, 8 September 1923; I. McMurtry to "Scotty" [A.F.D.], 28 August 1923. In McMurtry's reply is the hint of a woman's post-war critique of official military narrative. Jean Gunn, the president of the CNATN predicted the silence and may even have imposed it as early as 1919 with her public comment in *The Canadian Nurse*: "the record of their cheerfulness under every hard-

ship, the long hours of work with no time for rest during an active time on the front line, calling forth every bit of endurance each one possessed, their courage during air raids when hospitals were bombed, on the sea when ships were torpedoed, or the comfort they brought to our dying and wounded, will never be recorded." "The Services of Canadian Nurses and Voluntary Aids During the War," 1979.

37 Halifax *Mail Star*, 10 November 1997; Robert Duncan, "John McCrae's War," NFB documentary, 1998, and e-mail communication to S. Mann, 30 August 1999. See note 8 of the notes to the diary for 1915, which raises questions about the precise timing of her poetic entries.

38 On women's diaries, see Bunkers and Huff, eds., *Inscribing the Daily*; Buss, "'The Dear Domestic Circle,'" and *Mapping Our Selves*; Cline, *Women's Diaries*; Conrad et al., *No Place Like Home*; Lensink, "Expanding the Boundaries of Criticism"; Mann, "Domesticated Travel"; Wylie, *Reading Between the Lines*.

39 Although the diary entries become shorter in 1917 and 1918, Clare made time for writing many letters home, almost none of which has survived. Extracts from the few that I have been able to find are included in Appendix 3. The forbidding of cameras appears in a number of sources: Osler Library, Archibald Fonds, E.A. Archibald to daughter Margaret, 26 June 1915; NA, MG 30, E290, Sophie Hoerner Papers, Hoerner to Mollie, 31 December 1915; Fetherstonhaugh, *No. 3*, 230.

40 The War Diary for No. 3 records the speedy transferral of nurses away from venereal cases, 27 February 1919. On the winter of 1917, John McCrae is reported as commenting "To go to bed is a nightmare and to get up a worse one," 25 January 1917, quoted in Fetherstonhaugh, *McGill at War*, 52. See also Morton and Granatstein, *Marching to Armageddon*, 120.

41 *Montreal Star*, 11 October 1952.

NOTES TO DIARY 1915

1 Mina Margaret Grant (1871–1948), known as "Granty" throughout the diary, took Clare under her wing sometime between 1912 and 1914 when Clare contracted scarlet fever from one of her private duty patients. The doctor in charge of the case had assumed Clare would be

immune to the disease since she had had it as a student nurse. At the time of Clare's enlistment she and "Granty" were living in the same household on Tupper Street, likely where they met. According to the Montreal City Directory for 1914–15 and 1915–16, a Mrs F.E. Millward, widow, headed that household. Judging from a letter from Clare to her mother, dated 28 August 1915 (see Appendix 3), there may well have been other nurses living in the same house. This would fit an economic pattern of the time, when widows took in boarders to make ends meet. Grant, a devout Catholic, was secretary to the president of Cassidy's, a wholesale china company in Montreal. Information gleaned from archival sources and from conversations with nieces of Clare Gass: Elizabeth Anderson, Geraldine Brenton, Trudy Henderson, Roslyn MacPhee in Nova Scotia, April 1999, and from a telephone conversation with niece Mary Brown in Oakville, 16 January 2000; letters from G. Brenton to S. Mann, 6 June 1999, 21 January 2000.

2 Most of the women's names mentioned in the diary are those of Canadian nursing sisters with the same unit as Clare: No. 3 Canadian General Hospital (McGill) (No. 3 CGH). The naming pattern seems to reveal the nature of the friendship: a first name or a last name (occasionally rendered as a diminutive) appears to indicate closeness whereas the addition of Miss or Mrs establishes distance and perhaps a hierarchy of age and status. The naming pattern is likely a carry-over from Clare Gass's private schooling and nursing training where "Miss Gass" would be the required form of address. See Appendix 5 for a list of the original members of the unit.

3 Alice Mary Cooper (1881–19?) did her nursing training at the same time as Clare Gass: 1909–12. Her military file in the National Archives suggests an imposing woman: six years older than Clare, taller, considerably larger, and English by birth: National Archives of Canada (NA), MG 150, Acc 1992–3/166, Box 1965–45; attestation paper available via ArchiviaNet.

4 The initials M.A. were not easily decipherable in the original manuscript of the diary. They only became clear as the story of Martha Allan began taking shape from diary entries of 13 and 17 March. See notes 5 and 6.

5 The M.A. referred to here is the same one mentioned in the entry for 10 March and is, I believe, the unnamed subject of the letter in the *Tele-*

graph. According to that letter there was "disaffection in the ranks" of the McGill group of nurses then training in Quebec because of the reported presence of a "young lady" who was neither a trained nor a graduate nurse. The letter-writer, "Canadian," appalled that McGill might sanction incompetence (if in nursing, why not in surgery?), urged an end to "Mammon and Graft" in appointments; Quebec *Telegraph*, 13 March 1915: 7. The only M.A. on the list of original members of the unit (see Appendix 5) is Mrs Maud Austin but she is a graduate of the Royal Victoria Hospital School of Nursing and the "Mrs" would exclude her from being referred to as a young lady. She is in fact a clergyman's widow, described by another nurse of the same unit as "much older than I am" (NA, MG 30, E290, Sophie Hoerner Papers, S. Hoerner to "Dearest," 20 May 1915). On the subsequent list of reinforcements (Fetherstonhaugh, *No. 3*, 263), however, a Marguerite Martha Allan appears among the nursing sisters. I am convinced this is the same Martha Allan identified in note 6 below; in which case she would indeed be a young lady – age twenty in 1915 – too young even to be admitted to a nursing school much less graduate from one, and too young as well for the Canadian Army Medical Corps (CAMC). "Mammon and Graft" would then be a reference to the Allan family fortune and influence, part of which included close connections with the MGH, where, according to the *Annual Report* for 1913, Sir Montagu Allan (Martha Allan's father) was President of the Board of Management. Indeed it is unlikely that anyone but a member of such a prominent family would elicit a letter to a newspaper editor.

6 Martha Allan (1895–1942), daughter of Sir Hugh Montagu Allan, of Montreal shipping and banking fame shows up later in the diary with the McGill Hospital unit in France. From the comments of Clare Gass in her diary and those of Major (Dr) Edward Archibald in his letters from France to his wife in Montreal, Martha Allan seems to have been more of a nuisance than a help. She later had a significant place in amateur theatre in Canada as founder of the Montreal Repertory Theatre.

7 Judging from subsequent diary references Ruth Loggie (1883–1968) was Clare Gass' closest nursing companion during her years with the CAMC. They probably met during nursing training at the Montreal General: Ruth graduated in 1910 and Clare began in 1909. Ruth was

born in Burnt Church, New Brunswick, one of six children of Donald Loggie and Mary Jane Anderson, whose families had worked together as fish and general merchants. She and Clare kept in touch after the war; Ruth's name was listed at the same address as Clare's in the General Directory of the Overseas' Nursing Sisters' Association of Canada in 1931. NA, RG 150, Acc 1992–3/166, Box 5717–28, military file of Ruth Loggie; e-mail communication from Fred Farrell, manager, Private Sector Records, Provincial Archives of New Brunswick, 20 Dec. 1999; Jon Johnson and Colin Campbell, "Nursing Sister Ruth Loggie #3 Canadian General Hospital (McGill)," typescript, Chatham Public Library, Miramichi, New Brunswick; McGill University Archives (MUA), RG 96, Ctn. 437, file 854, "Wartime Nursing."

8 This homily, in poetic form, is the first of many to appear in the diary. The author is Howard Arnold Walter (1883–1918) and the piece was set to music (one of the versions is dated 1911) and sung as a hymn. *Canadian Youth Hymnal* (Toronto:United Church Publishing House 1939), hymn #99. Although the writing is clearly Clare's, it is nonetheless different in size and ink from that which precedes and follows it. She may have written the piece into the space later.

9 Sam Hughes (1853–1921) was minister of Militia and Defence (1911–16) in the Conservative Government of Robert Borden. His energy and enthusiasm for things military and imperial were matched by his autocratic tendencies, favouritism, and the occasional spectacular lack of judgment (notably in relation to the Ross Rifle, which jammed when used repeatedly, as equipment for Canadian soldiers). His knighthood, awarded in August 1915, appears to have been political recompense for his agreeing to allow the British to name senior military appointments. See Morton and Granatstein, *Marching to Armageddon*, 106–7; Haycock, *Sam Hughes*, 273. Clare's attaching a "Sir" to his name in May – she refers to him only as Sam on August 5 as does Fetherstonhaugh, *No. 3*, 21 – has to mean that she added this sentence later to the diary. The other clue is that the entries preceeding and following the one commencing with "Col Hughes" were originally written in pencil and overwritten in ink. That particular sentence is in ink only. The Colonel Hughes referred to is William St Pierre Hughes (1863–1940), younger brother of the minister and commanding officer of the 21st Battalion.

10 On 7 May 1915 the British passenger liner *Lusitania* was torpedoed by German U-boats off Ireland with a loss of life of close to 1200. The fact that Clare does not mention it until a week later could indicate the strength of military discipline, the control of rumour, or her own ability to suppress fear. Dr Archibald was aware of the sinking as of 8 May but "we were warned not to tell the nurses for fear of alarming them too much." He added "Of course this was quite useless. The next day one of the nurses asked me if I knew anything more definite about the sinking of the Lusit. The captain confirmed the report in a couple of days." (McGill University, Osler Library, E.A. Archibald to "Dear Girl" [wife Agnes], 10 May 1915.) From London, Clare does comment: "I cannot get over the fact that the Lusitania went to the bottom & we have arrived safely in England." (Postcard from C. Gass to Granty, 17 May [1915]; card in possession of E. Anderson).

11 Her mention of troops for the Dardanelles is a reference to infantry being sent to support what had initially been expected to be a purely naval attempt to secure the Straits between the Black Sea (Russian ports) and the Aegean-Mediterranean. With the landing of troops on the Gallipoli Penninsula, on the north-western shore of the Straits, the roles were reversed, the Navy providing support for the troops but doing so from a distance because of underwater mines and submarines. British naval ships therefore clustered in the relatively safe harbour of Mudros on the island of Lemnos. It was to this island that Canadian nursing sisters were sent later in 1915 (see Gass entry at 8 August) as the Gallipoli campaign turned into a disaster. It was abandoned in mid-December 1915.

12 This is a first trip to Europe for Clare Gass. To the usual list of London sights, she, as a military nurse, adds St Thomas Hospital, the home of the (Florence) Nightingale (1829–1910) Training School for Nurses.

13 Her mention of the Strathcona Horse is the first of many military units, facts and rumours that she will report. In this case her interest is personal – her brother Gerald was with the Strathconas. Trench warfare and mechanization rendered cavalry much less useful in the war. Cavalry members would therefore frequently serve as infantrymen. The instance noted in the diary was one such occasion. Gerald was later in the Signal Corps.

Majolica (from the island Majorca) is a glazed Italian tableware, originally white enamel with metallic colours. Clare may have known of it through Granty's work at Cassidy's china company in Montreal. Granty was so knowledgeable about china that one of Clare's nieces thought she had been a buyer for Cassidy's. Conversation with Mary Brown, 16 January 2000.

14 "Little Pelletier" is Juliette Pelletier (1891–1970) from Quebec City, daughter of career soldier and South African War veteran Colonel Oscar Charles Casgrain Pelletier and grand-daughter of Sir Charles E. Casgrain, lawyer, politician, senator, and lieutenant-governor of Quebec 1908–11. Juliettte studied at the Ursuline Convent in Quebec City before taking nursing training at the Montreal General Hospital, 1911–14, where she and Clare would undoubtedly have met. She argued her way out of her final stage of nursing training – that involving the diet kitchen (she claimed later that she never could cook because of that) – so that she could enrol as a nurse and go overseas with the first Canadian contingent in the autumn of 1914. Her father was not at all pleased with her decision. "Only trollops follow the army," he remarked and although he later regretted the comment she never let him forget it and it has come down the generations as family lore. During her nursing training, in the half-day off per week allowed the students, she met fellow Quebecer Stuart Ramsey, a McGill medical graduate of 1912. The two went overseas at the same time, though not on the same ship, and Captain Ramsey got round all sorts of army regulations so he could see her from his base in England and hers in France, with No. 1 Canadian General Hospital at Etaples. She was subsequently attached to No. 1 Canadian Stationary Hospital and sent with that unit to serve on Lemnos and in Salonika between August 1915 and February 1916. After a stint with a hospital in Brighton, England, she took on transport duty on a hospital ship to Canada and became the matron of the Valcartier Military Hospital from May 1917 to October 1918. She eventually caught up with Stuart in India after the war, marrying him the very day of her arrival, and the pair lived there before returning to Canada and settling in Montreal where Stuart became a prominent ophthalmologist and Juliette undertook extensive volunteer work. She was, for example, the founding president of the Overseas

Nursing Sisters' Association of Canada in 1929 and very active with the
St John Ambulance. The Second World War called her to a military role
again, this time with higher rank. She was a captain at the officers'
training centre at Ste-Anne-de-Bellevue and then a major and officer in
command of recruiting for Military District 4 (Montreal). My thanks
for most of this family information to Marguerite Ramsey Mackinnon
of Montreal, daughter of Juliette Pelletier, in a phone conversation 26
June 1999 and a visit 10 September 1999. She confirmed that her
mother was indeed "little" as Clare Gass describes her – five feet tall and
ninety-nine pounds – and she kindly showed me a scrap-book of press
clippings about her mother (primarily from the World War II but trac-
ing her prewar career) as well as two brief (10–15 pages) typescript
copies, one the World War I recollections of her father and the other a
sketchy diary of her mother's first year overseas. See also Canadian
Nurses' Association Archives (CNA), papers of the Nursing Sisters' Association of Canada; Nicholson, *Canada's Nursing Sisters*, 107, and Mac-
Dermot, *History of the School*, 59. Pelletier and Gass knew each other
long after the war: Elizabeth Anderson recalls visits by Pelletier to her
aunt's home in Montreal; telephone conversation, 4 February 2000.

15 Dr Kenneth Cameron later wrote a history of No. 1 Canadian General
Hospital in which he described the nurses from No. 3 CGH who arrived
on 22 May 1915 as "a carefully selected group of the most efficient
graduates of the Montreal General Hospital and the Royal Victoria
Hospital"; Cameron, *History of No. 1*, 176.

16 Sophie Hoerner wrote home the same day to tell of five seriously
wounded patients, likely not the three walking cases with whom she
and Clare had conversed. "There are five very bad cases, heart-rending,
and the stories they tell of what they see in the trenches are harrowing.
They are not boastful, any of them, but seem so glad to find someone
that is interested in them. They say that they like the Canadian Sisters
and that it is Heaven here. Nearly all of them want to go back to England just for a day and they would be quite happy to go back to the
trenches. They are all English." NA, Hoerner Papers, Sophie Hoerner
to Mollie, 8 June 1915.

17 Her mention of Festubert is a reference to a series of battles in that
neighbourhood during the spring offensive by the French and British

through May and again in mid-June 1915. The casualty lists Clare was reading on 3 June probably reflect the late May fighting.

18 "Hindous" is a reference to the Indian soldiers of the British Indian Army Corps, which served in France from September 1914 to October 1915. They had separate hospital facilities without nursing sisters; one of these hospitals was located in the former Jesuit College to which No. 3 CGH would move in January 1916.

19 Laurie is Laurence Gass, a cousin of Clare's whom she met in Montreal. This poem, with her notation, is the only extant documentary support for a family story that the two were in love. As a graduate mining engineer from McGill, Gass enlisted in the fall of 1915 as a lieutenant with the 165th Siege Battery; Conversation with E. Anderson, April 1999; NA, RG 150, Acc 1992–3/166, Box 3436–27, military file of Laurence Gass.

20 These two poems also appear to have been written into the diary at another time. The first, a well-known recital song of the time, was presumably what Captain Johnson was singing.

21 This poem does appear to match the day's record, both in penmanship and sentiment. Whether Gass is quoting or writing this unattributed piece, she is revealing a very early recognition – she had received her first patients on 31 May – that the male virtues of soldiering have been shattered. For a scholarly analysis of that shattering, see Leed, *No Man's Land. Combat and Identity in World War I*.

22 *Peeps into Picardy* is a charming history-cum-guide to the north-east region of France where Clare was located. Quite unlike modern *Guides Bleus* or *Michelins*, it is a small book written in essay style, full of legends, religion, and warfare, the latter mostly involving English and French on opposing sides. Clare took her sight-seeing seriously and *Peeps*, which she seems just to have acquired, became a constant companion. For example, a month earlier, on May 25, she recorded something which *Peeps* disputes, that the Church in Etaples was built by the English. And the spelling with which she records an outing to Hardelot Castle on 21 June suggests she has not yet encountered *Peeps*. A month later, however (see her entry for 29 July), she has clearly read *Peeps*, 74–6, before visiting the little church in Wirwignes. The copy of *Peeps* in the McGill library is signed H.S. Birkett, Camiers. From the state of the book, the

Commanding Officer of No. 3 CGH did not read it.

23 Captain (Dr) Reginald Malone of No. 3 CGH. In a tented camp, one might assume that the instrument he is playing is a violin. But in fact there was a piano in camp, first in the Officers' Mess and then in the nurses' Ante-room; NA, Department of Militia and Defence, RG 9, III C-10, vol.4571, folder 3, file 1, H.S. Birkett to H.B. Yates, 25 November 1915. In letters to his wife Major Archibald debated about having his violin sent over and finally decided against it. No. 3 CGH, after it was established more permanently at Boulogne in the early spring of 1916, eventually had a thirty-piece orchestra, all male; Fetherston-haugh, *No. 3*, 104.

24 Once again, the ink and writing suggest another time for the placing of this poem on the diary page of 7 July 1915.

25 The Reverend Allan P. Shatford was one of 447 Canadian chaplains who served overseas with the Canadian Expeditionary Forces (CEF). In France between 1915 and 1918 he was one of the more active chaplains, engaged in "social Christianity." Crerar refers to him as a "Montreal Anglican," but he had earlier been a resident of North Sydney, Cape Breton, and father of Sadie, an Edgehill pupil at the same time as Clare Gass; Crerar, *Padres in No Man's Land* 116, 119, 128, 162, 168, 178-9; Edgehill, "Register 1903-1904," *Calendar*, 1904-1905, 20.

26 Durbar tents were from India, a gift to the British War Office. Large enough to serve as a hospital ward, they had an outer and inner shell, each shell made of layers of material, the innermost and visible one of very decorative and coloured cotton. Clare was right to be concerned about their durability.

27 The "rumours of reverses" were true. On 30 July British troops near Hooge retreated when the enemy sprayed liquid fire (burning petrol) over the British trenches. The Russian "defeat" had been going on steadily since 18 July as German troops advanced eastward into Poland, which they continued to do until mid-August.

28 From the penmanship this poem too appears to have been written at some other moment in the space available on 1 August. The poet is Canon Frederick George Scott (1861-1944), the most well known of Canadian chaplains. The poem was initially published in *The Times* of London, 21 April 1915, (the day before the beginning of the Second

Battle of Ypres and the first use of chlorine gas) and subsequently in a tiny collection of Scott's wartime poems, *In the Battle Silences*, 10–11. Only in *The Times* version is there a reference to "Holy Week" during which time (28 March – 4 April 1915) Scott was in Estaires and Clare Gass not yet in Europe. In neither version is there a mention of Ypres, as suggested on the title line in the Gass diary. In Scott's collection the poem gives a location, Sailly, a tiny village south west of Cambrai, nowhere near Ypres. The poem itself certainly gives credence to Jonathan Vance's thesis in *Death So Noble*, notably ch. 2: "Christ in Flanders," where he argues that in memories of the war soldiers were turned into part of Christ's sacrifice, giving up their lives, as He had, to redeem humanity. Scott's own account, *The Great War as I Saw It*, expresses the same idea.

29 See note 9 re Sam Hughes. Clearly there was a family connection with Hughes even though the Gass family was staunchly Liberal. Clare's father Robert Gass was, among other civic undertakings, a recruiting officer in Shubenacadie in the early years of the war. Sir William Maxwell ("Max") Aitken (1879–1964), Lord Beaverbrook as of 1917, was a Canadian businessman who made his money in Canada but his political and newspaper career in England. During the war he was Hughes's personally appointed general representative for Canada at the front and took on the task of keeping Canadian war records. Morton and Granatstein, *Marching to Armageddon*, 108.

30 There was no major action near Hooge at this time.

31 Comfort bags, made by the thousands by women volunteers in Canada, were designed for general distribution to wounded soldiers. They could contain a variety of items: candy, chewing gum, chocolate, socks, handkerchiefs, bootlaces, cocoa, playing cards, tobacco, soup tablets, writing paper, sometimes even a personal (though anonymous) note; Wilson, *Ontario and the First World War*, lxxxv n.4.

32 By the war news not being good, she is referring to the success of German troops against Russia in eastern Europe and the fear that this would now permit Germany to fling all its strength westward. There were also British losses in Gallipoli in mid-August.

33 Her mention of eleven German ships being sunk may be an example of the frequent faulty reports that circulated. The only naval action in the Baltic anywhere near this date is the sinking of one German ship by a

British submarine on 19 August 1915.

34 A zeppelin, named for its German inventor, Count von Zeppelin, was a balloon-like rigid airship, originally used for reconnaissance and then to carry bombs. English and French versions were called dirigibles.

35 See Appendix 3 for correspondence of Clare Gass with her brother and her mother, in which she argues strongly against his enlisting. The family would have received the first plea, dated 24 July, but the second, dated 28 August, would have crossed this letter from her father announcing Blanchard's enlistment. According to the attestation paper in Blanchard's military personnel file, he enlisted in the 85th Battalion (the one to which Clare refers later) on 18 August 1915 and gave a birth date of 7 August 1897, which would give him the minimum age of eighteen required of the army; NA, RG 150, Acc 1992–93/166, Box 3436–15. All the references to his birthday in the Gass diary indicate that he was born 15 October 1898.

36 Margaret Clotilde Macdonald (1874–1948) was matron-in-chief of the Canadian Nursing Sisters as of September 1914. (See Introduction, xix). Her brother, Captain Ronald St John Macdonald, was a doctor with No. 3 CGH.

Lady Perry is likely the wife of Colonel Sir Allan Perry, the commanding officer of No.22 British General Hospital (Harvard), located nearby.

37 Sir William Osler (1849–1919) was an internationally known Canadian medical doctor and educator who trained and taught, initially at McGill and then at the University of Pennsylvania, Johns Hopkins, and Oxford. His knighthood was awarded in 1911. His son Edward Revere was with No. 3 CGH but transferred to the Royal Artillery and was killed in 1917. *Dictionary of Canadian Biography* (*DCB*) 14, 799–804. Fetherstonhaugh (*No. 3*, 25) has these visits happening on 8 September.

38 Captain MacMillan was one of the medical officers of No. 3 CGH. Lieutenant Colonel John McCrae, author of "In Flanders' Fields," was the officer in charge of medicine. See Appendix 5. A veteran of the South African War, McCrae was an outstanding physician in Montreal before the First War. His initial role with the Canadian Expeditionary Force was as brigade surgeon with the 1st Brigade, Canadian Field Artillery; *DCB* 14, 679–80.

Most of the men mentioned in the diary are the medical staff of No. 3 CGH, except for those she mentions during the shorter times she spent with other units. With an officer rank which she seldom omits (captain, major, colonel), they were all also doctors. Other men, to whom she refers by last name only (see, for example, the entry at 7 November 1915) were privates, mostly medical students, and subordinate in status to her.

39 Bluebird was the name given to the Canadian nursing sisters because of the colour of their uniform. The delight in pastoral settings could be interpreted as the contrast to the busy work world of the hospital and the nurses' own "lines." Leed comments on the pastoral motif in war accounts of soldiers; *No Man's Land*, 121–3.

40 Clare is identifying gas gangrene here, a particularly frightful form of toxic bacterial infection that could occur in a wound. The bacteria release carbon dioxide which, if unchecked (by opening the wound to air - and sometimes to maggots – or by amputating the limb) enters the bloodstream and kills the patient.

41 The Ypres battle to which she is referring is the Second Battle of Ypres, 22 April – 25 May 1915. The battle is particularly remembered for the first use of poison gas as a weapon. In this case the gas was chlorine, visible as a greenish-yellow cloud that was heavier than air and therefore sank into the trenches and shell-holes. Affected soldiers vomited, wept, and, in the most severe cases, suffocated. Later in the war phosgene and mustard gas added to the horrors. McCrae was present as a doctor during the fighting and the devastation was both the inspiration for his famous poem and the beginning of his own untimely demise in January 1918.

42 Sir George Makins (1853–1933), one of a number of surgeons- general with the British Royal Army Medical Corps, was consulting surgeon, based at Etaples. Major-General G.C. Jones (1864–19?), a Canadian, was the overseas director of Medical Services until 1916 when Sam Hughes fired him because of a scathing report on the Canadian Army Medical Corps (CAMC) by Dr Herbert Bruce. Morton and Granatstein elaborate in *Marching to Armageddon*, 137–8. The visits of prominent people to the hospital constituted a two-way street of mutual appreciation. Visitors encouraged the staff and patients while their favorable – and always quoted – comments served to keep the McGill unit in the

limelight and thereby the recipient of official favour in England and voluntary contributions from home. Both the official War Diary of the unit, in the National Archives, and Fetherstonhaugh, whose *No. 3* is based on that document, detail all these visits.

43 The surest news from and of the front was this order to evacuate patients from the hospital; it meant more were coming from another battle. In this case a major French and then British offensive was underway along the Champagne front 21–30 September and then again 6–11 October. Her references here and at 27 September 7, 10, 11 and 15 October are all to the fighting along this line. Her news of the war comes from newspapers, official communiqués and rumour. Rumour travelled faster than the papers and the communiqués but all three were notoriously unreliable. Whatever the source, the news was always at least a day or two, sometimes more, after the fact.

44 The date would suggest that the "curly-headed boy" can only be one or other of her two brothers then at the front, Gerald and Cyril. According to Gerald's daughter, Cyril had "kinky curly" hair wheras Gerald's was wavy; it would seem therefore that it is Cyril she is watching for. Letter from G. Brenton to S. Mann, 6 June 1999.

45 Harold Begbie (1871–1929) was a prolific, outspoken, and controversial British author and poet. He was already scorned by Canadian nurses for unfavorable comments about their uniform (Clint, *Our Bit*, 41) and they may well have kept an eye out for his barbs. I have hunted in vain for the source of his comment about the slight nature of wounds.

46 The 25th Battalion is brother Cyril's unit.

47 Wolsey [Wolseley?] Kit is a form of portable camp bedding, in all liklihood named for or designed by Sir Garnet Wolseley (1833–1913), whose brilliant career as a soldier was matched by his enthusiasm for army reform. It may be the same as the "Telescopic Camp Bedstead" mentioned as part of the camp kit for nurses when on active service. See appendix B in Appendix Two.

48 Hubert Neilson tents were Canadian designed hospital tents adopted by the British government. The designer was Canadian army physician Colonel John Louis Hubert Neilson (1845–1925).

49 McCrae's poem shows up here (with the same proviso noted earlier (notes 8 and 20) about the timing of her placing poems in the diary),

Ambulance train en route for Blighty (NA, PA 975)

in Sophie Hoerner's papers, and in the letters of Dr Archibald to his wife. Dr Archibald, a close family friend of McCrae's, kept an eye out for possible matches for bachelor McCrae among the nursing sisters. According to Archibald, McCrae could on occasion be rather stiff and domineering, and was not always liked by the nurses. He would then make amends and Archibald would cheerily report progress to his wife. Might it be possible that McCrae's poem, which appeared in print in *Punch* in December 1915 was a peace offering? McGill University, Osler Library, Archibald Fonds, E.W. Archibald to his wife, 26 November 1915, 28 December 1915. NA, Hoerner Papers, Sophie Hoerner to Mollie, 24 November 1915.

50 The *Sunday Observer*, subsequently *The McGilliken*, begun in October 1915, was the short-lived news sheet of No. 3 CGH. Put together by former members of the *McGill Daily*, the three page paper was initially typewritten. Once access to a printing press was possible, the paper became more substantial, the one copy in the McGill University

Archives, dated 15 February 1916, professionally printed. The editorial in that issue recounts the production of the paper. It consisted mostly of light-hearted reporting of the events of the hospital. See "Senior Meds. Returning," *McGill Daily*, 3 December 1915, and "News of McGill Hospital as Heard by 'McGilliken,'" *McGill Daily*, 7 December 1915 in which most of Vol. 1, no. 3 of *The McGilliken* is reprinted. Also MUA, RG 38, Faculty of Medicine, Container 14, File 259: "De Nobis," *McGilliken*, 15 February 1916, 4. After thirteen issues, the newspaper came to an end as mounting numbers of sick and wounded put demands on the entire hospital staff.

51 Blighty is the term used by the British army in India, adopted from Urdu slang, to refer to England. For a soldier to "have a Blighty" meant passage to England. Since the only way to get to England while on active service (except for leave) was to have a wound of sufficient severity to warrant the trip, the word also came to mean the wound itself.

52 This hearing and spreading of rumour (see entry for 29 November 1915) and the waiting for things to happen is the nurses' variant of soldiers' principal function: waiting (Morton, *When Your Number's Up*, 17). See introduction (xxxiii) and note 32, for the commanding officer's opposition to the nurses being billeted in Boulogne.

53 Clare tucked the sprig of flowers into her diary at this page where it survived until 1997.

NOTES TO DIARY 1916

1 Given that Clare was a fan of the much-heralded contemporary British author Rudyard Kipling (1865–1936) – she knew much of his poetry by heart and had brought a book of his with her from home – her matter-of-fact recording of this incident is odd. Presumably she was sleeping during his visit since she was on night duty at the time.

2 Marie Lohr (1890–1975) was an Australian-born actress whose English career began at age eleven at the Garrick theatre in London and continued until 1966 on stage and 1968 in film.

3 Colonel Yates was actually the second in command of No. 3 CGH, subordinate to Colonel Birkett, the commanding officer. Dr Archibald's letters to his wife suggest that Yates was the more congenial of the two.

4 Arthur Rackham (1867–1939), painter and watercolorist, was best known as an illustrator. Among the many books he illustrated was J.M. Barries's *Peter Pan in Kensington Gardens.* Given Clare's fascination with Peter Pan – Granty sent her a copy for Christmas 1915 (see Diary entry 28 Dec. 1915) and she once signed a card to Granty as "Peter" (2 Sept. [1917]; card in possession of Geraldine Brenton) – she probably knew that edition and hence recognized the trees near Taplow as Rakham-like.

5 Blanche Lefroy had been the "Lady Principal" at Edgehill between 1897 and 1905, years spanning Clare's schooling there. Miss Lefroy, formerly a teacher at the Cheltenham Ladies College in England, headed a staff of ten, among them another teacher with whom Clare maintained a friendship all her life. Dorothy Mills (1879–1966) had a lengthy post-Edgehill career as history head at Brearley School for Girls in New York, during which she published history texts. She visited Clare on numerous occasions in Montreal and the two were still corresponding at the time of Mills's death in England in 1966. Edgehill *Calendar*, 1904–5; notes from D. Mills to C. Gass tucked into a copy of Mills' text *The Middle Ages* (New York: Putnam's 1935) in the possession of Geraldine Brenton of Halifax.

The Provost uncle mentioned here would seem to be the Reverend John Richard Magrath, provost of Queen's College, Oxford, since 1878; Oxford University, *Calendar*, 1916; *Who's Who*, 1917.

6 The University of King's College, now in Halifax, was originally located in Windsor, Nova Scotia, close to Edgehill. It had both a collegiate school and a university. The program at Edgehill prepared senior girls to sit the examinations at King's for an "Associate in Arts"; Clare Gass took the exam in 1905. Despite the strict sexual segregation of the schools, Clare would have encountered some of the young men at King's. In the 1920s a fire destroyed the University. It was rebuilt in Halifax, but the boys' collegiate school remained in Windsor. In 1976 it amalgamated with Edgehill to form the present-day King's-Edgehill School, which, because of the King's connection, can advertise itself as Canada's first independent school founded in 1788. (Edgehill itself dates from 1891.) Information from Linda Davison-Landymore (and from her business card), director of Development and Alumni Affairs, King's-Edgehill School, April 1999.

7 An illustration of the strength of rumour during the war. It was a fire that destroyed all but the library of the original Parliament buildings on 3 February 1916. *The Times* of London carried the story.

8 Tobit is the main character and father of Tobias in the Book of Tobit, part of the Apocrypha which was included in the King James version of the Bible until the early nineteenth century. The story dates from the late pre-Christian era and was a popular subject with artists of the Middle Ages.

9 Mrs B. has me stumped. There was a reference in *The Times* the next day to a Mrs Baldwin charged with receiving stolen zinc from two schoolboys and fined 40s. It is surely not possible that such a tiny case – moreover not a trial – would interest Clare Gass.

10 After much fruitless sleuthing I concluded that Alex 1 must be the name of a ward in the hospital (like the F 1 that she mentions on 8 February). An obscure publication about the Canadian Red Cross confirms this conclusion. Queen Alexandra was so pleased with the hospital at Taplow that she allowed her name to be used for a ward. In nurses' parlance, one part of the Queen Alexandra Ward became "Alex 1"; Moore, *The Maple Leaf's Red Cross*, 92, 103 (note). Apparently something distressing happened in the ward on 13 February. The official War Diary of the Duchess of Connaught's Red Cross Hospital, Taplow, does not record anything for that day. Farther afield there was no bad war news out of Alexandria anywhere around this date. Nursing sisters from No. 1 Canadian Stationary Hospital were near Alexandria at that point, recovering from their time on Lemnos, but nothing in Mabel Clint's *Our Bit* suggests anything out of the ordinary around this date.

11 Along with the military wounded and sick, No. 3 CGH served the local population – presumably males only – in the surrounding area who required hospitalization.

12 Exposure to damp and cold can cause chilblains: hands and feet become inflamed, itchy, and sometimes ulcerated. There is no known cure; the condition disappears in time. Sophie Hoerner complained of them too; NA, Hoerner Papers, Hoerner to Mrs Nichols, 31 January 1916.

13 Standing for long hours with waterlogged boots and socks in the cold, muck, and corruption of the trenches (water, waste, rats, corpses) could literally erode the feet. The condition – numbness, infection,

even gangrene poisoning – came to be known as trench feet. In severe cases the only cure was amputation.

14 Daughter of Lt. Col. John Elder, the Officer in charge of surgery in the McGill unit. In November 1917 he became the commanding officer.

15 The shortlived "Easter uprising" in Ireland began on Easter Monday, 24 April 1916, when a "Citizen Army" led by James Connolly (1868–1916) and "Irish Volunteers" led by Padriac Pearse (1879–1916) took over the General Post Office in Dublin and proclaimed a provisional government for the Irish Republic. The "Irish question" had plagued British politics throughout most of the latter half of the nineteenth century, with debates over some measure of political autonomy for Ireland always encountering government procrastination and stubborn opposition from the northern part of Ireland. That the uprising was intended to take advantage of Britain's preoccupation with the war effort in Europe is clear from the involvement of Sir Roger Casement (1864–1916), who had arranged a shipment of arms from Germany to Ireland and had come to Ireland aboard a German submarine. He was arrested for treason before the uprising began. The uprising itself was snuffed out by British soldiers within five days. Most of the leaders, including Casement, Connolly, and Pearse, were executed. Clare Gass's report (see 30 April) that Connolly died of wounds is inaccurate.

16 Except for a Christmas salutation noted on 25 December 1916, this is the last poem to appear in the Gass diary. She may have been increasingly busy with less time for poetic reflection. Or the war may have begun to undermine the very security the poems seemed to offer.

17 Field post cards were printed cards with brief optional messages which a soldier merely ticked off, then added his signature. Designed as time-savers for weary soldiers and their anxious relatives, the cards also facilitated the censor's task.

18 Q.A. is short form for the name of the British nursing sisters' unit: Queen Alexandra's Imperial Military Nursing Service. These are the "Women of Britain, garbed in gray" of the poem at 1 March 1916.

19 The frightful battle near Ypres is that of Mount Sorrel, 2–13 June 1916, in which Canadians first lost, then regained, territory just east of Ypres. It is to this fighting that Clare is referring on 4 and 6 June as well. The only good that came of it all was the final recognition that the Ross

Rifle, with which Canadians were equipped, was useless.

20 The frightful battle in the North Sea is the battle of Jutland, 31 May –
1 June 1916.

21 Horatio Herbert Lord Kitchener (1850–1916), a career soldier in the
British Imperial service, served in the Middle East, South Africa, India,
and Egypt before being appointed secretary for War in the British Cab-
inet in 1914. He was responsible for raising huge numbers of soldiers
as part of the "new armies."

22 Here Clare has news on the very day: the major British and French
offensive of 1916 along the Somme began 1 July and continued until
18 November with horrendous loss of life. Her references on 5, 8, 10
July, 2, 16, 27 September, and 2 October are all to the on-going battles
of the Somme.

23 In a very busy day Clare nonetheless made time to write to Cyril enclosing a letter from their father. See Appendix 3, 7 July [1916] for some
indication of family traits and beliefs.

24 Had the Canadian military required or used women volunteers to the
extent the British did, drawing on an immense pool from the Voluntary
Aid Detachments (hence the name for the women: VADS), Martha Allan
would have been in that category. As an untrained Canadian woman of
considerable social and financial standing, she would have been the
Canadian equivalent of the most well-known of the British VADS, Vera
Brittain. Unfortunately she has not left us a *Testament of Youth* like Brittain's. Allan joined the CAMC through family influence and once there,
as the Gass diary suggests, she encountered the hostility of the graduate professional nurses. She flaunted her independence, disobeyed the
rules, dined with the Colonel, and resigned for reasons other than marriage or family illness. She would thus call into question the nurses'
sense of themselves as professionals, as military personnel, and as
women, a potent combination that had allowed them to get to Europe
and to the war in the first place. Sharon Ouditt's fascinating study of
British women and the war, *Fighting Forces, Writing Women*, notably chapter 1 "Nuns and Lovers," helped me clarify my thinking on the elusive
Martha Allan and the reaction of No. 3 CGH nurses to her. Clare Gass
herself may have been a bit ambivalent about Martha Allan: besides her
comments in the diary, there was a tiny newspaper clipping tucked into

the diary: a photo of "Miss Martha Allen" [sic] with the caption "who was with the R.A.M.C. in France, now doing war work in London." This may be a clipping from a Canadian paper, in which case it might have been sent to Clare, perhaps by Granty. Would Clare, on seeing it, have said "Humph" or "She'll be happier in that milieu"?

The Canadian VAD system, tiny compared to Britain's, is under investigation by Linda Quiney in a history Ph.D. thesis nearing completion at the University of Ottawa. Two contemporary references are Abbott, "Lectures on the History of Nursing," 149–50 and Gunn, "The Services of Canadian Nurses and Voluntary Aids During the War," 1977.

25 This "engagement," which really wasn't one, took place on 19 August with German ships advancing on awaiting British ships. No actual fighting took place.

26 Light duty patients were those well enough to be up and about and lending a hand on the wards but not sufficiently healed to be sent on to the convalescent camp, much less back to their fighting units.

27 The days and dates for the entries between 23 August and 30 August are the one occasion when Clare's placing of two years in the same diary book (see Introduction) becomes confusing for herself and for the reader. Likely her rapid departure for England, anxiety about her brother, hospitalized in Leicester, and the rush to pack and then catch the boat unsettled her.

28 The same day Clare sent a card home to her father. In it she was cheerier about Cyril's state: "Found Cyril looking fairly well." See Appendix 3, 26 August [1916].

29 Victor Lapp commented some weeks later on her visit to Leicester and presumed to interpret her feelings: "My I am glad you obtained your leave at such an opportune time and were able to visit your brother and make him happy. Poor boy. I am so sorry about his injury but how glad you must be that you still have him and it must be rather a relief to know that he will be safe." Victor Lapp to Clare Gass, 4 October 1916. Letter in possession of E. Anderson.

30 Records of hospital intakes and statistics re wounds and ailments and deaths were carefully kept. As of 1917 they appeared monthly in the unit's official War Diary. The death rate recorded for July is a percentage of the admissions. Presumably these figures had just been released; it is

Interior of Ward D (Pirie, *No. 3 Canadian General Hospital*)

the only time Clare records them. The McGill hospital prided itself on a low death rate, compared to the other hospitals in the Boulogne area.

31 Dr Ronald Playfair Campbell (1876–1916), a brilliant science and medical student at McGill, did post-graduate medical studies in Germany before being named medical superintendant of the MGH in 1904. Clare will have encountered him during her nursing training at the hospital between 1909 and 1912.

32 On 23 September German Zeppelins bombed London.

33 Trooper W.H. Blanch of the 9th Lancers fulfilled his promise in February 1917. The first entry in Clare Gass' autograph album is his lengthy description of "Xmas Day 1916 in Ward D No 3 Canadian General Hospital" – "the happiest day I have ever spent away from home & that is saying a lot." The autograph album, containing drawings (one is reproduced on pages 176–7) and poems and sentiments from the soldiers is in the possession of Geraldine Brenton.

285

NOTES TO DIARY 1917

1   Brother Athelstan (1901–75) was too young to be in the army. Like many other recruits (including his older brother Blanchard) he advanced his age and passed the initial screening in Canada. Once in England, however, his father intervened and insisted he return home. According to his daughters Trudy Henderson of Halifax and Mary Brown of Oakville, Athel was so annoyed over parental interference with his wish to be a soldier that instead of returning to Nova Scotia he went west and worked in the northern interior of Alberta and British Columbia for about ten years before coming back to live in Shubenacadie. The Second World War gave him the chance to be a soldier.

2   The grandfather mentioned here would have fought on the losing side in the Franco-Prussian War of 1870.

3   The 85th is brother Blanchard's unit, which was later commanded by the Major Ralston mentioned here. James Layton Ralston (1881–1948) is particularly known for his role as minister of National Defence in the government of Mackenzie King during the Second World War.

4   The Reg Gass here is not another brother although Clare did have one of that name (1904–95), much too young for military service. This Reg Gass is a distant cousin, the son of a cousin of Clare's father. Letter from G. Brenton to S. Mann, 6 June 1999.

5   The DI list marked a patient's condition as grave. Referred to as "the dangerous list" in Nursing Instructions, no. 51 (see Appendix 2), Clare's rendition may be either actual hospital usage ("dangerously ill") or an extension of the army classifications of men's fitness. Those categories, from best to worst, went from A to C with numerical gradations in between (hence the popular expression "A1" for being in top shape).

6   This may be part of the deliberate German plan to retreat, destroying as they went, a plan that was put into full effect in mid-March.

7   British troops occupied Baghdad on 11 March. The Turkish troops had left the city the day before.

8   Trouble had been brewing in Russia since at least the end of February 1917, with growing unrest over the war and dire economic conditions. Troops expected to quell mobs instead joined them in armed protest.

The rumours that Clare is recording probably precede the formation of the provisional government on 12 March.

9 The Czar abdicated on 15 March; it took three days for this news to reach northern France.

10 Clare's noting this arrival had me wondering whether it was Laurence ("Laurie") Gass's unit. But it is the 271st Canadian Siege Battery (McGill), the first combatant unit granted the right to have the university's name in its title. (Fetherstonhaugh, *McGill*, 25–6 has a different number for the unit but his recording of its going to France in March 1917 fits with Clare's notice of its arrival.) Laurence Gass was with the 165th Siege Battery. Moreover, judging by a letter from Victor Lapp to Clare Gass, dated 4 October 1916, in which he asks for details of her "cousin's" unit, she knew of Laurie's being in France as of late September 1916 although she makes no mention of it in her diary. (Letter in the possession of E. Anderson). Laurence's official military record in the National Archives has him in France as of 19 September 1916. Presumably it is the McGill connection of the unit that causes Clare to note its arrival.

11 Here rumour precedes fact: the Canadian attack on Vimy Ridge was planned for the early morning of 9 April, Easter Monday, 1917. What the rumour may be recording is the preliminary shelling that usually signalled an imminent attack.

12 The length of time for her to learn of these deaths is surprising. Lt Laurence Gass died of wounds received on 8 April and Lance Corporal Blanchard Gass was killed in action on 9 April, but she learns of Laurie's death only on the 18th and Blanchard's on the 20th. The *Montreal Star* reported the death of L. Gass on 17 April 1917 and the *McGill Daily* published an obituary on 26 November 1918 (with a picture the following day) as part of an irregular series "How They Died." That obituary contains the words of condolence sent to Gass's mother by his acting commanding officer. Even allowing for the hyperbole of such messages, it is clear that Laurence Gass was an exceptional young man, both intellectually and in terms of character. Clare Gass kept an undated copy of the obituary in her scrapbook, now in the possession of Trudy Henderson of Halifax, and the photo from the *Daily* was in the living room of Gass's apartment in Montreal as late as the 1950s. Elizabeth Anderson, who as Elizabeth Gass lived with her Aunt Clare between 1945 and

Lt Laurence Gass
(McGill Honour Roll 1914–18
[Montreal: McGill 1926], 41)

1953, reported the presence of the photo (conversation with S. Mann, 24 April 1999) and explained how she learned of the "Laurie" connection. During her nursing training at the now-defunct Reddy Memorial Hospital in Montreal, Elizabeth was asked by the business administrator of the school about her family name. Was she by any chance related to a Laurence Gass who had died in his arms near Vimy in 1917? Not knowing the answer, Elizabeth pursued the question with her aunt. Clare Gass, momentarily startled, revealed the story of the youthful romance. Phone conversation with E. Anderson, 2 January 1999.

Laurence Gass is buried in the Barlin Cemetery Extension, Pas-de-Calais, France (grave I.H.77) and Blanchard Gass is buried in the Canadian Cemetery No. 2, Neuville-Saint-Vaast, Pas-de-Calais, France (grave 1.B.38). Of all the deaths mentioned or hinted at in the Gass diary, these are the only two that could be identified and located via the Internet site of the Commonwealth War Graves Commission.

13 One can only assume the hollowness in Clare's heart and soul during these blank days of the diary. My reading of her photographs (see Introduction), in the possession of nephew John Gass, suggests a woman with less spunk as of these dates. Her diary entries also shrink.

14 On 7 June the British, having literally undermined the Messines Ridge with a series of explosive-laden tunnels, blew the Germans from their positions on the Ridge.

15 Like a number of the other junior members of No. 3 CGH (e.g., Victor Lapp mentioned at 4 April 1916 and Henry Fry at 25 June 1917), John Valentine had tired of serving as ward orderly and wanted to see more action by joining an infantry battalion. "Leaving his stripes on our desk" refers to his voluntarily choosing a reduction in rank and pay from a non-commissioned officer to a private in the infantry. The stripe indicating his NCO rank might literally – as seems to be the case here –

be cut off his uniform and left behind. Thanks to Desmond Morton for this and many other clarifications of military lore.

16 The "talk" she reports here will undoubtedly have included the death of their brother Blanchard at Vimy. Gerald had written to Clare a month earlier about the death: "when I say I expected what has happened you will think it funny, I could do nothing. But Clare I have seen many many fellows go & they have all given a warning of *some kind*. I may tell you lots of strange things someday." Letter from Gerald Gass to Clare Gass, 10 June 1917. Letter in the possession of Geraldine Brenton. Emphasis in the original.

17 An estaminet was a rudimentary café set up by enterprising local folk, often in their own home, anywhere in the vicinity of a soldier clientele for cheap wine, simple meals, coffee, conversation, companionship.

18 Although she gives no reason for choosing Scotland as a leave destination, Clare's family, on both the Gass and Miller sides, is of Scottish origin. Her friend Ruth Loggie had taken her leave in Scotland in the late spring of 1916. Clare was also well versed in Scottish history and romantic literature. The *Kidnapped* referred to is Robert Louis Stevenson's.

In her photograph album she mentions her travelling companion: Sara MacNaughton.

19 A Fifth Division of the Canadian Expeditionary Force was constituted in 1916, held in Britain for home defence and then, after considerable politico-military wrangling in the spring of 1918, broken up and used as reinforcements for the existing and seasoned 1st, 2nd, 3rd, and 4th Divisions of the Canadian Corps in France. Morton and Granatstein, *Marching to Armageddon*, 118, 196–7.

20 The stripe, to be attached to Valentine's uniform, recognizes his promotion from private to lance corporal.

21 The Italian Second Army collapsed as German and Austrian troops attacked Caporetto, 27 October 1917.

22 The official War Diary of No. 3 CGH records her leaving on 1 November 1917: "Nursing Sisters C. Gass and E.J. Giffin are struck off strength on proceeding to No. 2 Canadian Casualty Clearing Station. Both have done excellent work since the mobilization of this Unit two and a half years ago." The Clearing Station to which she went was near a railway depot at Remy Siding.

Canadian stretcher bearers bringing in wounded through mud.
Passchendaele, November 1917 (NA, PA 2367)

23 Passchendaele was the culminating point of the Third Battle of Ypres
that extended from 31 July – 6 November. Canadian troops were
assigned the task of taking Passchedaele across a bog of mud and did
so at tremendous cost between 26 October and 14 November.

24 The fighting to take Cambrai began 20 November and if any victory
could be recorded, that was the day. Thereafter, until early December
when fighting ceased, any British advances were met by German retali-
ation.

25 Her mention of voting is the wartime beginning of women's suffrage in
federal elections in Canada. Under the Military Voters Act of August
1917 she qualified to vote as a member of the armed forces; under the
Wartime Elections Act of September 1917 she qualified to vote as a

female relative (sister, mother, wife, daughter) of an overseas soldier. The purpose of both Acts was to garner support for the Borden government, which by October 1917 had attracted a sufficient number of former opposition members from the Liberal Party to create a coalition Union Government. The election in December gave the victory to Borden and to his policy of conscription – compulsory military service. With her first vote, therefore, Clare registered her support for a continuing supply of soldiers. Full women's suffrage for federal elections was accorded in 1918 and exercised in the first federal election after that in 1921.

26 The timing of her learning of these events is interesting. The new Bolshevik government in Russia had been talking of armistice since their taking power on 7 November 1917. The agreement with Germany to begin peace talks was on 27 November 1917. The short-lived military mutiny of Lavr Georgyevich Kornilov and Alexi Maximovich Kaledin

Poll for nursing sisters, No. 1 Canadian General Hospital, December 1917
(NA, PA 2279)

was on in September 1917. Kornilov, a high-ranking career soldier in the Russian army, had originally sided with the revolutionaries in the spring of 1917, but by the fall, when he was heading all the Russian forces, he despaired of the Kerensky government's pursuing the war effort. His revolt failed; briefly before his death in 1918 he mobilized an anti-Bolshevik White army.

27 The Halifax explosion occurred in the morning of 6 December 1917. Two ships collided in the harbour and the *Mont Blanc*, carrying explosives, blew up. The north end of Halifax was destroyed; 1600 people were killed, another 9000 injured.

NOTES TO DIARY 1918

1 Except for her title "The Cup of War," the passage is from the Bible (King James version), New Testament, Matthew 20, verse 22, with the phrase about baptism omitted.

2 This was her thirty-first birthday.

3 The German offensive was "long awaited" (Morton and Granatstein, *Marching to Armageddon*, 193) so presumably Clare knew of it. Or she might have penned the opening comment of this day's entry later. Only the spacing would suggest this latter possibility; the penmanship is the same.

4 Though the rumour was only partly accurate, it certainly was on time. That very day the British retreated from their line south of Peronne and the Casualty Clearing Station positions were captured. Both the wounded and the personnel of the CCSs had, however, been pulled back before the German advances. Macpherson, *Medical Services, General History*, in *History of the Great War*, 3: 210–213.

5 Clare wrote a poem entitled "Exodus from Remy" on this experience of the speedy evacuation of nursing personnel from a Casualty Clearing Station. In a letter from Matron-in-Chief to Nursing Sister Gass (dated 18 May 1921 and in the possession of Trudy Henderson), Margaret Macdonald asked for permission to publish the poem in the CAMC section of *The Canadian Nurse*. There is no record of a response to the request; the poem does not appear in that section of the journal; and the section's demise is announced in September 1922 with the immi-

nent retirement of Matron Macdonald from the permanent military nursing staff of the Department of Militia and Defence. Between February 1924 and December 1926 the section reappeared sporadically.

6 The air raid occurred during the night of 19 May causing extensive damage at No 1 Canadian General Hospital, the hospital where Clare served during her first weeks in France in the late spring and early summer of 1915. Three Canadian nursing sisters lost their lives.

7 As this is the only outing beyond Boulogne recorded for the summer of 1918, it may have inspired Clare to write

In the Poppy Fields

Blow summer winds
Across these fields of red,
Blow all the ruin and the guilt of war away,
And let we pray
The Guardian Angel "Peace"
To this dear sunny land
Return to stay

Signed LCG and dated 1918 France, the poem is recorded in a blank-page notebook entitled "The Scribble-in Book," in the possession of Geraldine Brenton. Clare's full name was Lelia Clare Gass.

8 The *Llandovery Castle* was torpedoed off the coast of Ireland on 27 June 1918 on a return voyage from Halifax. All fourteen sisters, along with most of the men, drowned. See the entry for Rena McLean, one of the victims, in *Dictionary of Canadian Biography* XIV: 723.

9 Until this point the hospital was known as No. 3 Canadian General Hospital (McGill). It is the disappearance of the latter bracketed name to which she is referring.

10 American soldiers, mentioned here for the first time, had been in Europe since the fall of 1917 and took part in their first major battle in late May 1918.

11 Abner Kingman was a prominent Montreal businessman and, among other positions, director of the Canadian Imperial Bank of Commerce and part of the brokerage firm McKenzie and Kingman. Clare would

have encountered him in his capacity as a member of the Committee, then Board, of Management of the MGH; *Annual Report of the Montreal General Hospital*, 1909–17; *McGill Daily*, 8 December 1915.

Sir William Peterson (1856–1921), a Scottish-born classicist, was principal of McGill University from 1895 to 1919. His knighthood was awarded in 1915.

12 The eight-mile Canadian advance to which she is referring took place on 8 August.

13 Morton and Granatstein (*Marching to Armageddon*, 200–3) provide full details of these thirty mile secret movements that took place between 1 and 8 August as well as the fighting itself on 8 and 9 August.

14 The tunnellers she is referring to here belonged to the Canadian Railway Troop (see diary entry 30 July 1918). There was also a Canadian Tunnelling Troop, part of the engineering corps, who constructed and maintained tunnels under trenches or wherever they were needed.

15 Transport duty meant doing nursing duty on a hospital ship or, after the war, on a troop ship from England to Canada, sometimes via Halifax and sometimes via Portland, Maine. The address in Ennismore Gardens was the London home of British M.P. Colonel Gretton, loaned to the Canadian Red Cross as of January 1918 as a rest home large enough to accommodate sixty nursing sisters; Moore, *The Maple Leaf's Red Cross*, 98–100.

16 Elsie is either a niece of Granty or a sister of Laurie Gass (information from Geraldine Brenton, in a letter to S. Mann, 6 June 1999.) If the niece, she became part of the family, visiting the apartment on Closse Street in Montreal that Clare shared with Granty from 1919 until Granty's death in 1948 and joining them for summer vacations among Clare's nieces and nephews on Martinique Beach in Nova Scotia.

Clare Gass's post-war household arrangements facilitated both her and Granty's professional lives. Without male "breadwinners" and with ambition – on Clare's part at least – to explore the new field of social work, the shared household provided both women with economic, emotional, intellectual, and social sustenance. It seems that Granty – the more reserved of the two – earned more than Clare and was a great cook. Information from nieces Mary Brown (conversation 16 Jan. 2000) and Geraldine Brenton (letter to S. Mann, 21 Jan. 2000).

66 Ennismore Gardens, Red Cross rest home for Canadian nurses
(NA, PA 5926)

The Gass-Grant household may be one glimpse along the twentieth-century path of economic and professional independence for middle-class women. That path, for Clare Gass, began with family, continued through boarding school, nursing training, war nursing, into co-operative housing arrangements. Later in the century there would be single-women home owners. I think the experience of war nursing was a significant step along that path.

17 CAMC Nursing Sister Vivian Tremaine nursed King George V, both in France and in England after he was injured during a troop inspection in France.

18 Canadian soldiers were involved in this advance, which took place between 26 August and 3 September.

19 The Segregation Camp at Rhyl in North Wales was a hospital for patients with venereal disease. When No. 3 CGH was turned into a venereal hospital in February 1919, the nursing sisters were sent to England; War Diary, No. 3 CGH, 27 February 1919. Presumably, therefore, the nurses at Rhyl dealt solely with influenza cases.

20 The abdication took place on 9 November. Once Clare is in England, as of early September 1918, she gives far less diary space to war news. Her patients were no longer the recently wounded but rather the convalescing, at Buxton, the sick, at Rhyl. Indeed, there is a slight sense that she may have filled in the entries leading up to 11 November after the fact.

21 If these unattributed words were placed as an epitaph to her journal, they constitute a provocative commentary on four years of hands-on healing. Exactly the same reflection appears, word for word, in Nellie McClung's *In Times Like These*, 122. It actually sounds more like Clare than Nellie and it is tempting to think that someone may have sent Clare *In Times Like These*, published in 1915, and that she appreciated the humour, the politics, and the forthrightness of Canada's foremost feminist. However, McClung had a habit of including unattributed material in her work, so it may be that both drew on some other contemporary source.

NOTE TO APPENDIX TWO

1 Official instructions dated 15 June 1917 and published as a pamphlet, Ottawa: J. de Labroquerie Taché Printer to the King's Most Excellent Majesty, 1918. *Source*: Canadian War Museum.

NOTE TO APPENDIX THREE

1 The cards and letters quoted here are in the possession of Geraldine Brenton of Halifax, niece of Clare Gass, except for the letter of 7 July 1916 and its enclosure, and the card of 22 July 1916 in the possession of John Gass of Hilden, Nova Scotia. Niece Elizabeth Anderson of Windsor, Nova Scotia, has a card from the war years and a few letters from the 1950s. These items constitute the only extant correspondence of Clare Gass.

NOTE TO APPENDIX FOUR

1 This item, including the prose preface which must date from 1919, was hand-written and tucked loose into the Gass diary. Everything suggests it

was written by Clare Gass: the writing, the sentiment, her location at a Casualty Clearing Station in 1917, and even the marginal numbering of the order of the stanzas that might suggest that stanza 4 was written after the others (or, more simply, that in transcribing it from what would surely have been rougher notes, she inadvertantly misplaced it). Besides her tribute to the "men," the poem is striking in showing the tenacity of her ideals in the face of the conditions of war.

NOTE TO APPENDIX FIVE

1 The list is taken from Fetherstonhaugh, *No. 3*, Appendix E, 258–61. He also has a lengthy list of subsequent reinforcements to the unit, which I have not reproduced (Appendix F, 262–9). I have been able to determine the nursing school Royal Victoria Hospital (RVH) or Montreal General Hospital (MGH) – and date of graduation and have added that information to the names of the nursing sisters.

NOTE TO APPENDIX SIX

1 The original article is in the papers of Matron-in-chief Margaret Macdonald at the National Archives as part of her uncompleted project for a history of the Canadian Nursing Services. This version, with Matron MacLatchy's name misspelled as McLatchey, appeared in the "C.A.M.C. Nursing Service Department" of *The Canadian Nurse* 18, no. 7 (July 1922): 414–18. I have corrected the spelling, using that of her autograph in a souvenir album belonging to Nursing Sister Marguerite Carr-Harris. Thanks to Professor Meryn Stuart of the University of Ottawa for showing me this album.

NOTE TO APPENDIX SEVEN

1 Chapter 14 of Clint, *Our Bit*, 110–19.

Sources and Further Reading

ARCHIVAL SOURCES
NATIONAL ARCHIVES OF CANADA
Government Documents
   Ministry of Militia and Defence
   Canadian Expeditionary Force – Military Personnel Files
   War Diary of No. 3 Canadian General Hospital (McGill)
Personal Papers
   Dorothy Cotton CAMC
   Frances Farmer American Red Cross
   Laura Gamble CAMC
   Sophie Hoerner CAMC
   Margaret C. Macdonald CAMC
   Francis-Xavier Maheux
   Ruby G. Peterkin CAMC (in Irene Peterkin Papers)
   Anne E. Ross CAMC

CANADIAN NURSES' ASSOCIATION ARCHIVES, OTTAWA
Canadian Nursing Sisters of World War I, Oral History Programme,
   Transcripts of Interviews
Alice Isaacson Papers
Nursing Sisters' Association of Canada Papers

CANADIAN WAR MUSEUM, ARCHIVES AND LIBRARY, OTTAWA

KING'S-EDGEHILL SCHOOL, WINDSOR, NOVA SCOTIA

Calendar of the Church School for Girls 1903–4; 1904–5

Manuscript Ledger 1902–3

Scheme of Work 1906–07

MCGILL UNIVERSITY ARCHIVES

Montreal General Hospital, School of Nursing

Hospital Unit [No.3 CGH], World War I

Montreal General Hospital, *Annual Report,* 1913–17

Royal Victoria Hospital, *Annual Report,* 1913–17

MCGILL UNIVERSITY, OSLER LIBRARY OF THE HISTORY
OF MEDICINE

Edward Archibald Fonds

PUBLISHED SOURCES

NEWSPAPERS AND PERIODICALS

The Canadian Nurse

McGill Daily

Montreal Star

Telegraph, Quebec

The Times, London

BOOKS AND ARTICLES

Abbot, Maude. "Lectures on the History of Nursing." *The Canadian Nurse* 19, no. 3 (March 1923): 147–51

Adami, J. George. *War Story of the Canadian Army Medical Corps.* Toronto: Musson 1918

Allard, Geneviève. "Les infirmières militaires canadiennes pendant la première guerre mondiale." MA thesis (History), Université Laval 1996

– "Des 'anges blancs' sur le front: le travail de soignante des infirmières canadiennes au cours de la première guerre mondiale." Paper presented to the annual meeting of the Institut d'histoire de l'Amérique française, Québec, 17 October 1998

Arnold, Gertrude. *Sister Anne! Sister Anne!* Toronto: McClelland and Stewart 1919

Beattie, Betsy. *Obligation and Opportunity. Single Maritime Women in Boston,*

1870–1930. Montreal: McGill-Queen's University Press 2000

Bongard, Ella Mae. Edited by Eric Scott. *Nobody Ever Wins a War: World War I Diaries of Ella Mae Bongard*. Ottawa: Janeric Enterprises 1997

Brooks, Alan A. "The Provincials by Albert J. Kennedy." *Acadiensis* 4, no. 2 (Spring 1975): 85–101

Bruce, Constance. *Humour in Tragedy. Hospital Life Behind Three Fronts*. London: Skeffington & Son n.d. [1918?]

Bunkers, Suzanne, and Huff, Cynthia, eds. *Inscribing the Daily: Critical Essays on Women's Diaries*. Amherst: University of Massachussetts Press 1996

Buss, Helen. "'The Dear Domestic Circle': Frameworks for the Literary Study of Women's Personal Narratives in Archival Collections." *Studies in Canadian Literature* 14, no. 1 (1989): 1–17

–*Mapping Our Selves: Canadian Women's Autobiography in English*. Montreal: McGill–Queen's University Press 1993

Cameron, Kenneth. *History of No. 1 Canadian General Hospital CEF*. Sackville: Tribune 1938

Cameron-Smith, J. "The Preparation of Nurses for Military Work." *The Canadian Nurse* 13 no. 9 (Sept. 1917): 556–8

Cline, Cheryl. *Women's Diaries, Journals and Letters: an Annotated Bibliography*. New York: Garland Publishing 1989

Clint, Mabel. *Our Bit. Memories of War Service by a Canadian Nursing Sister*. Montreal: Alumnae Association of the Royal Victoria Hospital 1934

Conrad, Margaret, Laidlaw, Toni, and Smyth, Donna, eds. *No Place Like Home. Diaries and Letters of Nova Scotia Women 1771–1938*. Halifax: Formac Publishing 1988

Craufurd, W.D., and Manton, E. and A. *Peeps into Picardy*. London: Simpkin, Marshall, Hamilton, Kent 1914

Crerar, Duff. *Padres in No Man's Land: Canadian Chaplains and the Great War*. Montreal: McGill-Queen's University Press 1995

Crofton, Eileen. *The Women of Royaumont: A Scottish Women's Hospital on the Western Front*. East Linton: Tuckwell Press 1997

Dictionary of Canadian Biography 14 (1911–20). Toronto: University of Toronto Press 1998

Didier, Béatrice. *Le journal intime*. Paris: Presses universitaires de France 1976

Duncan, Robert. "John McCrae's War in Flanders Fields." Documentary film co-produced by National Film Board of Canada and International Documentary Television Corporation 1998

Fetherstonhaugh, R.C. *McGill University at War.* Montreal: McGill University 1947

–ed. and comp. *No. 3 Canadian General Hospital (McGill) 1914–1919.* Montreal: Gazette Printing Company 1928

Gibbon, John. *Three Centuries of Canadian Nursing.* Toronto: Macmillan 1947

Grant, Amy Gordon, ed. *Letters from Armageddon: A collection made during the World War.* Boston: Houghton Mifflin 1930

Gullace, Nicoletta. "Sexual Violence and Family Honor: British Propaganda and International Law during the First World War." *American Historical Review* 102 (June 1997): 714–47

Gunn, Jean. "The Services of Canadian Nurses and Voluntary Aids During the War." *The Canadian Nurse* 15 no. 9 (Sept. 1919): 1975–9

Haldane, Elizabeth. *The British Nurse in Peace and War.* London: J. Murray 1923

Haste, Cate. *Keep the Home Fires Burning: Propaganda in the First World War.* London: A. Lane 1977

Haycock, Ronald G. *Sam Hughes. The Public Career of a Controversial Canadian 1885–1916.* Waterloo: Wilfrid Laurier University Press 1986

Higgert, Margaret R., Jenson, Jean, Michel, Sonya, and Weitz, Margaret C., eds. *Behind the Lines: Gender and the Two World Wars.* New Haven and London: Yale University Press 1987

Hoffman, Leonore, and Culley, Margo. *Women's Personal Narratives: Essays in Criticism and Pedagogy.* New York: Modern Language Society of America 1985

Holger, H.Herwig, and Heyman, Neil M. *Biographical Dictionary of World War I.* Westport, Conn.: Greenwood Press 1982

Kent, Susan Kingsley. *Making Peace: The Reconstruction of Gender in Interwar Britain.* Princeton: Princeton University Press 1993

Leed, Eric. *No Man's Land. Combat and Identity in World War I.* Cambridge: Cambridge University Press 1979

Lensink, Judy. "Expanding the Boundaries of Criticism: The Diary as Female Autobiography." *Women's Studies* 14 (1987): 39–53

MacDermot, Hugh Ernest. *History of the School for Nurses of the Montreal General Hospital.* Montreal: Alumnae Association 1940

Mackenzie, J.J. *No. 4 Canadian General Hospital.* Toronto: Macmillan 1933

Macphail, Andrew. *Official History of the Canadian Forces in the Great War, 1914–1919: Medical Services.* Ottawa: King's Printer 1925

Macpherson, William Grant. *History of the Great War. Medical Services General History.* Vol 3. London: His Majesty's Stationery Office 1924

Mann, Susan. "Domesticated Travel: Canadian Women 'Across the Pond.'" Unpublished paper presented at McGill Centre for Teaching and Research on Women, 22 October 1997

McClung, Nellie. *In Times Like These.* [New York: Appleton 1915] Toronto: University of Toronto Press 1972

McPherson, Kathryn. *Bedside Matters. The Transformation of Canadian Nursing, 1900–1990.* Toronto: Oxford University Press 1996

Moore, Mary Macleod. *The Maple Leaf's Red Cross. The War Story of the Canadian Red Cross Overseas.* London: Skeffington & Son 1919

Morton, Desmond. *When Your Number's Up: the Canadian Soldier in the First World War.* Toronto: Random House 1993

–and Jack Granatstein. *Marching to Armageddon. Canadians and the Great War 1914–1919.* Toronto: Lester & Orpen Dennys 1989

Munroe, Marjorie Dobie. *The Training School for Nurses. Royal Victoria Hospital 1894–1943.* Montreal: Royal Victoria Hospital 1943

Newell, M. Leslie. "'Led by the Spirit of Humanity': Canadian Military Nursing 1914–1929." MSc thesis (Nursing), University of Ottawa 1996

Nicholson, Gerald. *Canada's Nursing Sisters.* Toronto: Samuel Stevens, Hakkert 1975

Ouditt, Sharon. *Fighting Forces, Writing Women.* London: Routledge 1994

Pirie, A.H., ed. *No. 3 Canadian General Hospital (McGill) in France 1915, 1916, 1917.* Middlesbrough, England: Hood and Company 1918

Poplin, Irene S. "Nursing Uniforms: Romantic Idea, Functional Attire, or Instrument of Social Change?" *Nursing History Review* 2 (1994): 153–67

Scott, Frederick George. *The Great War as I Saw It.* Toronto: Goodchild 1922

–*In the Battle Silences. Poems written at the Front.* London: Constable 1916

Stuart, Meryn. "War and Peace: Professional Identities and Nurses' Training 1914–1930," in *Challenging Professions*, ed. Elizabeth Smyth et al. Toronto: University of Toronto Press 1999

Summers, Anne. *Angels and Citizens. British Women as Military Nurses 1854–1915.* London: Routledge and Kegan Paul 1988

Vance, Jonathan F. *Death So Noble: Memory, Meaning, and the First World War.* Vancouver: University of British Columbia Press 1997

Wilkinson, Maude. "Four Score and Ten." *The Canadian Nurse* 73, nos. 10, 11, 12 (October, November, December 1977): 26–9; 14–22; 16–23

Wilson, Barbara, ed. *Ontario and the First World War.* Toronto: Champlain Society 1977

Wilson-Simmie, Katherine M. *Lights Out. A Canadian Nursing Sister's Tale.* Belleville: Mika Publishing Company 1981

Wylie, Betty Jane. *Reading Between the Lines. The Diaries of Women.* Toronto: Key Porter Books 1995

MCGILL-QUEEN'S ASSOCIATED MEDICAL SERVICES
(HANNAH INSTITUTE)
Studies in the History of Medicine, Health, and Society
Series Editors: S.O. Freedman and J.T.H. Connor

Volumes in this series have financial support from Associated Medical
Services, Inc., through the Hannah Institute for the History of
Medicine Program.